Culture Wise GERMANY

The Essential Guide to Culture, Customs & Business Etiquette

Pamela Wilson

Survival Books • London • England

First published 2009

Survival Books Limited
26 York Street, London W1U 6PZ, United Kingdom
☎ +44 (0)20-7788 7644, 🖷 +44 (0)870-762 3212
✉ info@survivalbooks.net
🖳 www.survivalbooks.net

British Library Cataloguing in Publication Data.
A CIP record for this book is available from the British Library.
ISBN: 978-1-905303-33-5

Printed and bound in India by Ajanta Offset

ACKNOWLEDGEMENTS

My sincerest thanks to the many people who provided insights into German customs and culture that were outside my experience, including Alexandra Eberl, Mark Hogarth, April Müller, Nicole Roederer, Manuela Sessler, Claudia Schlegl, Victor Scicluna and Angelika Wittmann. I am also grateful to Manja Welzel for helping me to understand *Ossi* humour and culture, Sabina Lutz for help with the language, Chris Norville for sharing her expertise in German labour law and Elena Drexl-Schegg for her knowledge of *Wurst*.

I would also like to thank Joe Laredo for editing, Peter Read for proof-reading, Jim Watson and Di Tolland for DTP and photo selection, and Jim Watson for cartoons, maps and cover design. Finally a special thank you to all the photographers (listed on page 230) – the unsung heroes – whose beautiful images add colour and bring Germany to life.

THE AUTHOR

After obtaining a Master's degree in Art History, American-born, Pamela Wilson, worked as an archaeologist in Egypt and Waldgirmes, Germany, where she helped excavate an Augustan era Roman military camp. Moving on to Munich, she became an English teacher and the pedagogical supervisor for a language school. Pamela has written a monthly travel guide about Munich and Bavaria, and researched and edited a travel safety guide for travellers to Germany. She is also the editor of *Living and Working in Germany* (Survival Books).

Pamela met her future husband at the unlikely location of the Oktoberfest and they now have a son. After living for over ten years in Germany and surviving the various stages of culture shock, Pamela is well-qualified to share her knowledge on the subject with readers.

What readers & reviewers have said about Survival Books:

'If you need to find out how France works then this book is indispensable. Native French people probably have a less thorough understanding of how their country functions.'

Living France

'It's everything you always wanted to ask but didn't for fear of the contemptuous put down. The best English-language guide. Its pages are stuffed with practical information on everyday subjects and are designed to compliment the traditional guidebook.'

Swiss News

'Rarely has a 'survival guide' contained such useful advice – This book dispels doubts for first-time travellers, yet is also useful for seasoned globetrotters – In a word, if you're planning to move to the US or go there for a long-term stay, then buy this book both for general reading and as a ready-reference.'

American Citizens Abroad

'Let's say it at once. David Hampshire's Living and Working in France is the best handbook ever produced for visitors and foreign residents in this country; indeed, my discussion with locals showed that it has much to teach even those born and bred in l'Hexagone – It is Hampshire's meticulous detail which lifts his work way beyond the range of other books with similar titles. Often you think of a supplementary question and search for the answer in vain. With Hampshire this is rarely the case. – He writes with great clarity (and gives French equivalents of all key terms), a touch of humour and a ready eye for the odd (and often illuminating) fact. – This book is absolutely indispensable.'

The Riviera Reporter

'A must for all future expats. I invested in several books but this is the only one you need. Every issue and concern is covered, every daft question you have but are frightened to ask is answered honestly without pulling any punches. Highly recommended.'

Reader

'In answer to the desert island question about the one how-to book on France, this book would be it.'

The Recorder

'The ultimate reference book. Every subject imaginable is exhaustively explained in simple terms. An excellent introduction to fully enjoy all that this fine country has to offer and save time and money in the process.'

American Club of Zurich

'The amount of information covered is not short of incredible. I thought I knew enough about my birth country. This book has proved me wrong. Don't go to France without it. Big mistake if you do. Absolutely priceless!'

Reader

'When you buy a model plane for your child, a video recorder, or some new computer gizmo, you get with it a leaflet or booklet pleading 'Read Me First', or bearing large friendly letters or bold type saying 'IMPORTANT - follow the instructions carefully'. This book should be similarly supplied to all those entering France with anything more durable than a 5-day return ticket. – It is worth reading even if you are just visiting briefly, or if you have lived here for years and feel totally knowledgeable and secure. But if you need to find out how France works then it is indispensable. Native French people probably have a less thorough understanding of how their country functions. – Where it is most essential, the book is most up to the minute.

Living France

A comprehensive guide to all things French, written in a highly readable and amusing style, for anyone planning to live, work or retire in France.

The Times

Covers every conceivable question that might be asked concerning everyday life – I know of no other book that could take the place of this one.

France in Print

A concise, thorough account of the Do's and DONT's for a foreigner in Switzerland – Crammed with useful information and lightened with humorous quips which make the facts more readable.

American Citizens Abroad

'I found this a wonderful book crammed with facts and figures, with a straightforward approach to the problems and pitfalls you are likely to encounter. The whole laced with humour and a thorough understanding of what's involved. Gets my vote!'

Reader

'A vital tool in the war against real estate sharks; don't even think of buying without reading this book first!'

Everything Spain

'We would like to congratulate you on this work: it is really super! We hand it out to our expatriates and they read it with great interest and pleasure.'

ICI (Switzerland) AG

SWEDEN
DEN MA RK
Baltic Sea
North Sea
Kiel
Greifswald
Lübeck
Rostock
Hamburg
Bremen
Elbe
Havel
Ems
Berlin
POLAND
Osnabruck
Hannover
NETHERLANDS
Weser
Magdeburg
Munster
Spree
Harz Mts.
Elbe
Duisburg
Dortmund
Halle
Essen
Kassel
Leipzig
Düsseldorf
Dresden
Cologne
Erfurt
Bonn
Chemnitz
Aachen
Rhine
BELGIUM
Moselle
Weisbaden
Frankfurt-am-Main
Main
CZECH REPUBLIC
Mainz
Trier
Wurzburg
Mannheim
Saarbrucken
Heidelberg
Nuremberg
LUXEMBOURG
Regensburg
Karlsruhe
Stuttgart
Danube
Isar
Black Forest
Passau
FRANCE
Ulm
Augsburg
Munich
Freiburg
The Füssen Alps
Lake Constance
SWITZERLAND
Garmisch-Partenkirchen
AUSTRIA

CONTENTS

Neuschwanstein Castle, Bavaria

INTRODUCTION

If you're planning a trip to Germany or just want to learn more about the country, you'll find the information contained in ***Culture Wise Germany*** invaluable. Whether you're travelling on business or pleasure, visiting for a few weeks or planning to stay for a lifetime, Culture Wise guides enable you to quickly find your feet by removing the anxiety factor when dealing with a foreign culture.

Adjusting to a different environment and culture in any foreign country can be a traumatic and stressful experience, and Germany is no exception. You need to adapt to new customs and traditions, and discover the German way of doing things; whether it's sharing a few *Pils* and a game of *Knobeln* with your workmates at a local *Kneipe*, enjoying a *Bundesliga* match with your neighbours on a Sunday, or having a hearty dinner of *Wildbret* and *Mehlklöße* with some friends.

Germany is a land where many things are done differently: where the *Bundesbahnen* have no speed restrictions (which can be very disconcerting if you're used to driving sedately); where people drink beer made from wheat with fruit syrup and eat ham, cheese and *Wurst* for breakfast; and where the first stanza of the national song (*Lied der Deutschen*) is *verboten*.

Culture Wise Germany is essential reading for anyone planning to visit Germany, including tourists (particularly travellers planning to stay a number of weeks or months), business people, migrants, retirees, holiday homeowners and transferees. It's designed to help newcomers avoid cultural and social gaffes; make friends and influence people; improve communications (both verbal and non-verbal); and enhance your understanding of Germany and the German people. It explains what to expect, how to behave in most situations, and how to get along with the locals and feel at home – rather than feeling like a fish out of water. It isn't, however, simply a monologue of dry facts and figures, but a practical and entertaining look at life in Germany – as it really is – and not necessarily as the tourist brochures would have you believe.

A period spent in Germany is a wonderful way to enrich your life, broaden your horizons, and hopefully expand your circle of friends. We trust this book will help you avoid the pitfalls of visiting or living in Germany and smooth your way to a happy and rewarding stay.

Viel Glück! (good luck!)

Pamela Wilson

February 2009

vines alongside the River Mosel

1.

A CHANGE OF CULTURE

With almost daily advances in technology, ever-cheaper flights and knowledge about almost anywhere in the world at our fingertips, travelling, living, working and retiring abroad have never been more accessible, and current migration patterns suggest that it has never been more popular. But, although globalisation means the world has 'shrunk', every country is still a world of its own with a unique culture.

'There are no foreign lands. It is the traveller only who is foreign.'
Robert Louis Stevenson (Scottish writer)

Some people find it impossible to adapt to a new life in a different culture – for reasons which are many and varied. According to statistics, partner dissatisfaction is the most common cause, as non-working spouses frequently find themselves without a role in the new country and sometimes with little to do other than think about what they would be doing if they were at home. Family concerns – which may include the children's education and worries about loved ones at home – can also deeply affect those living abroad.

Many factors contribute to how well you adapt to a new culture – for example your personality, education, foreign language skills, mental health, maturity, socio-economic situation, travel experience, and family and social support systems. How you handle the stress of change and bring balance and meaning to your life is the principal indicator of how well you'll adjust to a different country, culture and business environment.

GERMANY IS DIFFERENT

Many people underestimate the cultural isolation that can be experienced in a foreign country, particularly one with a different language. Even in a country where you speak the language fluently you'll find that many aspects of the culture are surprisingly foreign (despite the cosy familiarity that may be engendered by cinema, television and books).

However long you live in Germany and however assiduous your study of German, as an adult learner you're unlikely ever to completely lose your foreign accent or be mistaken for a native speaker. This is something you should come to terms with sooner rather than later.

Germany is popularly perceived by the British as an easy expatriate option because it's practically 'next door' and so cannot possibly be that different from the UK. The fact that tens of thousands of Britons have made Germany their home suggests that settling there must be a straightforward process. Americans often make similar assumptions. They, and people from other countries, are often surprised and even shocked at how different Germany is from home – and from what they expected – and some survive only a year or two before returning home, disillusioned and disappointed.

Before you try to get to grips with German culture, however, you first need to adapt to a totally new environment and new challenges, which may include a new job, a new home and a new physical environment, which can be overwhelming. For example, you shouldn't underestimate the effects that the climate and weather can have on you, as Germany's often dreary and drizzly weather may affect your mood and cause 'winter depression' (also know as 'seasonal affective disorder' or SAD), caused by a lack of sunshine. There isn't much distinction between the seasons as it rains a lot all year round and it's a challenge to know when to put away your winter wardrobe because, because as soon as you do the weather is bound to change for the worse.

Those who move to a new job or attempt to start a business in Germany may encounter a (very) steep learning curve – indeed, even finding a job can be a struggle. The chances are that you've left a job in your home country where you held a senior position, were extremely competent and knew all your colleagues. In Germany, you may be virtually a trainee (especially if your German isn't fluent) and not know any of your colleagues. The sensation that you're starting from scratch can be demoralising.

Even if you move to a part of Germany with a well-established expatriate community, such as Berlin, Munich or Hamburg, things that you're used to and took for granted in your home country may not be available, e.g. certain kinds of food, opportunities to engage in your favourite hobby or sport, and books and television programmes in your language. The lack of 'home comforts' can wear you down. You'll also have to contend with the lack of a local support network. At home you had a circle of friends, acquaintances, colleagues and possibly relatives you could rely on for help and support. In Germany, there's no such network, which can leave you feeling lost.

The degree of isolation you feel usually depends on how long you plan to spend in Germany and what you'll be doing there. If you're simply going on a short holiday you may not even be aware of many of the cultural differences, although if you are it will enhance your enjoyment and may save you a few embarrassing or confusing moments. However, if you're planning a business trip or intend to spend an extended period in Germany, perhaps working, studying or even living there permanently, **it's essential to understand the culture, customs and etiquette at the earliest opportunity.**

> **'If you reject the food, ignore the customs, fear the religion and avoid the people, you might better stay at home.'**
>
> James A. Michener (writer)

CULTURE SHOCK

Culture shock is the term used to describe the psychological and physical state felt by people when arriving in a foreign country or even moving to a new environment in their home country (where the culture and in some cases language may vary considerably by region or social class). Culture shock can be experienced when travelling, living, working or studying abroad, when in addition to adapting to new social rules and values, you may need to adjust to a different climate, food and dress code. It manifests itself in a lack of direction and the feeling of not knowing what to do or how to do things, not knowing what's appropriate or inappropriate. You literally feel like a fish out of water.

Culture shock is precipitated by the anxiety that results from losing all familiar rules of behaviour and cues to social intercourse – the thousand and one clues to accepted behaviour in everyday situations: when to shake hands and what to say when you meet people; how to buy goods and services; when and how much to tip; how to use a cash machine or the telephone; when to accept and refuse invitations; and when to take statements seriously and when not to. These cues, which may be words, gestures or facial expressions, are acquired in the course of our life and are as much a part of our culture and customs as the language we speak and our beliefs. Our peace of mind and social efficiency depends on these cues, most of which are unconsciously recognised.

The symptoms of culture shock are essentially psychological – although you can experience physical pain from culture shock – and are caused by

the sense of alienation you feel when you're bombarded on a daily basis by cultural challenges in an environment where there are few, if any, familiar references. However, there are also physical symptoms including an increased incidence of minor illnesses (e.g. colds and headaches) and more serious psychosomatic illnesses brought on by depression. You shouldn't underestimate the consequences of culture shock, although the effects can be lessened if you accept the condition rather than deny it.

Stages of Culture Shock

Severe culture shock – often experienced when moving to a country with a different language – usually follows a number of stages. The names of these may vary, as may the symptoms and effects, but a typical progression is as follows:

1. The first stage is commonly known as the 'honeymoon' stage and usually lasts from a few days to a few weeks after arrival (although it can last longer, particularly if you're insulated from the pressures of 'normal' life). This stage is essentially a positive (even euphoric) one, when a newcomer finds everything an exciting and interesting novelty. The feeling is similar to being on holiday or a short trip abroad, when you generally experience only the positive effects of culture shock (although this depends very much on where you're from and the country you're visiting – see box).

2. The second (rejection or distress) stage is usually completely opposite to the first and is essentially a negative stage, a period of crisis, as the initial excitement and holiday feeling wears off and you start to cope with the realities of daily life – a life that is nothing like anything you've previously experienced.

   This can happen after only a few weeks. The distress stage is characterised by a general feeling of disorientation, confusion and loneliness. Physical exhaustion brought on by a change of time zone, extremes of hot or cold, and the strain of having hundreds of settling-in tasks to accomplish is a recognised symptom. You may also experience regression, where you spend much of your time speaking your own language, watching television programmes and reading newspapers from your home country, eating food from home

Top 10 Expatriate Gripes about Germany & Germans:

1. Bureaucracy
2. Customer 'service'
3. Brusque manners
4. High taxes
5. 'Can't-do' attitude
6. Short shop opening hours
7. Aggressive drivers
8. Lack of adequate childcare facilities and all-day schools
9. Conformity
10. Resistance to change

and socialising with expatriates who speak your language.

You may also spend a lot of time complaining about the host country and its culture. Your home environment suddenly assumes a tremendous importance and is irrationally glorified. All difficulties and problems are forgotten and only the good things back home are remembered. Some expats in Germany exhibit a 'we and they' mentality, in which 'we' (the foreigners) are constantly trying to educate 'them' (the Germans) about the 'right' way to do things – an endeavour which almost always results in disappointment.

3. The third stage is often known as the 'flight' stage (because of the overwhelming desire to escape) and is usually the one that lasts the longest and is the most difficult to cope with. During this period you may feel depressed and angry, as well as resentful towards the new country and its people. You may experience difficulties such as not being understood and feelings of discontent, impatience, frustration, sadness and incompetence. These feelings are inevitable when you're trying to adapt to a new culture that's very different from that of your home country, and they're exacerbated by the fact that you can see nothing positive or good about the new country and focus exclusively on the negative aspects.

   You may become hostile and develop an aggressive attitude towards the country. Other people will sense this and, in many cases, either respond in a confrontational manner or try to avoid you. There

may be problems with the language, your house, job or children's school, transportation … even simple tasks like shopping may be fraught with problems, and the fact that the local people are largely indifferent to these only makes matter worse. They may try to help but they just don't understand your concerns, and you conclude that they must be insensitive and unsympathetic to you and your problems.

   Relinquishing your old customs and adopting those of your new country is difficult and takes time. During this process there can be strong feelings of dissatisfaction. The period of readjustment can last six months, although there are expatriates who adjust earlier and a few who never get over the 'flight' stage and are forced to return home.

4. The fourth (recovery or autonomy) stage is where you begin to integrate and adjust to the new

culture and accept the customs of the country as simply another way of living. **The environment doesn't change – what changes is your attitude towards it.** You become more competent with the language and you also feel more comfortable with the customs of the host country and can move around without feeling anxiety.

You still have problems with some of the social cues and you don't understand everything people say (particularly colloquialisms and idioms). Nevertheless, you've largely adjusted to the new culture and are starting to feel more familiar with the country and your place in it – more at home – and you begin to realise that it has its good as well as bad points.

5. The fifth stage is termed 'reverse culture shock' and occurs when you return home. You may find that many things have changed (you'll also have changed) and that you feel like a foreigner in your own country. If you've been away for a long time and have become comfortable with the habits and customs of a new lifestyle, you may find that you no longer feel at ease in your homeland. Reverse culture shock can be difficult to deal with and some people find it impossible to re-adapt to their home country after living abroad for a number of years.

The above stages occur at different times depending on the individual and his circumstances, and everyone has his own way of reacting to them, with the result that some stages may last longer and are more difficult to cope with than others, while others are shorter and easier to overcome.

Top 10 Things Expatriates Like about Germany:

1. Slower pace of life
2. More annual leave and public holidays
3. Quality healthcare
4. Inexpensive beer and wine
5. Good motorways
6. Environmental friendliness
7. Strong local communities
8. Good trains
9. Bicycle friendliness
10. Clean cities and parks

Reducing the Effects

Experts agree that almost everyone suffers from culture shock and there's no escaping the phenomenon; however, its negative effects can be reduced considerably by the following – some of which can be done even before you leave home:

- **Positive attitude** – The key to reducing the negative effects of culture shock is a positive attitude towards Germany (whether you're visiting or planning to live there) – if you don't look forward to a holiday or relocation you should question why you're doing it. There's no greater guarantee for unhappiness in a foreign environment than taking your negative prejudices with you. It's important when trying to adapt to a new culture to be sensitive to the locals' feelings and try to put yourself in their shoes wherever possible, which will help you understand why they behave as they do. Bear in mind that they have a strong, in-bred cultural code, just as you do, and react in certain ways because they're culturally 'trained' to do so. If you find yourself frustrated by an aspect of the local culture or behaviour, the chances are that they will be equally puzzled by yours.

> **'Travellers never think that THEY are the foreigners.'**
> Mason Cooley (American writer)

- **Research** – Discover as much as possible about Germany before you go, so that your arrival and settling-in period doesn't spring as many surprises as it might otherwise. Reading about Germany and its culture before you leave home will help you familiarise yourself with the local customs and language, and make the country and its people seem less strange on arrival. You'll be aware of many of the differences between your home country and Germany and be better prepared to deal with them.

  This will help you avoid being upset by real or imaginary cultural slights and also reduce the chance of your inadvertently offending the locals. Being prepared for a certain amount of disorientation and confusion (or worse) makes it easier to cope with it. This book will go a long way towards enlightening you. For further details, there are literally hundreds of publications about Germany as well as dozens of websites for expatriates (see **Appendices B** and **C**). Many sites provide access to expatriates already living in Germany who can answer questions and provide useful advice.

  There are also 'notice boards' and 'forums' on many websites where you can post messages or questions.

- **Visit Germany first** – If you're planning to live or work in Germany for a number of years, or even permanently, it's important to visit the country to see whether you think you'd enjoy living there and be able to cope with the culture

before making the leap. Before you go, try to find people who have visited Germany and talk to them about it. Some companies organise briefings for families before departure. Rent a property before buying a home and don't burn your bridges until you're certain that you've made the right decision.

- **Learn German** – Along with adopting a positive attitude, overcoming the language barrier will probably be your most powerful weapon in combating culture shock and the key to enjoying your time in Germany.

  The ability to speak German isn't just a useful tool (allowing you to buy what you need, find your way around, etc.) but the passport to understanding Germany and its culture. If you can speak the language, even at a low level, your scope for making friends is immediately widened beyond the limited expatriate circle. Obviously not everyone is a linguist and learning a language can take time and requires motivation. However, with sufficient perseverance virtually anyone can learn enough of another language to participate in the local way of life. Certainly the effort will pay off, and expatriates who manage to overcome the language barrier find their experience in Germany much richer and more rewarding than those who don't.

  The Germans realise that their language is complex and are always honoured by a foreigner's attempts to use it. If you make an effort at communicating with the local people in their own language, you'll also find them far more receptive to you and your needs.

> **'I don't hold with abroad and think that foreigners speak English when our backs are turned.'**
>
> Quentin Crisp (English writer, actor & raconteur)

- **Be proactive** – Make an effort to get involved in your new culture and go out of your way to make friends. Join in the activities of the local people, which could be a religious holiday, local festival or social activity. There are often local clubs where you can play sport or keep fit, draw and paint, learn to cook regional dishes, make handicrafts, etc. Not only will this fill some of your spare time, giving you less time to miss home, but you'll also meet people and make new friends. If you feel you cannot join a local club, perhaps because the language barrier is too great, you can always participate in activities for expatriates, of which there are many in the most popular destinations. Look upon a period spent in Germany as an opportunity to redefine your life objectives and acquire new perspectives. Culture shock can help you develop a better understanding of yourself and stimulate your creativity.

- **Talk to other expatriates** – Although they may deny it, all expatriates have been through exactly what you're experiencing. Even if they cannot provide you with advice, it helps to know that you aren't alone and that the effects of culture shock lessen with time.

  However, don't make the mistake of mixing only with expatriates, as this will alienate you from the local people and make it much harder to integrate. Don't rely on social contact with your compatriots to carry you through, because it won't.

- **Keep in touch with home** – Keeping in touch with your family and friends at home and around the world by telephone, email and letters will help reduce and overcome the effects of culture shock.

- **Be happy** – Don't rely on others to make you happy; otherwise you won't find true and lasting happiness. There are certain things in life which only you can change.

  Every day we are surrounded by things over which we have little or no control but moaning about them only makes us unhappier. So be your own best friend and nurture your capacity for happiness.

Culture shock is an unavoidable part of travelling, living and working abroad, but if you're aware of it and take steps to lessen its effects before you go and while you're abroad, the period of adjustment will be shortened and its negative and depressing consequences reduced.

FAMILIES IN GERMANY

Family life may be completely different in Germany from what you're used to, and although you may not adopt the ways of a German family, you'll have to adapt to certain unfamiliar conditions. For example, your new home may scarcely resemble your previous one (it may be much more luxurious or significantly smaller) and the climate may be dramatically different from that of your home country. The stress of adapting to a new environment can strain family relationships – especially if they were under tension before you moved to

Germany. If possible, you should prepare yourself for as many aspects of the new situation as you can and explain to your children the differences they're likely to encounter, while at the same time dispelling their fears.

> **'And that's the wonderful thing about family travel: it provides you with experiences that will remain locked for ever in the scar tissue of your mind.'**
>
> Dave Barry (American writer & humorist)

In a situation where one spouse is working (usually the husband) and the other not, it's generally the latter (and any children) who is more affected by the change of culture. The husband has his work to occupy him and his activities may not differ much from what he had been accustomed to at home. On the other hand, the wife has to operate in a totally new environment, which differs considerably from what she is used to. She will find herself alone more often, as there will be no close relatives or friends on hand. However, if you're aware that this situation may arise, you can take action to reduce its effects. Working spouses should pay special attention to the needs and feelings of their non-working partners and children, as the success of a family relocation depends largely on the ability of the wife and children to adapt to the new culture.

Good communication between family members is vital and you should make time to discuss your experiences and feelings, both as a couple and as a family. Questions should always be raised and if possible answered, particularly when asked by children. However difficult your situation may appear at the beginning, it helps to bear in mind that it's by no means unique and that most expatriate families experience exactly the same problems, and manage to triumph over them and thoroughly enjoy their stay abroad.

A NEW LIFE

Although you may find some of the information in this chapter a bit daunting, don't be discouraged by the foregoing catalogue of depression and despair; the negative aspects of travelling and living abroad have been highlighted only in order to help you prepare for and adjust to your new life. The vast majority of people who travel and live abroad naturally experience occasional feelings of discomfort and disorientation, **but most never suffer the debilitating effects of culture shock.**

As with settling in and making new friends anywhere, even in your home country, the most important thing is to be considerate, kind, open, humble and genuine – qualities that are valued the world over. Selfishness, brashness and arrogance will get you nowhere in Germany or any other country. Treat Germany and its people with respect and they will reciprocate.

The majority of people living in a foreign land would agree that, all things considered, they love living there – and are in no hurry to return home. A period spent abroad is a wonderful way to enrich your life, broaden your horizons, make new friends and maybe even please your bank manager. We trust that this book will help you avoid some of the pitfalls of life abroad and smooth your way to a happy and rewarding future in your new home.

> **'Twenty years from now you will be more disappointed by the things you didn't do than by the ones you did do. So throw off the bowlines. Sail away from the safe harbour. Catch the trade winds in your sails. Explore. Dream. Discover.'**
>
> Mark Twain (American writer)

Heidelberg, Baden-Württemberg

2.
WHO ARE THE GERMANS?

The clichéd image of Germans among foreigners who have never visited Germany is of stoic and militaristic Teutonic people going about their lives with humourless efficiency, only occasionally letting their hair down, such as by donning lederhosen and swinging beer steins to polka music during Fasching or at the Oktoberfest. Like all such stereotypical images, this scarcely does justice to the people.

'The history of the world is also the sum of what might have been avoided.'
Konrad Adenauer (West Germany's first chancellor)

In fact, the Germans themselves are keen to distance themselves from it, as well as from the stigma of Nazism, and to reinvent their national identity – something they've had to do numerous times throughout their history. Few other countries can boast of having recovered from economic ruin (after the Second World War) and the division of their country (until 1990) within such a short time. Although they have many hurdles left to overcome, the Germans have proved themselves ready to face major challenges, to open themselves to change and accept globalisation.

As the Germans rebuild their country and its economic and political importance in Europe, they're also rebuilding their trust in themselves, their values and their way of life. But what are their values? How do they see themselves and others? To shed some light on the real Germans (and dispel some of the myths), this chapter provides information about Germany's history and demographics, and its people's preoccupations, humour, attitudes to foreigners and cultural icons.

A POTTED HISTORY

In order to gain an insight into the German people it's necessary to know something of their complex past. Germany was so named by the Roman historian Tacitus, but the nation state of Germany has existed only since 1871, and in its present form only since 1990. For much of its history, Germany has known discord and chaos, with frequent border changes and the dispersion of power among small principalities rather than a stable, centralised government – the antithesis, in fact, of the principal German *Sehnsucht* (longing): for order. The remnants of this patchwork of German kingdoms and states can be seen in the names and borders of the modern states (*Länder* – see **Geography** in Chapter 10 and the map in **Appendix F**).

> **Demographics**
>
> **Population**: 82.4m.
>
> **Population density**: 230 inhabitants per km² (598 per mi²). Berlin has a population density of 3,800 per km² (9,766 per mi²), Munich 4,272 per km² (11,000 per mi²).
>
> **Largest cities**: Berlin (3.4m), Hamburg (1.75m), Munich (1.3m), Cologne (986,000), Frankfurt (648,300).
>
> **Foreign population**: 7m.
>
> **Largest expatriate groups**: Turkish, Italian, Serbian and Greek.
>
> **State religion**: Germany is officially a secular state.
>
> **Major religions**: Christianity; 31 per cent Protestant (mainly in the north and east); 31 per cent Roman Catholic (mainly in the south and west) and 1.5 per cent Orthodox. Islam; 4 per cent.

First Arrivals

700,000BC – The earliest evidence of humans in what is now Germany.

500,000BC – The first signs of permanent settlement.

300,000-30,000BC – Neanderthal Man, *Homo* (*sapiens*) *Neanderthalensis* (it's still debated whether Neanderthal Man was a subspecies of *Homo sapiens* – modern humans – or a separate species), occupies Germany. The Neanderthals are highly developed and build complex structures, control fire and make tools such as spears and hammers.

2300-1700BC – Hunter-gatherer tribes (Celts) migrate from Asia and north-eastern Europe and settle in the Danube area. They use bronze tools and live from agriculture, mining and trading.

1700BC – A second wave of tribes, from southern Russia, migrates to Germany, eventually introducing the use of iron. These are believed to be the ancestors of the German-speaking people.

100BC – The Germanic tribes begin to occupy the north-eastern border of the Roman Empire and prove to be the Romans' greatest enemy.

9AD – Hermann (*Arminius* in Latin), a tribal chieftain, leads the tribes to victory over three Roman legions in the Teutoburg Forest (*Teutoburger Wald*).

410AD – German tribes sack the city of Rome.

The First Reich

772-880 – the Carolingian Empire: Charlemagne (*Karl der Grosse*), a Frankish king, rules over continental Europe and brings order in Germany by amalgamating the Germanic tribes and converting pagans to Christianity.

800 – Charlemagne is crowned Holy Roman Emperor by Pope Leo III.

814 – Charlemagne dies, the Empire is split and power is diffused over many principalities due to inheritance laws that divide property equally among sons.

962-1517 – German princes consolidate land and elect the succeeding Holy Roman Emperors until the 16th century, when succession becomes hereditary with the Austrian House of Habsburg.

The Reformation & Thirty Years War

1517 – The Augustinian monk, Martin Luther, protests against the Catholic Church's sale of indulgences (remissions of punishment for sins) to the people, inspiring the Reformation. Many northern principalities adopt Lutheranism, causing a major religious schism in Germany. Remnants of this north-south religious division are still visible today, with a predominantly Protestant population of the north-east and Catholics in the south-west. Even the national holidays differ between Protestant and Catholic states; for example, in the south it would be unheard of for Reformation Day to be celebrated.

1618-48 – The Protestant/Catholic conflict continues with the Thirty Years War, which greatly reduces the Holy Roman Empire's power. This causes Germany to remain a hodgepodge of small, autonomous principalities, duchies, kingdoms and free cities for nearly two centuries.

1806 – Napoleon dissolves the Holy Roman Empire.

The Rise of Prussia & the Second Reich

1224 – Prussia in north-eastern Germany is formed by a group of monks, the Teutonic Knights, a subsidiary of the Knights Templar, whose mission is to convert Baltic peoples to Christianity. Their capital is at Marienburg, modern-day Malbork in Poland.

1525 – The knights convert to Protestantism and secularise the Order, eventually becoming landowners and forming an aristocracy.

1701 – Prussia forms a kingdom. Its military might is a stabilising force in Europe.

1815 – Prussia greatly contributes to the downfall of Napoleon at the battle of Waterloo. A German Confederation of States is founded, which includes Prussia and Austria.

1866 – Prussia's Chancellor, Prince Otto von Bismarck, finally unifies Germany after a battle with Austria.

1870-71 – After defeating France, Kaiser Wilhelm I is named emperor of a united Germany. This new sense of organisation and order in Germany spills over into its economic endeavours, allowing the country to achieve rapid industrialisation with military precision, rivalling the economic growth of Britain and the US.

First World War & the Weimar Republic

1914-18 – Kaiser Wilhelm I's successor, Wilhelm II, leads Germany into the First World War.

1919 – Germany is forced to sign the Treaty of Versailles, admitting responsibility for the war, and make huge reparations, and the country's borders are reduced.

1919-33 – A new democratic constitution is drawn up at Weimar, beginning the Weimar Republic. Resentment towards the new measures and a crippled economy lead to widespread dissent, which is exploited by the National Socialist (Nazi) party.

1932 – The Nazi party wins the election.

1933 – Adolf Hitler becomes Chancellor and Head of State of the Third Reich.

The Third Reich

1933-45 – The first goal of the Nazi party and its leader (*Führer*), Hitler, is to provide the people with work and bread (*Arbeit und Brot*). The country's economic problems having been solved, the next goal is to expand its borders, which precipitates the annexation of the Rhineland and the invasion of Austria, Czechoslovakia, Poland and parts of Russia.

Hitler's idea of making Germany great includes the creation of a 'master race' of blond, blue-eyed 'Aryans' – and the extermination of all undesirables, including Jews, Romanies, homosexuals and dissidents, among others. Genetic manipulation and experimentation are also used to reach this goal. Atrocities are committed in concentration camps, built in central and east Europe, which later turn into extermination camps. During the 'Holocaust', between 1939 and 1945, an estimated 12m people are killed, around 6m of whom are Jews.

Post-war Germany & Division

1945 – Once the war is over, the allied powers of the US, the UK, France and the Soviet Union have to agree on how to keep Germany 'in line' for the future.

Papiermarks

Unfortunately, there's a difference of opinion between the three Western allies and the USSR, which leads to a division of the country.

1949 – The three western occupied zones become the Federal Republic of Germany, and the communist-controlled eastern zone becomes the German Democratic Republic (GDR). Both halves of Germany begin to rebuild, and by the '70s West Germany is the world's third-largest economic power.

1953 – Russia builds fences and walls between East and West Germany following a civil rights uprising in East Germany.

1961 – The Berlin Wall is erected during the night of 13th August, dividing the city. Those who try to escape from the East are shot on sight.

1961-89 – As West Germany flourishes, with the help of America's Marshall Plan, East Germany's economy stagnates. This, combined with the government's iron grip and repression, compels thousands to attempt to escape to the West.

Reunification

1989-90 – The Berlin Wall is breached then demolished, and Germany is officially reunified on 3rd October 1990.

'They came, they saw, they did a little shopping.'

(graffiti on the Berlin Wall referring to the influx of East Berliners into West Berlin after travel restrictions were lifted.)

1998 – For the first time since 1949, a German government, the conservative CDU/CSU/FDP coalition led by Helmut Kohl, is voted out of office by the electorate (rather than by a vote of no confidence within the German parliament). This event is also significant because the party had been in power for 16 years and was the Federal Republic of Germany's most liberal coalition in its short history. The SPD/Green Party, led by Gerhard Schröder, is voted in.

1999 – Germany moves its political capital from Bonn to Berlin, its former capital, providing a sense of closure to the division of Germany.

2002 – The euro replaces the Deutsche Mark. The unemployment problem leads to the creation of the Hartz commission to make labour reforms, referred to as the Hartz reforms, which are brought about in a series of four enactments between 2002 and 2005. The most significant and controversial Hartz reform restricts unemployment benefit (in both the amount and duration) and creates a backlash leading to court cases.

2005 – The CDU party wins a slight majority in the election and is forced to form a coalition with its great rival, the SPD, with Angela Merkel as Chancellor. A Bavarian cardinal, Josef Ratzinger, is elected Pope (see Icons below).

2006 – Germany hosts the football World Cup (they are defeated in the semi-final 2-0 by the eventual winners, Italy.)

2007 – Germany hosts the Group of Eight conference (G8), chaired by Angela Merkel.

THE PEOPLE

The turmoil and reversals of fortune that Germany has endured, particularly during the 20th century, have had a profound effect on the values and attitudes of the German people. Every country has regional differences, but few are as pronounced as those of the patchwork nation of Germany. Because of this diversity, there's little centralisation, and each state is in many ways like a separate country, with its own dialects and traditions.

There's also a noticeable gap in attitudes between the young and old as a result of the post-war generation's

moral shift (*Wertewandel*), which accelerated after the end of the Cold War, spurred on by increasing globalisation. German society as a whole is becoming more open to change, with increased emphasis today on the individual and self-development, and less on the family. The younger generation hasn't experienced the same hardship as the old and is more open to diversity and taking risks. Although the moral shift has been a gradual process, young Germans often seem to be a completely different people.

Despite these disparities, Germans have many unifying values and characteristics, and understanding these is important to anyone visiting or living in Germany.

Order

The most important thing to know about Germans is that they long for and need order. *Ordnung muss sein* (there must be order) is a frequently used expression, meaning that society relies on everyone following the rules. This is true at a national level, as the Germans try to re-structure their land, which has seen little peace and order, and to change the world's negative view of it by acting as a role model; at an individual level, every upstanding citizen feels it's his duty to bring order to the surrounding disorder. For example, if your shoelace is untied or you drop your glove, you're may be told quite sternly about it, as if being scolded for disorderly conduct! Crossing the road on a red light is a big no-no and offenders are soundly reprimanded.

The upside of this rigid rule-following is that many things still operate on the honour system – such as using public transport and buying newspapers – and it works. If you don't follow the system you appear stupid and/or rude.

Punctuality

Linked to this love of order is the importance of time-keeping. You should be on time for a business meeting – 'on time' meaning several minutes early – and are unacceptably late 15 minutes after the appointed time. There's a time for everything, including meals and house-cleaning, and disruption of the schedule is frowned upon. Inviting someone out should be done well in advance; if you ask at the last minute, you'll be refused, as that evening will already be planned – even if the plan is to stay at home and watch television.

Knocking-off or quitting time (*Feierabend*) is not to be toyed with. Arriving at a shop a few minutes before it closes will earn you brusque, unfriendly service (often the case anyway) or worse, a refusal to serve you altogether. Official closing times mean that you must have finished your business by then, so you should arrive at a government office at least half an hour before closing time to obtain a number,

or you run the risk of the ticket machine being switched off.

Despite Germany's reputation for trains you can set your watch by, the German rail service is becoming increasingly unreliable, although it's still quite punctual in comparison with most other European networks.

Clarity

From the German perspective, someone who smiles a lot at strangers automatically warrants suspicion. People who are friendly right from the start are superficial – or are flirting. You must get to know people before you're allowed to show that you like them – and that may take years.

Germans are renowned for their bluntness, but they themselves would prefer the words 'directness' or 'straightforwardness'. You need clarity (*Klarheit*) to create order, and that requires plain speaking. If you do something Germans disapprove of, they will tell you so without any qualifiers or circumlocutions. As far as they're concerned, they're saving you and themselves the trouble that can result from misunderstanding, which is what inevitably happens when too much subtlety or tact is used with Germans. Such criticism can hurt, but at least you always know where you stand. Being wishy-washy when criticising is considered weak and unhelpful. The number one complaint of German students learning English is that their teachers are too soft.

The German language itself is blunt and direct, with little subtlety, something of which Germans are not only aware, but also proud. The expression '*Jetzt werde ich mit ihm Deutsch reden müssen*' (Now, I'll have to speak to him in German – i.e. tell him in no uncertain terms) illustrates this nicely. It's significant that when Germans wish to be vague, as in marketing and advertising, they often use English words.

When Germans speak to you in English, they tend to translate literally, which comes out sounding extremely brusque. For example, if you ask the way, you're likely to be told, in a loud voice: 'You must go straight ahead and you must turn left and then you must turn left again ...'

Tips for dealing with German bluntness:

- Never take it personally; it's for your own good (or they think it is).
- Be direct (without being downright rude) in return. It will be appreciated as you're helping them to improve themselves.
- Don't soften your criticism; it will only create confusion and possibly make you look weak or incompetent.
- Avoid giving compliments to German business partners as it can cause embarrassment.
- Above all, don't expect a German to read between the lines.

Efficiency

Germans are known the world over for their efficiency and reliability.

The northern half of the nation is particularly famous for its work ethic (though the southern half has the lowest unemployment rate), which is said to come from its militaristic Prussian background and the Lutheran influence. Germans undoubtedly work hard while they're at work. However, with around 13 public holidays a year, an average of 30 days' annual holiday and a set of strong labour laws that protect them from being overworked, they aren't at work that often compared with people from most other countries. Nevertheless, they seem to use their time wisely and get more done in a day than many southern Europeans achieve in a week, earning their 'right' to pursue hobbies in their ample leisure time.

Thoroughness & Correctness

A typical German attitude is that if you aren't going to do something properly, you shouldn't do it all. This belief encompasses everything from running a car to drinking beer. Germans often refer to books and manuals on how to do even the most trivial things. Starting a new hobby involves reading all the available literature on the subject, and buying a new soap powder requires checking the latest consumer report (Stiftung Warentest). A German friend was given some Spanish wine for his birthday and before opening it downloaded a several page-long PDF file from the internet on the correct way to do so. There's no relying on common sense in Germany.

In conversation, being knowledgeable and credible is more important than being entertaining. Whatever the subject of conversation – be it football, politics or holiday resorts – it's acceptable to disagree utterly with your host, but you had better know your stuff and be able to make a good argument.

Pessimism

> **'Sleep is good, death is better; but of course the best thing would be never to have been born at all.'**
> Heinrich Heine (poet and writer)

Germans seem to enjoy wallowing in self-pity and anxiety (*Angst*). Newspaper headlines are often negative and hyperbolic. They focus not only on things that are going wrong, but also on the possibility of things going wrong.

Climate change is bringing us to the verge of disaster; taxes are about to rise (again); it's impossible to find work; pesticides in food will kill us all; the German 'race' is dying out because of a low birth rate, etc. The last few years have seen an economic recession, and this 'woe is me' mentality has done little to boost consumer confidence. Taking risks or 'living for today' are not popular ideas.

Germany is the land that brought us the gloomy works of Goethe and Wagner and Nietzsche's nihilism. A pessimist is seen as being an intellectual, a profoundly critical thinker, while optimism is a sign of naiveté. This doesn't mean that Germans don't know how to have fun, but it tends to be mandated fun, 'turned on' during their numerous fairs and **festivals**, rather than spontaneous.

Hypochondria

A major Angst of most Germans concerns their health – or lack of it, which they often blame on weather conditions. These can cause the ubiquitous *Kreislaufstörung*, which literally means 'circulatory disorder' but is used to refer to headaches, fatigue or depression – and is often used as an excuse to take a day off work. This obsession with the effect of the weather on health has led to newspapers including a 'bio-weather' (*Biowetter*) report alongside the conventional weather forecast. This serves as a kind of hypochondriac's horoscope, listing all the weather-related health problems you can expect to suffer that day. The most common 'causes' are barometric pressure, the sun (or lack thereof), winds (especially the Föhn – see *Climate* in Chapter 10), humidity and ... fresh air.

A major paradox among Germans is their love-hate relationship with air. Fresh air (*frische Luft*) is essential, and rooms must be aired (lüften) frequently – even when the temperature is sub-zero and heating costs are going through the roof. German windows can be tipped as well as swung open in order to achieve the ideal airing. On the other hand, a draught is considered deadly and on a train on a sweltering day someone is sure to come by muttering '*es zieht*' (it's draughty) and close all the windows.

National Humility

Mostly as a reaction to the excessive nationalism of the Nazi era, the post-war generations have suppressed any sense of national pride. Not only are there constant reminders in the press and on film that Germans are 'bad', but in the political arena other countries are only too ready to play the 'Nazi' card whenever it suits them – or at least that's what Germans fear will happen. There's no flag waving or national anthem singing, and children are forced to endure endless history lessons about how cruel their grandfathers were and to visit the concentration camp memorial sites on regular field trips. It's a permanent debt they must pay, financially as well as emotionally, irrespective of whether they were even alive at the time of the atrocities.

And there's the more recent legacy of Germany's division. The destruction of the Berlin Wall was a highly emotional moment in the country's history, when families torn asunder a generation earlier were suddenly reunited, their joy and tears watched by the world. But nearly 20 years later there's still a schism between the 'two Germanies' – on economic, social and psychological levels. The Easterners (*Ossis*) haven't yet reached economic parity with the Westerners (*Wessis*), who resent the financial burden reunification has placed on them.

The most positive change in Germany's self-identity in recent years came when the country hosted

the football World Cup in 2006. Great efforts were made to make visitors feel welcome, the authorities instigating campaigns to promote good manners and friendliness to foreigners – which were well received. Germans were on their best behaviour, and for good reason: their team had low expectations but finished third. The feeling of national pride was unprecedented. German flags were everywhere, and a year later some people still hadn't taken them down.

World Cup Baby Boom

Around nine months after Germany hosted the 2006 World Cup and its national team did surprisingly well, hospitals reported as much as a 15 per cent increase in the number of births, some complaining that there weren't enough beds to meet demand as expectant mothers came pouring in.

Regional Pride

Perhaps because of the historical lack of national unity, pride is more evident on a regional level – and it's free of negative associations, except for the occasional neighbour-state rivalry and stereotyping, such as 'the penny-pinching Swabians' or the 'beer-guzzling Bavarians'. You'll often see state flags rippling in the wind and being used as tablecloths, as if the region were a country in its own right. In fact, Bavaria is still considered a free state.

Stoicism

Germans don't wear their hearts on their sleeves, and you rarely witness anyone expressing strong emotion, except maybe anger at rule-breakers. In some families it's usual for parents and children to greet each other by shaking hands. At the dentist's you may be asked if you want Novocain before the drilling begins; it often isn't enough, but any reaction from the patient is considered dramatising. Women are usually advised at birthing courses not to request any painkillers during labour, and they're expected to comport themselves in a ladylike manner during the whole process.

Privacy

There's no privacy or 'personal space' outside the home, as you and your actions affect those around you.

If you open a newspaper on the underground (*U-bahn*), for example, you can expect to find several people unabashedly reading over your shoulder. In fact, the moment you get on the train, you're scanned from head to toe to see if you conform to society's standards or if you're a potential disruptor of order. Many Germans feel it's their duty to watch others around them to make sure they're keeping order. Some even sit looking out of their window all day waiting for someone to commit an offence so they can report them. At first, such behaviour might make you feel unnerved, alienated or even paranoid, but staring back or smiling and waving should help to 'break the ice'.

Almost every time you take your children out you must endure an inspection as to whether they're dressed warmly enough, have the 'right' haircut, are the 'right' weight, etc. Expect unsolicited advice or admonition rather than admiring glances or overt approval such as a smile or a nod, which are mainly reserved for children under two. From this age, children become an annoyance, as they disrupt order.

> **Queuing**
> **The German love of order unfortunately doesn't extend to queuing. Elbowing and pushing your way to the front is acceptable, and if you hesitate in deciding what you want or your attention wanders for a split second you've lost your place and it's your own fault. Keeping your place in a queue (if there is one) takes enormous concentration in Germany.**

Self-centredness

There's a vast difference between the way many Germans treat strangers and the way they treat family and friends. For example, on a train or bus in the rush hour, Germans often take up as much space as possible with their bags and coats and relinquish their 'right' to more than one seat with great resentment. On the other hand, if you're taking up an extra space with your bag, they will often simply sit on it without giving you a second to remove it. When going through a doorway, Germans don't look behind to see if they're about to slam the door in someone's face, but straight ahead as if they have tunnel vision (a common affliction among waiting staff). The opposite is true among German friends, who are normally conscientious and loyal.

Political Incorrectness

Simply put, 'political correctness' doesn't exist in Germany. This isn't because Germans are all racists but because they value plain speaking (see above). Using euphemism and circumlocution in order not to cause offence is an alien concept to them. Germany doesn't have the immigrant culture (not to mention a history of native extermination and slave exploitation) of countries such as the US, and Germans therefore have less experience of dealing with integration problems. Outright racial insults are, of course, unacceptable, but coddling people of other ethnic groups or minorities would be considered ridiculous.

SENSE OF HUMOUR

Germans have a reputation for being mirthless and dour. This is due in part to cultural and linguistic factors; English is far more flexible language

which is the basis of a good bit of English humor, a concept nearly non-existent among Germans. German jokes often contain wordplay that doesn't translate into other languages, and cultural humour – often based on stereotypes – that doesn't travel well. This means that newcomers to Germany rarely understand German humour or, if they do, don't find it funny. By the same token, foreign humour is frequently unappreciated.

The literal-minded German will take sarcasm completely seriously. For example, saying 'nice weather' on a rainy day normally elicits the response, 'No, it isn't. It's raining!' East Germans tend to be an exception.

There's a time for humour, just as there's a time for everything else, so when you catch a German unawares with a joke, you're met with a blank look. The traditional separation between work and private life has encouraged Germans to reserve jokes for the pub, among friends, and to avoid them in the workplace and with strangers. This attitude is softening, however, and business people are starting to lighten up.

German humour stems from traditions that are unknown in the UK or the US, such as cabaret, which is a combination of satire, cross-dressing and risqué songs. Slapstick comedy is often seen on German television and in carnival and festival shows. East Germany developed its own brand of humour as a way of coping with life under communism, coming up with a wealth of biting, sarcastic jokes based on shortages (especially the lack of bananas), the *Stasi* (secret police), Trabant cars and the *Wessis* (referred to as *Besserwessis*, a play on the word *Besserwisser*, which means 'know-it-all').

GDR Jokes

'What do you get when you cross an *Ossi* with a *Wessi*? An arrogant unemployed person.'
'How do you double the value of a Trabant? Fill up the tank!'

In the south, Germans have a dry wit and are famous for political satire. Every year the Nockherberg beer hall in Bavaria hosts the famous Stark Beer Festival (*Starkbierfest*), inviting Germany's politicians and making fun of them in a four-hour-long comedy show. In the Rhineland, playing tricks on people is popular.

Some other staples of German humour are: Fritzchen (little Fritz) jokes, which involve a boy catching out authority figures in witty repartee; blonde and Opel Manta-driver jokes, which are similar to English blonde jokes but include her low-class, car-obsessed boyfriend; anti-jokes, which have the structure of a joke but are illogical; and the ever-popular stereotype jokes, which make fun of different nationalities, particularly the 'penny-pinching' Scots. The last are often juvenile and can be offensive. German attempts to imitate British humour or American stand-up comedy routines often fall flat.

Germans are able to laugh at themselves through caricatures of famous people (*Promis*). They tackled the daring and controversial topic of Hitler for the first time in 2007 in the satirical film *Mein Führer: The*

education than by his family background or occupation. Although schools are open to everyone, it's still difficult for immigrant children and those from poor backgrounds to get ahead, as only children who receive lots of help from their parents or have private tutors really have a chance to succeed academically.

Truly Truest Truth about Adolf Hitler, although it received mixed reviews. Several successful comedies have come out of the *Ostalgie* genre, based on life in the GDR.

It takes a while to develop the linguistic skill needed to understand most German jokes, and it's best to wait until you have before trying to tell jokes in German yourself.

THE CLASS SYSTEM

There's no apparent class system in Germany, as it was officially dismantled in 1918, with the abdication of the emperor. Before this only the elite were educated in a *Gymnasium*, for example. The few descendents of the old aristocracy get little publicity, and you can live in Germany for many years without finding out who they are. Everyone seems to belong to the middle class (*Bürgertum*) and the Biedermeier period (1815-48), characterised by the huge expansion of the middle class, is something Germans are proud of.

Today, Germans determine a person's 'class' more by his level of education than by his family background or occupation. Although schools are open to everyone, it's still difficult for immigrant children and those from poor backgrounds to get ahead, as only children who receive lots of help from their parents or have private tutors really have a chance to succeed academically. Professors and others of high academic achievement are the most respected members of society. This means that in the job market, the person who looks the best on paper (e.g. has the best degree) is invariably preferred to someone who has other attributes, such as experience, skills and charisma.

But social status is also based on wealth, as in Germany earning your money from hard work is the ideal. It's harder for women to get into university and to get a high-level job – or to be taken 'seriously' by society; as a result women in Germany have second-class status.

Experts predict a German population decline of 17 per cent by 2050.

CHILDREN

Are the Germans dying out? A recent newspaper headline in Germany asked this very question. Chemnitz – a former East German city – had the lowest birth rate in the world in 2005, with 6.9 births per 1,000 inhabitants. The nationwide average was not much

Attitudes toward babies and toddlers are generally warm and welcoming, but parents accompanying noisy, 'undisciplined' youngsters are sometimes treated icily and accused of giving them a poor upbringing (*Erziehung*).

In German cities, navigating your pushchair through crowds and on and off public transport can be extremely trying. People seldom disguise their annoyance at having to share the limited space on a bus or underground train with a pushchair, and sometimes grudgingly move out of the way so that you can board – or refuse to do so at all. When travelling with children, it's best to avoid using public transport during rush hours and shopping on Saturdays.

Restaurants that cater to children are few, but large department stores usually have excellent facilities, including, nappy-changing rooms, high chairs and play areas. Otherwise, you may be restricted to changing a nappy in a public toilet.

When travelling with a pushchair on the underground, always check that the station you're planning to use has a lift or escalator. You can find out on the transport website or pick up a brochure at a transport counter.

better at 8.2 – the lowest in Europe. And these figures include those of non-German ethnic origin, so the number of 'true' Germans is dwindling even faster, though as a general rule the wealthier parts of Germany have a slightly higher birth rate.

Most people attribute the declining birth rate to economic factors, especially the increasing number of women seeking careers. It's still frowned upon for females to be both mothers and 'career women', and they often experience discrimination. The government is trying to change this attitude by offering attractive financial benefits for working mothers and passing job security laws. The other major obstacle facing working parents is the lack of day care and nursery schools; to get a place for your children, you need to register them before birth.

There are also social factors. In Germany, children should be seen but not heard – or preferably kept at home. In public, children receive unwanted scrutiny from passers-by.

ATTITUDES TO FOREIGNERS

Germans tend to be sceptical of foreigners and could be considered xenophobic, especially in relation to those who belong to other ethnic groups, as the subconscious distinction between a German and a foreigner (*Ausländer*) is mostly based on ethnicity. In Germany, foreigners are foreigners – and remain so. It's difficult to acquire German citizenship unless you have at least one German-born parent even if you were born in Germany and your parents have lived here for several years. Bavarians are particularly vocal in their disapproval of *Ausländer*, though their attitude is considered a sign of regional pride rather than of xenophobia or racism. In its campaign to win the Hesse state election in 2007, the country's majority political party, the CDU, used the slogan 'Kick out all foreign criminals'.

Whenever there's talk of building a mosque (in any part of Germany), there's a public outcry and construction is either cancelled or postponed. Foreign Jews, however, are untouchable: if they make a fuss about something, officials cave in immediately. At least two Carnival parades had to be cancelled in 2008 because they fell on Holocaust Memorial Day.

On the other hand, there's strong support for immigrant integration courses on foreigners. Germany's ageing population and low birth rate mean that the country needs immigrants to contribute towards the rising cost of social security. Those of European background are usually accorded the highest status, although eastern Europeans are regarded with suspicion, as most Germans fear that they will come and live off state handouts. If you're of Asian or other non-European origin, on the other hand, don't be surprised to face questions as to where you're 'from' – even if it's the UK or US.

Turkish Guest Workers

Germany doesn't have a long history of immigration, and it isn't a cultural 'melting pot'. Many foreigners choose to live a separate lifestyle, and even after many years of living in Germany may feel like Ausländer. The most blatant example of this is the Turks, who were originally invited to Germany in the '60s and '70s and arrived in droves as 'guest workers' (*Gastarbeiter*) to compensate for the low male population. As the name implies, their stay was considered short term. They lived in meagre accommodation and performed mainly

manual labour and were supposed to return to their home country at some unspecified time in the future. Many of these *Gastarbeiter* now have grandchildren and even great-grandchildren who were born in Germany and are here to stay.

The highest concentration of Turks is in Berlin, which has the second-largest Turkish population of any city in the world after Istanbul. And most of them haven't integrated into German society; many don't even speak German. Happily, there have been no racial conflicts on the scale of the infamous 2005 riots in France, but there's tension, a major cause of which is religion.

The vast majority of German Turks are Muslims, but German officials are still at a loss as to how to integrate Islam with Christianity. Should Muslims have to pay church tax (as do Christians and Jews) and, if so, how would the money be distributed among the different Muslim groups (who often disagree with each other)? Should Muslim women teachers and students be allowed to wear a headscarf to school? Should Muslim children take a separate religion class in school – instead of the standard Christian class – and, if so, on which type of Islam should it be based?

Almost half a century after guest workers began to arrive in Germany, these questions have still not been adequately answered. For more on this topic see **Religion** in Chapter 10.

Turkish-isms are becoming quite popular among the younger generation in Germany, thanks in large part to the comedians Erkan and Stefan, among others, who have built up the image of the Turkish-German as a cool underdog, speaking a dialect commonly referred to as *Kanak Sprak*.

Neo-Nazism

Primarily in the former East German states and Berlin, resentment against 'foreigners' living in Germany has led to the formation of neo-Nazi groups, who blame them for the country's social and economic ills. There have been attacks on people of non-German ethnic origin, mostly in these areas.

These (and other) groups have the right to hold 'peaceful' demonstrations, but you're advised to keep well clear. It's forbidden to display the swastika, wear Nazi uniform or perform a Nazi salute, the consequences being huge fines and imprisonment. When a neo-Nazi demonstration occurs, the police presence nearly always outnumbers the demonstrators – as on some occasions do 'anti-demonstrators', who have been known to steal the show.

ICONS

Like every country, Germany has its icons – people, places, food (and drink) and symbols – that are uniquely German and have special significance to the German people. The following list includes German national icons as seen by the German people and the outside world (which are not always the same). The author apologises for the many famous people who are missing from this list due to lack of space; it's a tribute to Germany that is has so many outstanding people worthy of the title 'German icon'.

Icons – People

Konrad Adenauer (1876-1967) – German statesman whose political career spanned sixty years, most famous for his role as the first Chancellor of West Germany from 1949–1963 and chairman of the Christian Democratic Union from 1950 to 1966. He was the oldest Chancellor ever to serve Germany, leaving office at the age of eighty seven.

> ***'Die Weltgeschichte ist auch die Summe dessen, was vermeidbar gewesen wäre.'* (The history of the world is also the sum of what might have been avoided.)**
>
> Konrad Adenauer
> (West Germany's first Chancellor)

Karl Albrecht (b 1920) – Entrepreneur who founded the Aldi supermarket chain (with his brother Theo). He is the wealthiest man in Germany and one of the richest in the world, worth an estimated $27bn.

Johann Sebastian Bach (1685-1750) – Baroque composer and organist who produced some of the greatest Western classical music – and had 20 children.

Franz Beckenbauer (b. 1945) – Possibly the greatest defender in football history, he played in three World Cups, captaining the triumphant 1974 side and also managing the 1990 winning team. He chaired the organisational committee for the 2006 World Cup, which took place in Germany.

Boris Becker (b. 1967) – Former world number one male tennis player, who won Grand Slam singles titles and an Olympic gold medal and is (to date) the youngest ever men's Wimbledon singles winner at 17. More recently he has been in the headlines for his scandalous personal life.

Ludwig van Beethoven (1770-1827) – Another of history's greatest classical composers, whose music spanned the transition between the Classical and Romantic eras. The theme of the fourth movement of his ninth symphony, the 'Ode to Joy', is the European Union anthem.

Hildegard von Bingen (1098-1179) – A nun who lived in the Rhineland in the 12th century. She's said to have had visions from the age of eight, and in her adult life she recorded them in illuminated manuscripts. She invented her own alphabet, wrote at least eight musical compositions and had powerful political connections with popes and

statesmen. Although her canonisation was never completed, she's considered a saint by many.

Dieter Bohlen (b. 1954) – Singer and producer of questionable talent who headed the '80s group *Modern Talking*. Although virtually unknown to the rest of the world, he often hits the headlines in Germany, usually thanks to his sordid 'love' life or his antics on the jury of the TV show *Pop Idol*.

Willy Brandt (1913-92) – Chancellor of West Germany during the cold war, who promoted improved international relations with East Germany (GDR) and other eastern block countries. He was awarded the Nobel Peace Prize in 1971. He was forced to resign as Chancellor in 1974, when it was discovered that one of his closest aides was an East German secret service spy.

Albrecht Dürer (1471-1528) – Artist and mathematician, most famous for his prints and engravings.

Marlene Dietrich (1901-92) – An entertainer and singer who started her career in the '20s in cabarets in Berlin. She later became a Hollywood actress, starring in films such as *The Blue Angel* and *Morocco*, for which she was nominated for an Oscar.

Albert Einstein (1879-1955) – Considered the most brilliant theoretical physicist of all time and winner of the Nobel Prize for his Theory of Relativity. Einstein's name is synonymous with the word 'genius'.

> **'If my Theory of Relativity is proven successful, Germany will claim me as a German and France will declare that I am a citizen of the world. Should my theory prove untrue, France will say I am a German and Germany will declare that I am a Jew.'**
>
> Albert Einstein (theoretical physicist)

Johann Wolfgang von Goethe (1749-1822) – Germany's legendary man of letters – writer, poet, philosopher and artist, whose most famous work was a two-part poem, Faust (which took him 26 years to complete). His tragic, semi-autobiographical book, *The Sorrows of Young Werther*, inspired a string of suicides.

Steffi Graf (b. 1969) – Former world number one female tennis player who won 22 Grand Slam singles titles and is to date the only player (male or female) ever to win the 'Golden Slam', capturing all four Grand Slam singles titles and the Olympic gold medal in one year. She is married to US tennis star, Andre Agassi.

The Brothers Grimm (Jacob 1785-1863, Wilhelm 1786-1859) – Professors Jacob and Wilhelm Grimm created an anthology of fairy and folk tales in the early 19th century which are now among the world's best known children's stories, including *Snow White, Rumpelstiltskin, Cinderella* and *Hansel and Gretel*.

Jürgen Klinsmann (b. 1964) – Played in the German national football team which won the World Cup in 1990 and later managed the team, leading it to third place in the 2006 World Cup.

Helmut Kohl (b. 1930) – German Chancellor from 1982 to 1998 – the longest tenure since Otto von Bismarck. He helped bring about the end of the cold war and signed the Maastricht treaty, which created the European Union.

Martin Luther (1483-1546) – priest who inspired the Reformation and made one of the most influential translations of the Christian Bible. Today, the Lutheran Church he formed has millions of followers worldwide.

Karl Marx (1818-83) – Philosopher, political economist and revolutionary, Marx is said to be the father of communism.

Max, Moritz & der Struwwelpeter – Traditional characters in children's literature that represent what happens to little girls and boys when they misbehave. Max and Moritz are a famous pair of mischief-makers who meet a sticky end in a children's book written by Wilhelm Busch – said to be the first comic strip. Der Struwwelpeter, or shock-headed Peter, is a nasty boy who doesn't cut his fingernails or comb his hair from a book by Heinrich Hoffmann, first translated into English by Mark Twain.

Angela Merkel (b. 1954) – The first woman and first former East German citizen to become Chancellor of Germany and the second woman to chair the G8 (after Margaret Thatcher). She is considered the most powerful woman in the world.

Nena (b. 1960) – '80s singer who performed one of the few international German-language hits, the New German Wave song, *99 Luftballons*, in 1982. She made a comeback in Germany in 2002.

Friedrich Nietzsche (1844-1900) – Philosopher who wrote *Thus Spake Zarathustra* and popularised the ideas of the *Übermensch* and nihilism.

Adam Ries (1492-1559) – 16th-century mathematician who wrote three books on calculation and one on algebra in German (rather than Latin) in order to reach the common people – though the algebra book wasn't published until 1992.

Claudia Schiffer & Heidi Klum (Schiffer b. 1970, Klum b. 1973) – 'Aryan' beauties who have both made their mark as supermodels; they are adored by

Volkswagen Beetle

Brandenburg Gate, Berlin

the German public (and others) and have successfully balanced careers and motherhood.

Michael Schumacher (b. 1969) – recently retired Formula One racing car driver and record seven times world champion. He was the world's first billionaire sportsman.

Richard Wagner (1813-83) – Romantic composer who wrote lengthy dramatic operas about legendary German characters. The Bavarian King Ludwig II (see **Neuschwanstein** below) sponsored his work and there's a famous Wagner Opera Festival (*Wagner Festspiele*) in Bayreuth held annually.

Icons – Places & Structures

Black Forest – A wooded mountain range, bordered to the west and south by the Rhine valley in Baden-Württemburg. It's known as the Black Forest (*Schwarzwald*) on account of the predominance of pine trees. Although it has suffered some damage in recent years from acid rain, the Black Forest is considered the most beautiful in Germany. In addition to its spectacular views, the region is renowned for its cheesy (kitschig) cuckoo clocks, Black Forest cake, honey and Black Forest ham. Freiburg is the largest city in the Black Forest.

Brandenburg Gate (***Brandenburger Tor***) – Nike, goddess of victory, drives a chariot atop the neoclassical Brandenburg Gate in Berlin, the symbol of reunified Germany. It appears on the reverse of the 50, 20 and 10 cent coins. In the past, German armies began their parades there.

Cologne Cathedral (***Kölner Dom***) – A Roman Catholic cathedral officially known as the *Hohe Domkirche St. Peter und Maria*, it's the largest gothic church in northern Europe and has the third-highest spire in the world. As a UNESCO World Heritage Site, it's one of the most visited buildings in Germany. Its construction was begun in 1248 and took over 600 years to complete, as there were a number of interruptions.

Hofbräuhaus – The world's most celebrated beer hall, in Munich, where Bavarian food and Hofbräu beer by the litre (*Maß*) are served while an oom-pah band plays traditional and modern songs.

Neuschwanstein Castle – Construction of the fairytale castle began in 1869, when King Ludwig II let his obsession with German folklore and legend run away with him – and with the Bavarian bank – and was unfinished when Ludwig was declared insane in 1886 and arrested. Spectacularly located in Bavaria's breathtaking mountainous region, the Allgäu, it's the most photographed castle in Germany and one of the most famous in the world, having provided the inspiration for the Disneyland castle. Many Bavarians were sorely disappointed when the castle wasn't voted one of the Seven Wonders of the modern world in 2007, alongside the Taj Mahal and the Great Wall of China.

Reeperbahn – A street in Hamburg's St. Pauli quarter famous for being a red-light district. In addition to legalised prostitution and sex shops, the area boasts numerous bars, clubs and theatres, one of which features live-sex shows.

Reichstag – Germany's neoclassical house of parliament and a major tourist attraction in Berlin. Built in 1894, it was set on fire soon after Adolph Hitler assumed power in 1933. The fire was blamed on communists and was used as an excuse to suspend civil rights and vest more power in the Führer. It was restored and became the home of the German parliament, the *Bundestag*, in 1999.

Semper Opera House – Built in Dresden in 1841 in early renaissance style, destroyed during the Second World War and re-built. The Semper is one of the most famous and best loved opera houses in the world.

Zugspitze

Germany's highest mountain at 2,962m (9,717ft) above sea level, located on the Austrian border in Garmisch-Partenkirchen, Bavaria. At the summit is a centuries-old weather station that is still operational.

Icons – Symbols

Autobahn – Germany's motorway network covers 11,500km (7,132mi) but, although you're permitted to drive at breakneck speeds, it's often so congested that Germans refer to it as a 'gigantic car park'. Contrary to popular belief, Autobahn construction began during the Weimar Republic – before the Nazis came to power – although it was greatly accelerated by Hitler. For more information see **Chapter 7**.

BMW – Bayerische Motoren Werke (BMW) AG is one of Germany's leading automobile manufacturers and has a high reputation around the world. The company was founded in 1916 as a producer of aircraft engines but was forced to change direction after the First World War and began manufacturing motorbikes and, later, cars. During the Second World War, BMW resumed aircraft engine production using forced labour from

Cologne Cathedral

the Dachau concentration camp. Today BMW employs over 100,000 people and produces almost 1.5m cars annually, including Minis and Rolls Royces.

Cars – The automobile (*Auto*) is an important status symbol in Germany – provided it's German. It's considered respectable to drive a BMW (see above), Audi or Mercedes, while Porsche drivers are flashy and Volkswagen owners barely reputable. Foreign cars, especially Asian models, are for the lower classes. Driving a German car also greatly increases your chances of survival on the *Autobahn* (see above).

Der Spiegel – The country's best-selling and most influential weekly magazine, *Der Spiegel* is renowned for uncovering political scandals and running provocative articles.

Eagle – The German *Reichsadler* or *Bundesadler* is one of the oldest heraldic symbols in Europe, symbolising God, the emperor and invincibility. The eagle, in the colours of the national flag, appears on official seals, buildings, standards, federal flags and coins (euro and *Deutschmark*).

Edelweiss – *Leontopodium alpinum* is an endangered alpine flower with small yellow blooms surrounded by white petals in a star formation. It blooms between July and September at altitudes of around 2,000m (6,600ft). It's the symbol of the German alpine societies, mountain rescue service and, previously, mountain infantry. During the Third Reich, anti-Nazi youth groups wore edelweiss badges. Edelweiss is used in folk medicine to treat abdominal and respiratory disorders.

KaDeWe – Short for *Kaufhaus des Westens* (Department Store of the West), Berlin's KaDeWe is the largest department store in continental Europe (London's Harrods is larger). It was founded in 1907, is now owned by Arcandor AG and welcomes up to 50,000 customers per day (100,000 per day during Advent). The store is on seven floors and the liveried porter welcomes and directs customers in seven languages.

Lederhosen

Leather shorts with suspenders, worn with long socks. The stereotypical German garment, popularised by the Oktoberfest (see below), is in fact particular to Bavaria and even there normally worn only on special occasions.

Oak tree – The oak is Germany's national tree and appears on the 1, 2, and 5 cent coins.

Oktoberfest – The largest beer festival in the world takes place in Munich and draws around 6m people each year – over four times the population of the city. For more information see **Festivals** in Chapter 8.

Railways – The first German railway was opened in 1831 and used a horse-drawn car to transport coal; steam engines were introduced four years later. Nowadays, Germany's trains are all electric and operated by Deutsche Bahn, which was until recently a public limited company but is now planning semi-privatisation. Deutsche Bahn's flagship train, the Intercity Express (ICE), can reach speeds of up to 320kph (200mph). German trains have a reputation for being reliable and employing the latest technology. For more information see **Trains** in Chapter 7.

Volksmusik – German folk music reflects regional and local lifestyles. Songs are sung in dialect and involve harmonising or yodelling. Instruments employed include alpine horns, zithers, accordions, violas, guitars, harmonicas and brass.

Volkswagen Beetle – the rear-engined 'peoples car' was designed by Ferdinand Porsche and produced from 1938-2003, during which period 21,529,464 were built worldwide.

Icons – Food & Drink

Apfelstrudel – A traditional Bavarian dessert (also claimed by Austria) consisting of apples and raisins baked in pastry and served warm with vanilla sauce.

Beer – Germany is famous the world over for its excellent beer, brewed in accordance with an ancient 'purity law' (*Reinheitsgebot*), which permits only three ingredients: hops, malt and water. One exception is wheat beer (*Hefeweizen*), which contains yeast and wheat. Each region favours different beers: in Bavaria lager (*Helles*) and wheat beer (which Bavarians call *Weissbier*) are preferred, whereas people in the north and the east prefer pilsner (*Pils*) and in the Cologne area *Kölsch*, a pale brew with little effervescence.

Bread – Little known to non-Germans is the German obsession with bread. The first complaint most Germans have on visiting a foreign country is the lack of good *Brot*, which comes in countless varieties in Germany. Black bread, made from dark sourdough, is especially popular and is usually bought fresh rather than in the plastic packets it's usually exported in.

Hamburger – The most famous German food isn't in fact considered by Germans to be German at all, but American. Nevertheless, as its name suggests, the hamburger derives from the Hamburg steak, a slab of pounded beef commonly served in Hamburg in the mid-19th century.

Lebkuchen – A traditional Christmas cake containing honey, ginger, cinnamon, nutmeg and cloves, and similar to American gingerbread cookies. It was made famous by the witch's house in *Hansel and Gretel*.

Mixing drinks – Despite their love of order and purity, Germans love to mix their drinks: for example, beer with lemonade (lemon-lime soda), called *Radler, Alsterwasser* or *Russn* depending on the type of beer, or cola (*Diesel or Neger*); cola with orange soda (*Spezi*); apple juice (or other juices) with sparkling water (*Apfelschorle*); and wine with water (*Weinschorle*).

Potatoes – Open the menu of any German restaurant and you'll find that almost every dish comes with potatoes, whether in the form of dumplings (*Knödel* or *Kloß*), mashed (*Pureé*), chipped (*Pommes*), fried, roasted, baked, or served cold with mayonnaise.

Pretzels – *Brezel, Breze* or *Brezn* are soft knots of bread coated with coarse salt, a speciality of southern Germany and Austria. Eaten with meals, beer or as a snack, pretzels can be served plain, with mustard (*Senf*) or with butter (*Butter*).

Sauerkraut – A favourite side dish consisting of cabbage (*Kraut*) fermented in lactic acid bacteria and then boiled – rather more appetizing than it sounds.

Schnitzel – A breaded veal cutlet served with a lemon wedge and, inevitably, potato. Although traditionally veal, schnitzel is often made with pork.

Wurst – Germany's favourite food, sausage is most popularly served with mustard in a bread roll. There are more than 1,500 kinds of *Wurst* including ground veal and pork (*Bockwurst*), finely chopped pork, beef and/or veal (*Bratwurst*), liver sausage (*Leberwurst*) and blood sausage (*Blutwurst*).

'Eating in Germany is easy, because there is basically only one kind of food, called the *wurst*.'

Dave Barry
(American writer & humorist)

Hall of Mirrors, Herrenchiemsee Schloss, Bavaria

Landsberg am Lech, Bavaria

3.
GETTING STARTED

One of the most frustrating things you're faced with when moving to a new country is bureaucracy and the attendant paperwork – especially when it's in a foreign language – but the exasperation you feel when plodding through the necessary forms and dealing with smug civil servants can be lessened. Forewarned is forearmed, as they say, therefore if you're well prepared before tackling the red tape it might not be quite as bad as you feared.

This chapter is designed to help you overcome the challenges of arriving and settling in Germany, such as obtaining a residence permit, finding accommodation, renting or buying a car, opening a bank account, registering for taxes, obtaining healthcare, council services and utilities, finding schools for your children, getting online and staying informed.

'One German makes a a philosopher, two a public meeting, three a war.'

Robert D. MacDonald (Scottish playwright)

As laws are continually changed and updated, always check with your local consulate or embassy or the relevant German government website, which often provide information in foreign languages, including English, about the latest regulations.

IMMIGRATION

Upon arrival in Germany you must go through passport control and customs. If you come from an EU country, the US, Canada, Australia or New Zealand you'll almost certainly get through without a second glance. If you come from an Arab, Asian, African or eastern European country (especially the former Yugoslavia) you may be interrogated and may even be handed over to the passport control officer's supervisor. Your passport will be thoroughly checked and stamped and your luggage may be searched. However, provided you have all the necessary documents and haven't broken any regulations, you can expect a positive outcome, but the procedure may be a bit nerve-wracking. The officers may be brusque but shouldn't be unfair, and it's in your interest to remain calm and civil.

Residence Permits

Visas aren't necessary: for EEA and Swiss nationals, although nationals of Iceland, Liechtenstein and Norway need to obtain a residence permit for stays of longer than three months. EU nationals planning to live in Germany must register their residence at the Registrar's office (*Einwohnermeldeamt*). This is quite a quick procedure involving the completion of a simple form. When registering your residence, be aware that those declaring themselves as Christian or Jewish will be levied a church tax on their income.

Citizens of Australia, Canada, Israel, Japan, New Zealand, South Korea and the US may enter Germany without a visa and stay for up to three months as tourists; to remain longer, they must apply for a residence or work permit.

Visas are necessary: to enter Germany for nationals of Russia, Asia, Africa and some South American countries, which can then be converted into residence permits upon settlement (see details below).

Nationals of the following countries who plan to stay in Germany longer than three months don't require an entry visa, but a residence permit must be obtained in advance: American Samoa, Andorra, Argentina, Bermuda, Bolivia, Brazil, Brunei, Chile, Cook Islands, Costa Rica, Croatia, El Salvador, Guam, Guatemala, Honduras, Hong Kong (HK-SAR only), Macoa (RAE only), Malaysia, Mexico, Monaco, Nicaragua, Niue, New Caledonia, New Zealand, Panama, Paraguay, San Marino, Singapore, Uruguay, Vatican City, Venezuela and the US Virgin Islands. It's forbidden to change your status from tourist to employee, student or resident once in Germany.

You're required to carry personal identification (including your residence permit and passport) at all times; if you're stopped and found without identification, you can be fined or arrested.

BUREAUCRACY

Germans are great rule-makers and -followers, therefore to make your time in Germany successful and enjoyable you must learn and obey all the relevant rules. Residing in Germany (as in any country) involves a profusion of forms, letters and certificates; everything must be in writing (*schriftlich*) to be officially recognised. Being shunted from one office (Amt) to another for essential paperwork, obtaining a number and waiting endlessly are standard procedure, no matter how prepared you think you are.

The 'Catch-22' system for getting some things such as a work permit (you need

> **Tips for dealing with German paperwork:**
>
> - Always find out exactly what you need in advance from an official source.
> - Always take a duplicate of everything.
> - Expect not to have the right paperwork the first time (no one ever does) and count on two or three visits to accomplish your goal.
> - Double-check the opening hours of an office and ensure the date of your planned visit isn't a public holiday (national, regional or local).
> - Arrive at least 30 minutes before closing time.
> - Allow most of the morning or day to make an application.

a job before you can get a work permit and a work permit before you can get a job) can be mind-boggling.

Brief opening hours (0800-1130 four days a week) and the slow, communist-style work ethic of civil servants also hinder the efficient processing of documents. The good news is that once you've acquired the proper paperwork, your residence permit is usually provided the same day and a work permit within eight weeks (sometimes much sooner).

You can save yourself a lot of time by downloading documents from official websites. Some particularly helpful sites include: 💻 www.bund.de (the main German government website, which provides information in English on visa requirements, living, education and working in Germany); 💻 www.germany.info (the site of the German consulate and the most helpful website for English speakers, containing downloadable forms in many languages); and 💻 www.ifa.de (the Institute for Foreign Relations', also in English). Other good sources of information are chambers of commerce, town halls and expatriate support groups (also a good place to obtain emotional support).

Civil Servants

Civil servants (*Beamter*) include teachers, police, forest rangers, postal workers and employees in government offices. They have privileged status in Germany – short working hours, regulated breaks, annual salary increases, generous benefits and protection from dismissal – and have been known to take advantage of this.

Having acquired their position, many civil servants become complacent and some develop an intimidating air, conscious that they wield the power to approve or decline your permit or other request. Some may enjoy making you squirm, while others are reasonable and helpful. On the whole, however, *Beamter* embody the worst traits of the German character: even other Germans complain about them.

When you settle in Germany, you're assigned a 'case worker' (*Sachbearbeiter*) in accordance with the first letter of your last name and, in most cases, you're stuck with this person for life (or until they retire or die). When your *Sachbearbeiter* is on holiday or sick, you may be out of luck: where two or more *Sachbearbeiter* share a position, you may find that the paperwork you've meticulously prepared for the first isn't what the second one wants and you must go away and find yet more documents.

Remember that however provocative and rude civil servants may be, they're bound by the rules and will eventually give you what you've requested – provided, of course, that you've followed all their procedures. Being excessively friendly and polite does no good, as you're likely to be regarded as desperate – or a criminal. It's best to be civil and business-like in your bureaucratic dealings. By the third visit at the most you should have accomplished your goal.

Getting Round Bureaucracy

It's a commonly held belief among Germans that visitors to their country should speak their language. You therefore shouldn't expect to be welcomed with open arms if you don't speak a word of German. If you have at least basic German, your effort is normally appreciated. But however good your command of German and however endless your patience, it's recommended to take the following steps to mitigate the worst excesses of German bureaucracy.

Friends & Colleagues

If you don't speak any German, it's best to find a German-speaking friend or colleague who can help you compete your application, accompany you to the relevant office and act as your interpreter. If your friend is German, it will greatly speed up the process.

Lawyer

In most cases you should be able to handle German bureaucracy alone or with a German-speaking friend, but if you're from a poor country, have a police record or are expecting to come up against obstacles of any kind, you should hire a lawyer (*Anwalt*). People who have been refused residence permits might try engaging a lawyer to submit an application on their behalf – it's important to find one who specialises in *Ausländer-Asyl Recht* (foreign/asylum law). Immigration lawyers are usually on good terms with many civil servants, as their job brings them into daily contact with officials. You can easily find one via the yellow pages or the internet, but your best bet is to choose one who has been recommended by other foreigners who have been granted permits. For a single application, a lawyer should only charge between €50 and €100, depending on how difficult the case is, and he should process it within a week.

ACCOMMODATION

Apartments are usually rented unfurnished and bare means exactly that; there's no kitchen – not even a sink – and no light fittings.

Rented Property

Finding a property to rent in Germany can be very difficult, depending on your nationality or race and where you wish to live. Some landlords refuse to let their property to foreigners (*Ausländer*), and it isn't unheard of to be hung up on or to be told to leave the premises as soon as you divulge your country of origin – or even before.

This isn't necessarily a sign of racism or xenophobia. Tenants have extensive rights and are almost impossible to get rid of once they've signed a contract – even if they refuse to pay the rent. And foreigners are considered high-risk tenants, not least because they may have an unreliable income or may leave the country at a moment's notice.

In any case, in the major cities, the housing shortage is so great that 30 people may turn up to view any affordable accommodation. You'll then be asked to complete detailed forms about your financial status and habits, such as smoking, pet-loving and musical activity. *Ausländer* and large families are always at the bottom of the list. Many people tire of competing for privately advertised accommodation and resort to using estate agents, even though they charge a commission of two to three months' rent plus value added tax.

Finding Rental Accommodation

The following tips may help you secure a rented home in Germany – or at least avoid a nervous breakdown in the process:

- Allow yourself plenty time (it can take up to six months in larger cities). This may mean taking short-term accommodation while house-hunting.
- Word of mouth is the best way to find a good and hassle-free deal.
- Check local newspapers and the websites 💻 www.immobilienscout24.de and 💻 www.immowelt.de for rental offers (*Mietangebote*), which are in German but are the most comprehensive.
- For cheaper and short-term housing, check the notice boards at local universities.
- Take along proof of income, work contract and residence permit to all viewings and meetings with prospective landlords and agents.
- If possible, have a German-speaking person make calls to set up viewings and to accompany you to meetings.

Deposits

You're normally required to pay a security deposit equivalent to three months' rent for an apartment or house. In order to get your security deposit back you should:

- Insist on a receipt, especially if you're paying in cash.
- Take a German-speaking friend with you when signing the contract to make sure that you've understood everything.
- Read the conditions of your contract carefully; any breach of contract can mean you forfeit your deposit.
- Request an annual account statement (landlords are required to place your security deposit in an interest-earning account in your name).
- Make sure you carry out the (usually extensive) repair and renovation when vacating the property; if you don't, the costs will be deducted from your security deposit.
- If your landlord refuses to return your deposit without grounds, obtain help from the local renter's association (*Mietverein*).

Contracts & Payment

There are two main types of contract: short-term (*befristet*) and permanent (*unbefristet*). Short-term contracts can be renewed if the landlord agrees, whereas permanent contracts give you the right to stay indefinitely and the first refusal to buy the property if the landlord decide to sell it.

Contracts, in typical German fashion, have strict terms and conditions and include a list of 'house rules' (*Hausordnung*) concerning noise and cleanliness, among other things. Your contract also states the regular maintenance necessary and what repairs must be made before moving out.

Rent payment is almost always made by direct debit, and your bank statement is regarded as a receipt. If your landlord is the trusting kind, you may be allowed to pay your rent by bank transfer, cheque or in cash, for which you should always obtain a receipt.

Landlords

Your landlord may be a private person or a company. In general, renting from a company is preferred, because companies don't take a personal interest in your activities, provided you don't do

anything that damages the property or costs them money.

A company is also more likely to give you your deposit back when you move out and to handle any maintenance and repairs promptly.

Getting on the good side of your landlord should be no problem if you pay on time, follow the house rules and keep the property in good condition. **If you wish to make any improvements or repairs, inform the landlord first; not only is it required under your contract, but the landlord may reimburse you for some or all of the costs.**

Buying a Home

The procedure for finding a home to purchase is similar to that for finding rented accommodation (see above). Local newspapers and websites such as 💻 www.immobilienscout24.de and 💻 www.immowelt.de also advertise property for sale (*Immobilien*).

Before committing yourself to a purchase, you should consider the following:

- Fees associated with a purchase add around 10 per cent to the cost, which means you need to own a house for up to three years simply to recover the associated fees.
- Prices are calculated according to the size of a property in square metres (*Quadratmeter*) and its age, condition and location.
- German banks expect a deposit or down payment (*Eigenkapital*) of at least 15 to 25 per cent.
- Banks have stricter requirements for foreigners applying for a mortgage and will generally refuse your application if you or your spouse is self-employed or has a short-term job contract (unless you can provide collateral).
- Once you've arranged a mortgage (if necessary), the purchase moves quickly and you may be able to move in within a month. Some of the legal paperwork with the notary (*Notar*) and the property ledger (*Grundbuch*) may be completed after purchase.
- If you buy an apartment, you need to pay monthly community charges (*Hausgeld*), which are deposited in a general fund. Some of this money covers monthly costs such as heating, water and maintenance of the communal areas (including windows, doorways, facades, stairwells, entrances, courtyards and grounds), while the rest accrues interest until you and the other owners agree to make improvements to the property.

Richtfest

A *Richtfest* is an impromptu party to celebrate the completion of the structure of a house. It's decorated with a wreath or fir tree, and both the builders and the future homeowners toast its completion with beer and food.

BUYING OR HIRING A CAR

Car Hire

To hire (rent) a car in Germany you must be 19 or older – depending on the model – and hold a driving licence that has been valid for at least a year.

You don't need a German licence if you've been in Germany for less than

six months or are renting for tourist purposes. Payment is easiest by credit card because of the €200-300 deposit required. If you don't have a credit card, you must make the deposit in cash. You also need identification such as a passport. You can usually hire accessories such as child seats, snow chains/tyres and ski/luggage racks.

Buying a Car

New Cars

When buying a car in Germany, it's important to note that you must pay more than the list price. Extra charges include 19 per cent VAT (*Mehrwertsteuer*), shipping charges, dealer preparation fees, and, after purchase, registration fees and insurance premiums. The list price is often non-negotiable, but it's worth haggling to try to get a few extras included. Shop around different dealerships for the best deal, financing terms and guarantees.

Used Cars

Buying a used car in Germany isn't quite as risky as in some countries, as vehicle inspection standards are stringent, meaning that cars are generally well maintained and in good condition. In fact, you rarely see 'old bangers' on German streets.

Nevertheless, it pays to be cautious, especially when buying privately.

Make sure that a vehicle has valid safety inspection and emissions test certificates, and that the vehicle identification number on the chassis matches the number on the registration document.

Before buying a used car, always check that the price corresponds roughly to the value given on the ***Schwacke Liste*** (standard used car price list), which can be checked online (www.schwacke.de).

For information about driving in Germany see **Chapter 7**.

EMERGENCY SERVICES

Germany has efficient and reliable emergency services. In the event of an emergency, dial the national police or fire brigade number (see opposite) and a squad car or ambulance will be sent as appropriate. Telephone operators may not speak English, therefore you should be prepared to explain briefly in German the type of emergency and your location (see opposite).

HEALTH SERVICES

Thanks to (or despite) continual reform of the health service, the quality of healthcare in Germany is excellent,

Emergency Numbers

Number	Service
112	Fire brigade (*Feuerwehr*) & ambulance (*Krankenwagen*)
110	Police (*Polizei*)
19222	Mountain and water rescue services
0180-222 2222	Vehicle breakdown service (ADAC)
0800-111 0333	Child abuse hotline
0761-19240	Poison control
116116	Emergency credit card cancellation from a mobile phone (for all kinds of credits cards)
030-4050 4050	Emergency credit card cancellation from a fixed line

Emergency Phrases

(car) accident – (*Auto*) *Unfall*
allergic reaction – *allergische Reaktion*
(armed) attack – (*bewaffnete*) *Angriff*
it's bleeding (a lot) – *es blutet* (*viel*)
broken arm – *gebrochener Arm*
broken leg – *gebrochenes Bein*
burglary – *Einbruch*
fire – *Feuer*
heart attack – *Herzschlag*
I need an ambulance – *Ich brauche einen Krankenwagen*
I need a doctor – *Ich brauche einen Arzt*
intruder – *Eindringling*
mugging – *Überfall*
not breathing – *atmet nicht*
(I am) on the road to x – (*Ich bin*) *auf dem Weg zu x*
overdose – *Überdosis*
unconscious – *bewusstlos*
wounded – *verwundet*

and the German government makes a huge investment in its health system in comparison with most other governments.

State Healthcare

You have your pick of health insurance companies; conditions vary only slightly between them and you can generally count on receiving good service. Most insurance companies require you to make a quarterly €10 'co-payment' for each visit to a doctor (who should make referrals to any other doctors or specialists you wish to visit in that quarter, so that you can avoid additional co-payments). There are no co-payments for children.

If you'd like to have the extra services provided by private insurance but don't meet the salary requirement, you can take out supplementary insurance (***Zusatzversicherung***) for a monthly fee.

Private Healthcare

Statutory health insurance is compulsory unless you earn over

around €4,000 a month, in which case you may take out private cover. However, there isn't a huge difference in quality between statutory and private healthcare services in Germany, and there are no waiting lists for treatment for the state insured. Nevertheless, those with private insurance are given a private room, treated by the head doctor during hospital stays, may be entitled to 'alternative' treatment, and have a greater choice of doctors (some doctors accept only private patients as they earn more).

Choosing a Doctor

You have the freedom to choose any doctor, specialist or hospital, whether you have statutory or private insurance. If you'd like a doctor who speaks your native language, your consulate or embassy can provide you with a list; otherwise you can obtain recommendations from friends, colleagues or expatriate support groups. A doctor may recommend specialists, but you aren't obliged to take his advice.

Making an Appointment

To make a doctors' appointments, simply check the surgery times (*Sprechstunde*) and 'phone them. You should be able to obtain an appointment within a week for a general practitioner (GP) and a few weeks for a specialist, depending on how 'high profile' he is. Most surgeries close for lunch and are closed on Wednesdays or one other day each week. If you need a doctor and your GP is on holiday, he will leave the details of another (locum) doctor on his answerphone.

Visiting the Doctor

When you arrive at a surgery, inform the receptionist, take a seat and wait until your name is called. At some practices you may have to wait up to an hour and a half, at others less than 15 minutes. Going on a Monday morning usually means you must wait longer.

Consultations are quite formal and to get the most out of them you should be prepared to describe your symptoms and wishes exactly. Normally, you sit across a desk from your doctor fully clothed, and there's no bodily contact except a handshake at the start. Neither your blood pressure nor your temperature is taken, nor is any other examination performed unless you specifically request it. If you say you have a cold, the doctor takes your word for it, gives you a prescription and writes you off sick. If you think you have a serious illness, do some research beforehand and tell your doctor exactly what you think you have, and what tests you want carried out. You'll then be referred to the appropriate specialists.

Waiting room etiquette

It's typical to greet the other patients in a waiting room when you arrive. After that, you should keep quiet: there should be no loud conversation and mobile phones should be turned off.

Emergency Treatment

All state hospitals offer emergency treatment, and emergency departments are often full to bursting point. After ascertaining how urgent your case is, you're seen by a doctor. If you have a medical problem outside your doctor's surgery hours, you can go to the local *Bereitschaftsdienst* – an office open only 'out of hours' with a rota of doctors and specialists such as paediatricians, gynaecologists and orthopaedists. However, these are often crammed with unhealthy people, therefore you should go there only in an emergency.

Medicines

Germans are sceptical about medicines in general, and you need a prescription for almost any type of medication, although you can obtain aspirin or throat lozenges from a chemist's (*Apotheke*). Most doctors will prescribe or recommend herbal preparations before medication, and antibiotics are avoided like the plague. Germans are also averse to taking tablets and capsules, preferring soluble medicines. Vitamins in tablet form are practically unheard of and you must normally dissolve them in water to make a fizzy, orange-flavoured drink, which leaves a sickly after-taste.

Prescribed medications are pre-packaged and available immediately (should the chemist have them in stock) rather than made up while you wait. Prices are reasonable – usually under €5 – and if you have a regular prescription, a pharmacist will make out a 'standing order' for you.

Essential medications are free for children, the disabled and pregnant women, provided you have a prescription. However, you must always pay for over-the-counter medicines.

Hospitals

Hospitals provide rooms with one to four beds with en-suite bathrooms. Visiting hours must be adhered to and noisy guests aren't tolerated.

Mobile phones are forbidden, but a television (TV) and telephone are usually provided; to use the phone you need a prepaid card, from which the cost is deducted automatically. You aren't usually provided with a hospital gown – except for surgery – therefore it's up to you to bring your pyjamas and dressing gown. You also need to bring your own toiletries. Food is usually palatable, unless you're put on a diet, and you can sometimes choose from a menu. There's little privacy in German public hospitals, therefore you shouldn't be surprised if you're expected to use a bedpan, receive injections or have your blood drawn with staff and other patients looking on. Privately insured patients are accommodated in private rooms and receive hotel-like service – with toiletries and towels provided.

Nursing Care

German nurses are highly qualified and professional, but you might find them quite cold and impersonal at times. As with doctors, when dealing with nursing staff, you must be firm and direct about your wishes to get results.

Should you or a family member need home nursing care, it's covered by a separate statutory insurance (*Pflegeversicherung*), which is automatically deducted from your salary.

Medical Procedures

It isn't usual for patients to question medical procedures in Germany. If your doctor says you need a particular treatment, you're expected to accept and grin and bear it. If you have questions, you need to be assertive to get satisfactory answers. Doctors seldom make bed visits at hospitals unless you're privately insured; if they do, they may be harried and have an entourage of worshipping underlings. You may have better luck with the nurses, whom you'll see quite often.

Childbirth

Expectant mothers receive excellent treatment in Germany and have a wealth of options open to them. During pregnancy, you have regular check-ups and ultra-sounds, and your condition is closely monitored. If there's the slightest risk to you or your unborn child, you're given bed-rest in a hospital. For prenatal check-ups you may visit a gynaecologist or midwife, which is covered by state insurance. A midwife will visit you at home during your pregnancy, accompany you to the hospital for the birth and make home visits for the first few months after the birth. Hospitals often have a list of midwives in the local area.

Birth preparation classes are covered by your insurance and are highly recommended, as you'll learn about the procedures normally used and the options open to you. Usually, you choose a hospital according to the services it offers, which may include water births, birthing balls,

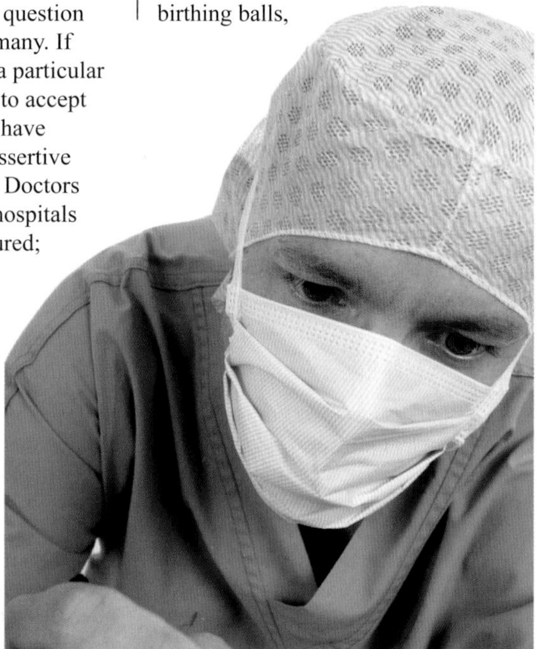

acupuncture, epidurals, etc. Homebirths are also possible. Be warned: birthing class teachers are often biased against pain relief during labour and may try to talk you out of an epidural. This same 'stoic' attitude may rear its head in the delivery room, unless you bring your own midwife with you. Voluntary caesarean sections are discouraged.

Partners are allowed to be present during the birth and during caesarean section unless you're under full anaesthesia. You're expected to care for your baby full time after birth.

If you suffer complications or are incapacitated after being sent home (e.g. in recovering from a caesarean section), housekeeping services are covered by your health insurance.

Post-treatment Care

You're normally allowed full convalescence in hospital, especially after giving birth, and might have to beg to be sent home. After being discharged, it's up to you to organise any necessary check-ups. If you've given birth, you can arrange home visits by a midwife.

INSURANCE

Compulsory insurance for individuals in Germany includes:

- health insurance (*Krankenversicherung*), unemployment insurance (*Arbeitslosenversicherung*), social security (*Rentenversicherung*) and nursing care insurance (*Pflegeversicherung*) for the employed;
- third party car insurance for car owners;
- third party property liability insurance for homeowners and tenants;
- life insurance for mortgage holders.

Other optional (but highly advisable) insurance includes, car breakdown, life, travel and household insurance and legal costs.

Health Insurance

Only the employed are eligible for statutory health insurance in Germany; everyone else must take out private health insurance. If you're moving from another EU country, you should apply for a European Health Insurance Card (EHIC), which will cover you for necessary treatment until you're eligible for German health insurance. If you take up a job in Germany, you can choose a statutory insurance company (*gesetzliche Krankenkasse*), which will provide the necessary registration form for your employer.

Car Insurance

EU regulations allow you to insure your car with any EU insurer, but if your vehicle is licensed in Germany, it must be insured with an insurer registered in Germany. Insurance documents must be carried in the car at all times, as you can be fined for not having them.

Household Insurance

Contents insurance in Germany usually covers your property in the event of damage by fire, burglary, vandalism, storm and water, and usually replaces items at their current value, up to certain limits. If you have especially valuable items, such as antiques or jewellery, you may need to take out additional insurance. Policies may also cover hotel or transportation costs incurred as a result of property damage.

Exterior areas usually aren't covered and there may be other exclusions, therefore it's important to check a policy carefully before you sign.

Claims

German insurance companies accept only written and fully documented claims. If a claim is for stolen goods, they require a copy of the police report.

EDUCATION

Choosing the right education for their children is one of the most challenging and important decisions parents need to make upon relocating to Germany.

To make the right decision it's essential that you research the different types of school – and think long term. The German system offers little flexibility: once you've committed to one type of school, there may be no turning back, therefore your choice will have lasting consequences for your child.

> **International Schools**
>
> **Germany has 28 international schools. In most cases, lessons are taught in English and follow the American educational system.**

German or International School?

If you're able to choose between a German and an international school, the following pros and cons of each will help you to make the best choice for your child.

International Schools

International schools are among Germany's elite schools and offer an English-language education. Your child is exposed to cultural and ethnic diversity, as pupils are from all over the globe, although most international schools have a high proportion of American and British students. The obvious downside is that they are extremely expensive, costing between €600 and €1,000 per month. There's a rapid turnover of pupils as parents are often re-located, and schools are isolated from the German

system (they may also be a long way from where you live), meaning that your child may have little exposure to the German language and culture (although German is part of the curriculum).

If you're planning to stay in Germany for five years or less, it's worth considering an international school as the system may be more like that of your home country, and it will be easier for your child to adapt to the teaching methods and to re-adapt when they return home (or move on to another country). Should you later choose to stay longer in Germany, however, the inflexible German school system may not accept the international educational standard and your child may need to make up any 'deficient' subjects.

Germany's PISA (Programme for International Student Assessment) results show that not only are children from migrant and lower-class families less successful than others, but the inequality is greater than in any other industrialised nation.

State Schools

If you're going to live in Germany indefinitely, or are considering it, a state school may be the best option. Those with German school backgrounds have better job prospects (in Germany) and an easier time getting into a German university. Another reason for choosing a state school is that it gives your children the chance to integrate more fully into the German way of life, including the language and culture, and to have German friends. A state school will also be closer to home and part of the local community.

On the other hand, the older your children are, the harder it will be for them to adapt to the German system – both academically and socially – particularly the language. German schools expect a lot of parent involvement and help with homework, which may be difficult for you if your German isn't good.

Bi-lingual Schools

If you're planning to stay in Germany for a long time and would like your child to be exposed to the German language while still having lessons in your native language, a bi-lingual private school might be the best option.

Bi-lingual (i.e. English-German) private schools are becoming more popular in Germany, especially in the major cities. They aren't international schools, which means they follow the German curriculum, but unlike state

schools offer extra-curricular activities, such as sports and music. Private school fees are calculated on a sliding scale according to your income, so a bi-lingual school may be cheaper than an international school.

German schools require students to study religion (usually Christianity) or ethics. Some schools have introduced classes on Islam, aimed at Germany's increasing Muslim population.

The German Education System

Each state devises its own education programme, but although information below applies to most states. Primary school (*Grundschule*) starts between the ages of five-and-a-half and six-and-a-half, depending on the month your child was born. In some states, children are held back a year if they don't speak sufficient German or are considered immature.

There are three main types of secondary school, which pupils progress to in accordance with their academic performance. *Hauptschule* is more for pupils who are less gifted academically, *Realschule* for those of average achievement and *Gymnasium*, which is equivalent to a British grammar school, for those who plan to attend university.

Most *Hauptschule* graduates do an apprenticeship in a manual trade or continue studying at a vocational school, while *Realschule* graduates normally go on to do an apprenticeship in a commercial trade or medical profession. *Gymnasium* concludes with the *Abitur* examination, which comprises four subjects and is a university entrance qualification.

Most schools finish by 1pm and offer no lunch, but there has been huge pressure on the government to introduce more all-day schools (*Ganztagsschulen*) to accommodate the needs of working parents and to improve educational standards. The government has pledged €4bn to create around 10,000 *Ganztagsschulen* by 2009 and had already opened 6,400 by the end of 2007. All-day schools include more extra-curricular activities and tutoring with homework. Lessons continue until 4 or 5pm and there may also be evening activities.

One of the greatest shortcomings of the German school system is that a child's academic (and career) future is practically set in stone at the age of 10 or 11. Other important points to note about German education are:

- Instruction is mostly academic (e.g. maths, science, German), and extra-curricular activities are rarely offered. The onus is on parents to arrange social, creative and sports activities for your children.
- A lot of learning is done by rote and students are expected to memorise huge chunks of text and lists of facts.
- Learning isn't about developing the individual, but rather following the programme as a group.
- All subjects have textbooks, which are followed to the letter.
- Primary school classes are mixed ability, therefore both gifted and weak pupils must adapt to the pace.
- The system has little tolerance of non-German speakers and few teachers speak English except in bi-lingual schools.
- Students can be required to repeat a year if they don't meet the required standard; if they still aren't up to scratch after a repeated year, they're sent to a lower-level school (if applicable).

If you're fortunate enough to have a choice of *Kindergärten*, ask yourself the following questions:

Location – Is it near your home or workplace?

Hours – Are the hours convenient and do they fit in with your schedule? (Note that many are only open until 12 or 1pm and close for school holidays).

Teaching methods & atmosphere – Do you agree with the teaching methods? Do you think your child would like it?

Cost – Can you afford it? The youth office (*Jugendamt*) offers subsidies of up to around €360 per month (depending on your income) for *Kindergarten* costs. Details are available from local social services offices (*Sozialbürgerhaus*), listed in the yellow pages. Be aware that getting a subsidy takes times and involves completing lots of paperwork

- Homework is excessive (a minimum of two hours' a night) and parents are expected to help their children with it.

University

- Degree courses last at least four years.
- Many students take longer than programmed to achieve their degrees, finishing as late as the age of 28.
- Only students with the highest *Abitur* grades may choose the university

they wish to attend. Others are allocated places.

- There are no grants, but student loans are available.

In some areas, crèche and nursery school places are extremely limited, irrespective of whether they're state or private facilities. Children are often put on several waiting lists before they're even born.

Day Care & Pre-schools

Nursery schools (*Kindergärten*) take children from around the age of three, or when they're toilet-trained, and crèches (*Kinderkrippen*) from six months. There are state and private schools as well as parent-run 'initiatives' (*Elterninitiativen*), which are partially subsidised by the state. Elterninitiativen give parents more say in their child's education, but also involve extra work and inconvenience. You may be asked to provide meals and a washing service or to step in if a teacher is ill; if you take a place on the management board, it's like a full-time (unpaid) job.

You may not have much choice of pre-schools or day care centres, as there simply aren't enough of them in some areas. The best way to get a place is to put your child's name on as many waiting lists as possible immediately – they're non-binding and free. You might have a better chance of finding a place at a bi-lingual *Kindergarten*, as they must have a certain German-foreigner ratio.

COUNCIL SERVICES

Refuse Collection

Refuse (garbage) collections are weekly or fortnightly, depending on the arrangement you or your landlord has made with the local *Stadtverwaltung*,

except for Sundays and public holidays. You put your rubbish in a sealed plastic bag and deposit it in a bin on the street or in the courtyard behind your building. You aren't permitted to put your rubbish in a neighbouring bin or to leave rubbish bags lying around if a bin is full.

If you have bulky items to dispose of, such as furniture or appliances, they must be taken to a *Sperrmüll* centre in your area; there's normally no charge. You may also dispose of rubble there.

The German comedian, Otto, summed up the German obsession with recycling (and the recycling process) when he explained how a tea bag should be recycled in one of his stand-up routines: the bag itself as 'compost', the string as 'material', the label as 'paper' and the staple that holds them together as 'metal'.

Recycling

Germans are serious about recycling, but the procedure is somewhat complicated. Paper and organic rubbish (e.g. leftover food and coffee grounds) can be thrown in the paper (*Papier*) and organic (*Bio*) recycling bins designated for your building, but cans, glass, plastic and other packaging material must be put in the grey communal bins in your area (not necessarily near your building). Batteries must be recycled at supermarkets and drugstores, which have a collection box near the entrance. Mobile phones can be sent back to the manufacturer.

When you purchase anything, the shop is required to recycle the packaging for you, and they normally have a bin for this purpose. If you order large items, such as furniture or household appliances, the company must take the packaging away on delivery.

You may see local newspaper advertisements for a free collection service for old furniture and electrical equipment, which are either sold in aid of charities or 'recycled'. There are also regular collections of old clothes, announced by leaflets and posters.

UTILITIES

Germany is one of the world's largest consumers of energy and costs are high.

Electricity

Electricity supply (*Strom*) has been privatised and there's an array of 'brokers' that purchase energy from the generating companies and sell it to consumers in a variety of 'packages' and 'plans'. It's therefore worthwhile shopping around for the best deal. A useful website where the various offerings are compared is 💻 www.verivox.de/power (in German only).

Germany has an excellent infrastructure and you shouldn't encounter any major supply problems. In some rural areas, the supply is somewhat unreliable, in which case you may wish to install surge protectors and battery backup for your computer and other sensitive appliances.

Gas

Mains gas is generally available only in main towns and cities, and there's a limited range of suppliers. For a list

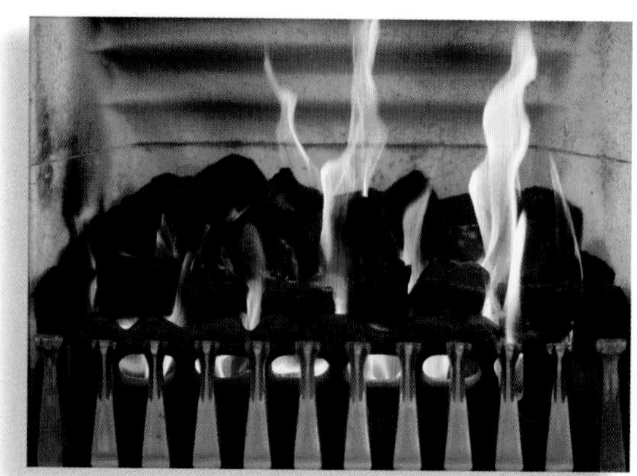

appliances regularly to prevent damage.

Despite the high quality of the tap water, Germans insist on drinking carbonated mineral water. In restaurants you don't usually receive water with your meal, unless you pay for bottled mineral water.

Telephone

Fixed and mobile telephone services are available practically everywhere

of local gas suppliers, look in the yellow pages under *Gasversorgung*. Even where it's available, there isn't normally a cooker connection as almost all German cookers are electric, and it usually isn't possible to have gas installed in a single apartment within a building.

Water

Water costs are included in the communal charges of all apartments and most 'community' houses; individual houses are metered. Costs are based on usage and you have no choice of provider. Washing machines and dishwashers have only a cold water connection and heat the water internally, therefore it's no good bringing machines with you that require a hot water intake.

Water quality and hardness (i.e. lime content) vary with the area, but tap water is filtered rather than chlorinated and is safe to drink throughout Germany, except perhaps in small rural communities supplied from wells and springs. Bavarian tap water comes from alpine springs and is considered to be of the highest quality in Europe, but it has a high lime content and it's necessary to decalcify coffee machines and other

from the big brother of all telephone companies, Deutsche Telekom, which owns over 90 per cent of German telephone lines and rents them to smaller companies (there are also from a number of other providers).

You're usually offered a 'package', e.g. internet plus phone, including unlimited use for a fixed monthly fee (*Flatrate*). As with electricity, it's advisable to shop around for the best deal. Don't be seduced by attractive offers without reading the small print; for example, 'unlimited' calls may in fact be limited to your local area or to Germany, and long-distance calls and calls to mobile phones may cost an arm and a leg – in some cases, local calls are only free if you call someone with the same provider.

Contracts are usually for at least 12 months, and you're required to give three months' notice of cancellation. Being over-charged and receiving unannounced tariff changes isn't unheard of. If a complaint gets you nowhere, you should contact the consumer protection agency (*Verbraucherzentrale*).

Installation & Connection

To have a phone line installed you can go to a Deutsche Telekom T-com shop or register online at 💻 www.t-com.de. Installation costs around €60, although if you're taking over the line of a previous owner or tenant you pay a reduced 'connection' fee of €30. Bills are sent out monthly and can be paid by direct debit or at banks.

Internet

The internet is very popular in Germany, where there's a huge number of internet service providers (ISPs) and an abundance of access packages. ISPs may offer the following types of internet connections:

- **Analogue** – the slowest and least efficient but adequate for people who don't use the internet for more than around 20 hours per month;
- **ISDN** – a digital connection that allows you to use the telephone and the internet simultaneously;
- **ADSL** – a broadband digital connection over the telephone line with higher data transfer speeds than ISDN (as high as 24,000 kilobits per second);
- **Cable** – a broadband connection that can send up to 30 megabits per second.

Deutsche Telekom's internet service, T-Online (💻 www.t-online.de), is the most popular and offers a variety of tariffs depending on the kind of connection you choose. An ADSL (or DSL as it's called in Germany) connection costs between around €15 and €30 per month for unlimited access (Germany has over 10mn DSL customers). The best deals usually involve a combination of telephone and internet connection (dubbed 'call and surf') and cost from around €40 per month (unlimited), depending on the line speed.

Other major service providers include AOL (💻 www.aol.de) and there are also dozens of smaller ISPs who advertise in local newspapers and magazines, and on TV and radio.

STAYING INFORMED

Television

German TV could hardly be called quality entertainment – and you have to pay a licence fee of around €200 a year to receive it. Programmes generally consist of quiz shows, chat shows, 'reality' shows, live courtroom shows ... and football, alongside news programmes and documentaries. Investigative reporting is quite popular and usually reflects the anxiety (*Angst*) the average German feels, covering such topics as food scares, holiday disasters, shoddy builders and crooked estate agents.

Soft- and hard-core pornography is shown on some channels in the evening, and even during the day some programming features partial nudity. The kids' channel Kika shows appropriate programmes for school-age children, and in the evening the beloved Sandman sends the children to sleep – provided, of course, they have a TV in their bedroom.

Cable and satellite TV offer a wider choice of channels, including free-to-air (FTA – free and unencrypted) English-language stations such as MTV, CNN and Sky News, but not the BBC or ITV channels, for which you must pay. Almost half of German households have access to cable services and almost as many have satellite dishes.

Caution

As soon as you've registered your residence in Germany you must license your TV and radio with the *Gebühreneinzugszentrale* (*GEZ*) – both are included in the €200 annual fee. You can obtain the necessary form when you register your address at the registrar's office or at any bank, or you can register online at 💻 www.gez.de. If you don't, you'll receive a call and, although in theory you aren't obliged to let a *GEZ* representative into your home, in practice it's usually impossible to keep them out!

Radio

Many radio stations in Germany are syndicated and therefore virtually indistinguishable; they're also highly commercial, broadcasting not only lots of advertisements but also 'sponsored' programmes. They often mix rock, country, jazz, etc., but designate one hour per week to a specific period, such as '70s or '80s. 'Classical' stations often play film soundtracks in addition to Bach and Beethoven. Most stations broadcast news flashes and traffic reports, and in some cases listeners call in to warn other drivers where the police have set up a *Blitz* (speed) camera. If German radio is too indiscriminating for your taste, you can receive radio broadcasts from your home country via the internet.

The Press

There are essentially two types of German newspaper: serious/intellectual and sensationalist/mindless. The interesting thing is that no one is ashamed to be caught reading the 'gutter' press. In fact, you rarely see anyone reading anything else on the underground (*U-Bahn*).

The main national newspapers are the following:

- ***Bild Zeitung*** – the most widely read and therefore most low-brow paper – with a photo of a topless woman on the front page. Its official circulation is around 3.5m (the highest newspaper circulation in Europe and the sixth-highest in the world), but it's estimated that one in six Germans read it – or at least the front page. As well as the national edition, there are 32 'regional' editions published from Monday to Saturday. The focus is on celebrities, but articles also play on the public's fears and prejudices, with huge, exaggerated headlines.

- ***Frankfurter Allgemeine Zeitung*** – the second-largest national/regional daily after the *Süddeutscher* (see below), with a circulation of around 365,000, and liberal-conservative;

- ***Der Spiegel*** – a weekly news magazine published online at 10pm on Saturdays and on paper the following Monday (Sunday in the major cities), selling 1.1m printed copies per week throughout

Europe. Costing a whopping €3.50 per issue, *Der Spiegel* is famous for its criticism of public figures, including politicians, and for uncovering corruption, and it's said to have a significant influence on government. Founded in Munich before the First World War, it was shut down by the Allied forces soon after the Second World War (because of its criticism of their policies) but reinstated in 1947. Recent surveys indicate that it has lost its political edge, however, and one-third of Germans feel that the Süddeutsche Zeitung (see below) now has greater influence.

- ***Süddeutsche Zeitung*** – the largest national/regional daily in Germany with a circulation of around 450,000. The SZ contains thought-provoking editorials of liberal bias, as well as extensive sections on culture and the arts, rather like the British Guardian newspaper.
- ***Die Welt*** – a conservative daily selling around 265,000 copies. *Welt am Sonntag* is the Sunday version and *Welt Kompakt* a condensed version aimed at younger readers.

In an effort to help the poor earn some money in a respectable manner and avoid social isolation, some cities 'employ' the homeless to sell magazines. Prices are negotiable and vendors are allowed to keep around 40 to 50 per cent of the revenue but must follow certain rules, such as no drinking of alcohol or begging (while selling, that is ...).

BANKING

German banks are modern and efficient. Although the trend is towards online banking, many Germans still make teller transactions and use service terminals inside and outside banks. German banks are conservative, even with long-term customers and especially with foreigners.

The following is a summary of German banking and payment practices that may be unfamiliar to newcomers:

- **Bank charges** – Charges vary from bank to bank, so before opening an account you should ask the following questions: Is the bank affiliated with any other bank so that you can use their cash machines without being charged? Are there fees for transfers, bank statements, etc. and, if so, what are they? Is there an automatic monthly 'service' fee (most banks have one)? If not, what are the requirements for free banking? Most banks require a minimum monthly deposit of €1,000 or your monthly salary must be direct-deposited each month; some charge a fee unless you bank only online.
- **Bank managers** – Every time you need to make a significant change

to your account (e.g. on changing jobs), you should go to the branch where you opened the account and speak to your bank manager directly. German bank managers are usually friendly and helpful, but may try to sell you insurance policies and savings plans; do some research before signing up for anything.

- **Cash** – In order to withdraw cash over the counter, you need photo identification in addition to your bank or credit card.
- **Cash machines** (ATM) – If the machine (*Geldautomat*) is marked 'international', instructions are available in a number of languages. If you make a cash withdrawal from a machine that doesn't belong to your bank, there may be a charge of around €5, although many banks have agreements with other banks that allow you to withdraw from their machines free of extra charge.
- **Cheques** – German banks (and other institutions) are moving towards paperless transactions, therefore cheques are rarely used. Banks don't offer cheque books and if you order a bank cheque (or draft), you must pay a fee.
- **Credit cards** – Germans are cautious with their money – and so are banks – so credit cards normally allow you to delay payment for only four weeks, after which the entire amount is debited from your account. Revolving credit – credit that you pay off in monthly instalments – isn't popular and may be difficult to obtain by those without a credit history in Germany. There's also an annual fee of between €20 and €100 for all credit cards, depending on the level of service provided. What's more, credit cards aren't widely accepted in Germany; the main exceptions are large department stores, hotels and some flashier shops and restaurants. MasterCard and Visa are the most popular, followed by American Express and, occasionally, Diners Card.
- **Debit cards** – Payment by debit card (EC Karte) is popular in Germany and they're accepted in most shops and supermarkets. Some shops require you to enter your PIN, others need your signature, and they occasionally request identification.
- **Direct debits** – In Germany, people trust the 'authorities' such as telephone and energy companies, and it's usual to

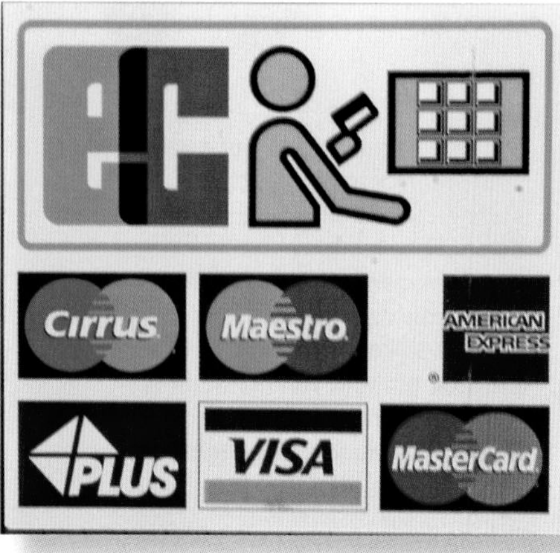

give them permission to debit your account directly (such authorisation is known as *Einzugsermächtigung*). They send you a paper bill by post detailing the charges, and then debit the amount automatically a week or so later. It's wise to request a detailed bill when you sign any contract and to check charges as soon as you receive it. If you find a mistake, you can stop payment.

- **Money changing machines** – There are machines in tourist areas that change foreign notes to euros.
- **Opening hours** – Banks are typically open from 8.45am to 4pm on Mondays, Tuesdays, Wednesdays and Fridays, and until 6pm on Thursdays. They're closed at weekends and on public holidays. Small branches and branches in small towns normally close for lunch between 12.30 and 1.30pm.
- **Service terminals** – You can access service terminals in bank foyers 24 hours a day (with your bankcard and PIN) for all sorts of transactions, including bill payment.
- **Standing orders** – The preferred method of payment in Germany for regular bills, where the amount is the same every month (e.g. rent), is by standing order (*Dauerauftrag*). You can set up or cancel an order in minutes at a service terminal, online or over the counter. If you wish to stop payment, you should inform your bank at least two weeks in advance.

Fraudsters tamper with cash machines in order to steal cards and security numbers – if your card is lost in an ATM, your should contact your bank immediately and, if necessary, cancel your card.

Banking Security

- When entering your PIN, always use your other hand to cover the keypad so that no one can see or record your number.
- If you see anything suspicious about a cash machine, such as plastic applied to the keypad, don't use it, and report the irregularity immediately. All machines display an emergency number to call outside banking hours.
- Never give personal or financial information by email to anyone, even if the email appears to be from your bank. **A bank will NEVER send you an email asking for your confidential security details.**
- Never click on links included in emails claiming to be from your bank.
- Keep your anti-virus programme regularly updated.
- Only use confidential information, such as your user name, password and PIN, when using your bank's secure website.

TAXES

If you're employed, income tax (*Einkommensteuer*) is deducted automatically from your salary and you don't need to file a tax return unless you have another source of income or are expecting (or hoping) to get a tax refund. Most goods and services attract value added tax (*Mehrwertsteuer/MwSt or Umsatzsteuer/USt*), the standard rate being 19 per cent. There's no wealth tax in Germany and most capital gains are untaxed, but there are inheritance (estate) and gift taxes.

Getting Help

Getting used to a new tax system is always difficult (the one you were used to was probably complicated enough), but Germany is blessed with many sources of support for taxpayers. If you need to file a return – which is required of all self-employed people – it's advisable (at least the first time) to hire a tax adviser (*Steuerberater*). A tax adviser usually charges per hour, so it's best to have all your paperwork in order before the clock starts ticking. The tax office (*Finanzamt*) rarely disputes returns submitted by tax advisers and you're less likely to have audits.

US citizens must file tax returns in Germany and in the US.

If you aren't self-employed but want to file a tax return (e.g. you're expecting a refund), you can save money by becoming a member of a taxpayers' association (*Lohnsteuerhilfeverein*) for an annual fee of around €100 for a single person, or €150 for a married couple filing jointly. Your annual fee includes tips on what deductions you can claim, and an adviser completes all the paperwork and files it for you. You'll be given an estimate of your tax credit or charge on the spot, which is usually accurate. If you wish to renew your membership, your adviser will save your information, making subsequent tax returns easier to complete.

Tax Fraud

Tax evasion is a serious crime in Germany and isn't worth the risk. The tax office has the right to monitor your bank account to obtain data from banks overseas. If you're caught working 'on the black' (i.e. without declaring your income for tax), you can be expelled from the country, not to mention that you won't have access to health insurance, social security benefits or workers' rights.

If you do any freelance work that requires an invoice, the paper trail will eventually catch up with you, so it's best to declare it.

COST OF LIVING

Germany has a high standard of living and high wages, but prices and taxes are also high. The average cost of living for a small German household is around €2,300 per month. In the major cities you can expect your cost of living to be significantly higher, due mainly to the cost of rents or property. Munich is the country's most expensive city, where rents are around twice as high as in eastern Germany.

However, Germans are avid bargain-hunters and there are plenty of low-cost retail outlets and regular sales. You can, of course, save a lot by buying online, e.g. on (German) eBay and on the websites of the large mail-order companies, such as Neckermann (💻 www.neckermann.de), Quelle (💻 www.quelle.de) and Otto (💻 www.otto.de), the last being the world's largest. Neckermann, Otto and Quelle also have stores in most German cities and maintain agencies in smaller cities and towns, where customers can consult catalogues and place orders. Most small items are delivered within 24 hours and even larger appliances and furniture are usually delivered quicker than by local stores, e.g. in a matter of days rather than weeks. For more information on shopping see **Chapter 9**.

For services, such as telephone and internet connection and energy supplies, it's advisable to shop around and read the small print before buying.

4.
BREAKING THE ICE

One of the best ways of making yourself at home in Germany, and easing the pains of homesickness and culture shock, is meeting and getting to know Germans. Making new friends anywhere can be a challenge, but the language and cultural barriers you'll face in Germany make it even more difficult. This chapter provides information about important aspects of German society and the expatriate community, and advice on how to behave in social situations, topics to steer clear of in conversation and ways of dealing with confrontation.

It isn't true that the Germans have no sense of humour; it's just that nobody but a German can understand it.

COMMUNITY LIFE

The German countryside consists of closely-knit communities that have remained settled in one village or region for generations, where outsiders (including German outsiders) may not feel welcome straightaway. The onus is on you to introduce yourself to the neighbours, and even then it might take a while for people to warm to you. Germans place a great deal of value on order and privacy and don't always take kindly to outsiders, who they may believe will disrupt things.

In small towns many people live in semi-detached homes or other shared housing, according to strict rules (see below), and newcomers are scrutinised to check that they abide by those rules. In cities, as in most countries, there's a high degree of anonymity and you may go years without getting to know – or even seeing – your neighbours.

As everywhere in the world, you'll find that some people are open and friendly and that there are some hard nuts to crack. Bear in mind that, as a newcomer, you're the one who wants and needs to make friends, which isn't necessarily the case for your neighbours, who may already have a wide circle of friends. You might feel a small sense of accomplishment when after a few attempts your greeting is answered with a friendly '*Hello*'. On the other hand, if you greet people regularly and still get the cold shoulder, it's probably best to give them up as a bad job.

Introducing yourself should be done in an unobtrusive manner, as people enjoy their right to privacy, therefore instead of knocking on neighbours' doors it's best to wait until you see each other in the lift or entrance hall, or on the way to work. Shopping at local stores, going to local libraries and community centres, and joining in local activities are good ways of becoming a part of the community – and improving your German.

Community Rules

When visiting the German countryside, you're likely to be enchanted by the picturesque, almost fairytale villages, with their homogeneous architecture and colour schemes. This homogeneity is due, in part, to strict community rules (*Hausordnung*). Community rules concern communal areas, such as patios, gardens, entrance halls and parking spaces, and private areas visible from outside e.g. balconies and facades. If you wish to make any alterations to the exterior appearance of your property, e.g. the colour of awnings and facades, the type of roof tiles, and the style and positioning of satellite dishes (which are often not allowed at all) – especially if your building is under a preservation order – you must obtain approval or face the consequences, which may include lawsuits, trumped-up 'charges' and even physical attack!

To help you get off on the right foot with your neighbours, here are some rules to watch out for:

- **Laundry** – Rules govern the use of communal laundry rooms and the hanging of laundry (which is often prohibited on balconies).
- **Noise** – Buildings often impose a quiet time from 1 to 2pm and from 10pm to 7am, when no loud noise such as drilling or even vacuuming is allowed.
- **Pets** – Pets may not be allowed at all; if they are, there will be restrictions and clean-up rules.
- **Rubbish** – Rules govern how, where and when rubbish must be dispsed of.
- **Storage** – There will be rules telling you where you can (and cannot) store bicycles and pushchairs.

SEXUAL ATTITUDES

Germans have an extremely open attitude to sex and nudity – too much so for some. Pornographic television programmes and topless shots on front pages of daily newspapers are commonplace, while ads for hygiene products often show 'tasteful' nudity. Not only do women sometimes go topless at the pool or on beaches, but letting it all hang out in the park and on the beach isn't uncommon, even in places where it isn't officially permitted. Saunas are often mixed and you're out of place or unwelcome if you wear a swimsuit.

statue, Schloss Sans Souci, Potsdam

Naturism (*Freikörperkultur*) is alive and well among all age groups and body shapes in Germany, with an estimated 10m Germans a year taking naturist holidays. There's even a German travel agency offering nudist flights: passengers remove their clothing after boarding and start their holiday as they mean to go on. Nudism isn't considered a display of sexuality, rather an expression of oneness with nature. Now and then you may wish that some people would leave their clothes on, but at least the Germans cannot be criticised for being ashamed of their bodies (although some should be!). In any case, it isn't polite to stare, no matter what you see.

There are government-regulated red-light districts in many German cities. Prostitutes' income is subject to tax and they're eligible for health insurance and social security benefits.

Men

Men's and women's roles are still quite sharply divided in Germany. Many men live at home until the age of 25 or even 30, their mothers doing their laundry, housekeeping and cooking, and when finally they marry, their wives (or a paid housekeeper) take over this role. According to the Federal Statistics Office's 'Time Budget Survey', German women spend ten hours per week more than men on housework and gardening.

Although half of the workforce in Germany is made up of women and attitudes are changing, the general view is that men are the breadwinners and women are expected to give up their careers when they become mothers.

When a boy's father dies, he may be told that he's now the man of the house, and when he becomes a father himself, he's expected to work even harder than before in order to be a good provider for his family. When a couple applies for a loan at a bank, most questions are directed at the man, as the assumption is made that he's the main breadwinner of the family and head of the household.

Men's Day

Father's Day falls on Ascension Day, which is a bank holiday in Germany, and an occasion for certain 'traditions' to be perpetuated in men's clubs – mainly involving drinking and playing cards. Typically, there are certain rules to be observed; for example, each man must wear a flower (sometimes a lilac) in his hat or isn't allowed to speak to any woman on that day unless she's a waitress. Customs vary from club to club.

The tradition of a men's day in Germany goes back to the 19th century in the Berlin area, when young men gathered to go carousing and smoke cigars, while others dragged carts full of beer up the mountains for parties. Nowadays, some fathers put their day off to better use: to take the family out, for example.

Women

There isn't much of a grey area for German women, who are expected to be either career women or mothers – and a woman who tries to be both may be considered a *Rabenmutter* (raven mother, meaning like a raven, which leaves its young to fend for themselves), although the term isn't

used in polite conversation. Giving up her career is often a conscious choice a woman makes when she becomes a mother, and many German women accept this role in society. However, a growing number of women choose to forego marriage and motherhood in order to remain successful, unrestricted career women.

Only a generation ago, almost all women were housewives, whose major duties were to raise children, carry out household chores and help care for elderly family members. Some of that traditionalism persists today, but other factors that influence whether a mother quits working include the extent of government benefits and the availability of childcare facilities.

Nursery school (*Kindergarten*) places need to be reserved before a child is even born in some cases and even then applicants are means tested. A woman who's on her second pregnancy can be turned down on the grounds that she will now have to stay home to take care of her children anyway. Even if you find a place for your child, most nursery schools (and primary schools) are finished for the day by 1pm, giving a mother little or no free time for work.

A new child benefit scheme encourages parents to stop working or reduce their work time to under 30 hours per week, in return for which they receive two-thirds of their former pay for 12 or 14 months. Although it's usually mothers who claim the benefit, it has also led to an increase in the number of stay-at-home fathers. According to the Federal Statistics Office, 10.5 per cent of benefit applicants in 2007 were men, up from 3.3 per cent in 2006 (under the former, lower-paying system).

Unlike in rural France, for example, it's socially 'acceptable' for women to go out alone or with other women in Germany and doesn't imply promiscuity. In fact, the sexes are quite independent and couples sometimes prefer to take holidays separately or to have separate nights out; they don't feel the need to everything together.

Because of Germans' essentially private nature, the best way to meet a potential girlfriend or boyfriend is through other friends. German men don't usually randomly chat up women at a bar, for instance, and if they do, it's probably not because they're looking for a serious relationship. Many young men aren't interested in long-term commitment, whereas women are often searching for a stable relationship; if they aren't getting the right signals from their partner, they will ask the dreaded question: 'Where is this relationship going?' If she doesn't like the answer she gets, she will waste no more time on him. Many young German women find older men more ready to commit.

Homosexuals

Although it's widely known that homosexuals were persecuted during the Third Reich, the gay community is an accepted part of modern Germany. Same-sex couples can register their 'union' under the Life Partnership Act (*Eingetragene Lebenspartnerschaft*) and enjoy many of the same rights as married couples, including social security benefits, inheritance, alimony and adoption. They don't receive the same tax benefits as a married couple, however. The civil ceremony is carried out by a notary in some states and by a justice of the peace in others. Berlin has the highest number of registered same-sex couples.

Legal considerations notwithstanding, the general attitude of Germans is live and let live, and many gays don't have difficulty 'coming out of the closet' (if they were ever in one), socially at least. Nevertheless, it's wiser not to discuss your sexual preferences at a job interview.

Gay pride events are frequent and are officially supported by the mayor in most towns and cities. The current mayor of Berlin, who is himself gay, has been known to march in parades with his constituents. Major cities – especially Berlin, Cologne, Dusseldorf and Hamburg – have thriving gay scenes. In Berlin and Munich, gay men and women have separate 'scenes', whereas smaller cities and towns have close-knit, integrated communities. Smaller towns and villages may be more conservative and less welcoming of an 'alternative lifestyle', though people in the former East Germany are in some ways more tolerant, as they haven't had the same religious upbringing as some strict Catholic communities.

A useful resource for newcomers is *Spartacus* magazine, which is available internationally and describes the gay scene in each city in a number of languages and highlights the best places to meet people. Regional guides can be found at news kiosks and gay bars, while the internet is also a good way to investigate Germany's gay scene.

MEETING PEOPLE

Meeting people isn't easy in Germany – even for Germans. Natives who move from one city or region to another often complain that it's hard to make friends.

There are a few reasons for this. Until recently Germany didn't have an 'immigrant culture' (unlike the US and Australia, for example), therefore the majority of Germans didn't need to mingle and make new acquaintances, as most already had a network of close friends. Another reason is that Germans like to separate their public and private lives and don't readily open the door to their personal life. As a foreigner, of course, there's the additional language and culture barrier; unless you find people who speak your language, how can you begin to communicate with them? If you can communicate, can you find something in common, considering your different values and experience?

The following list offers some advice on how to meet Germans and other expatriates:

- **At work** – Your work environment may contain lots of potential friends, though if your company is of the more conservative type, it may take a while to break the ice. People who address you as Sie (see **Chapter 5**) are keeping a respectful distance; work is work and private is private.

  If you're on a first name *du* basis (and in some companies this is the norm), there's a better chance of getting to know someonTry asking a friendly colleague to lunch or for a coffee and see how it goes. German companies usually organise parties at Christmas and on other occasions, which are a good opportunity to make friends. If your company is international and English-speaking, this will obviously help you overcome cultural and language barriers. In fact, many companies in Germany use English as their official language, which makes the atmosphere quite different from a company in which only German is spoken. For one thing, there's no *du* and *Sie* distinction, which cuts down on the formality, and your colleagues have probably visited the headquarters in the US, UK or another country often enough to understand something of the culture – or at least to appreciate that other countries may have very different cultures. In any case, people in such a company are likely to be more laid back, which means you'll be more comfortable about inviting your colleagues for a coffee or a beer and getting to know them.

- **Expatriate networks** – There's no shortage of expat clubs and activities in the major cities, and they also exist in small towns; expat networks are a great source of information, support and often friends. In some cases, there are groups that cater specifically to singles or families.
- **Further education courses** – The German *Volkshochschule*, a national network of schools, offers a wide variety of evening courses, which is a great way to meet people with similar interests; local schools can be found via : www.vhs.de.
- **Language lessons** – The German language is one of the major barriers to making German friends, therefore enrolling in German classes is the best place to start, particularly as language schools usually organise social events as well as formal lessons. If nothing else, you'll meet other foreigners who are going through a similar experience. Another possibility is to arrange 'language exchange' sessions with Germans who want to learn English.

> **How charmed I am when I overhear a German word which I understand!**
> Mark Twain (American writer)

- **Clubs** – Germans love joining clubs, such as singing and sports clubs, and there should be plenty in your area. Ask at the town hall (*Rathaus*) or look in local newspapers for details.
- **Religious services** – If you belong to a religion, a good way to meet people is to go to the local church, mosque or synagogue. Churches, in particular, organise a wide range of social activities.
- **School or childcare facilities** – Schools and *Kindergärten* (nursery schools) often arrange social activities and have parents' associations; check the school notice board or ask other parents. Try to get to know other parents when you take your children to school and collect them. As you have a common interest – children – it's easy to break the ice.
- **Irish pubs** – There are Irish pubs in most German cities, which are a good place to meet friendly English-speaking people.
- **Beer halls or beer gardens** – If you're in southern Germany and you like German beer (if you don't, what are doing in Germany?), go along to a beer hall or garden and sit on a bench with a pint or a *Maß* (litre) and you'll soon be chatting to the people squashed up against you and swaying with the oom-pah-pah music.

Where & When to Meet

A good place to meet is at a café, restaurant, pub or beer garden –

but make sure you're on time, as punctuality is important in Germany. It isn't usual to invite people to your home until you know them well. On the other hand, if you're invited to a German's home, you should consider it an honour.

Paying the Bill

You should pay for exactly what you've consumed. At a pub, the waiter marks your beer mat to keep track of your drinks and, when you ask to pay, adds up the bill at the table. Elsewhere, make sure you keep track of how many you've had. You should round up the total to provide a tip.

It isn't usual to buy rounds unless it's your birthday, when you're expected to pay for your friends' drinks.

INVITATIONS

Receiving Invitations

Receiving an invitation to a German's home is symbolic of being let into their private sphere, and indicates that they consider you a friend. Such an invitation is therefore not to be taken lightly and you should feel privileged. Your host will have gone to a lot of trouble to make the house spotless and orderly, and, if a specific time was fixed, arriving on time is essential as it shows respect for your host. If you're invited at around 3pm, you can expect to be served coffee and cake.

You won't be invited for aperitifs, as, for example, in France; a lunch invitation will normally be for midday and a dinner invitation for around 7pm. The invitation normally extends to your spouse or partner, but may not include your children unless specifically mentioned. If your host has children, they're likely to have been sent off to their grandparents or to friends for the evening.

Dress Code

What you wear depends on the occasion and the other people at the event. If it's a work party or an important occasion such as an engagement, dressing up is called for. If it's a casual dinner at home with a few friends, smart casual should be fine.

Gifts

It's a good idea to bring a gift to show your appreciation for the invitation. A bottle of wine (not German wine unless it's exceptional), a box of chocolates, a bouquet of flowers or something from your home country are all acceptable gifts. In some regions there are superstitions about flowers and, although young people may not worry too much, it's better to be safe than sorry: an odd number of flowers is traditional (but not 13, which is considered unlucky) for aesthetic and superstitious reasons; avoid white chrysanthemums and carnations, which are for funerals, and red roses (for lovers). You should remove the wrapping paper before presenting the bouquet. Germans like flowers (which are relatively expensive), and there are florists at most underground (*U-Bahn*) stations and busy street corner, so if you're in a hurry to get to a party you can easily pick some up on the way.

The Meal

Lunch is the main meal of the day in Germany and there's usually a soup or salad to start, and a meat dish (normally pork) with potatoes for the main course. Dessert is often unnecessary as the portions are huge.

It's acceptable to eat seconds and polite to leave a clean plate. If you cannot or don't want to eat something, you should tell your host and explain why. Vegetarians or those with special dietary requirements should inform their host well in advance to avoid embarrassment. Dinner is generally lighter than lunch and you may be offered only cold meats with bread, cheese, boiled eggs and raw vegetables.

Making Invitations

If you invite Germans to your home for a meal, you should state the time clearly and (if there is one) the occasion. Expect your guests to be punctual – even a few minutes early.

What to Serve

Unless your guests are elderly or extremely old fashioned, they will be curious to try some of your native cuisine. It's better to cook something you know well than to try cooking a German dish and botching it. If your home cooking is highly spiced, make sure you tone it down a bit, as spicy food may not be to your guests' taste.

Offer beer (especially in Bavaria) or wine before and during the meal, and coffee afterwards. German or Italian white wine is acceptable, as is imported red wine. Prepare a lot of food and offer second helpings.

RESPECTING PRIVACY

Although they don't mind asking you about yourself, Germans usually don't like to be asked about their private life. For example, it isn't uncommon for colleagues at work to get married or have a baby (men, that is) without telling anyone at work about it.

The Germans have a saying '*Dienst ist Dienst und Schnaps ist Schnaps*' (literally, duty is duty and brandy is brandy), meaning that work or public matters should be kept separate from socialising and private life. Germans are private people and often wish to keep themselves to themselves unless they're with close friends or family.

People rarely discuss private issues outside their 'inner circle', and you shouldn't enquire about personal matters or you may offend. By the same token, you shouldn't discuss your personal problems as it might cause embarrassment. Discretion is highly prized, and if someone confides in you it should be kept secret. Similarly, you can usually trust a German to keep something confidential.

You should also respect a German's personal space by not visiting unannounced or phoning at inappropriate times, such as after 10pm.

TABOOS

There are certain things that are highly disapproved of by many Germans, and although they will be more than happy to point out your transgressions, it's better to avoid making them. Here are a few things to avoid doing:

- Crossing on a red light (especially if there are children present), which will be greeted with disdain and possibly earn you a fine;
- Standing on the left side of an escalator, which marks you as an *Ausländer*;
- Calling a stranger *du*;
- Arriving late without a good excuse;
- Being indiscreet;
- Driving a gas-guzzler (unless it's a Porsche);
- Doing environmentally unfriendly things (except throwing cigarette butts on the ground) and being wasteful.

Conversation

Starting a conversation with a German isn't always easy, as many dislike or aren't adept at making 'small talk'. First conversations can be awkward, as they usually involve your facing a barrage of questions aimed at finding out if you conform to your nationality's stereotype (e.g. gun-toting American or fish-and-chips-eating Brit) and to ascertain your reason for visiting or moving to Germany (most Germans cannot believe that foreigners would want to live in their

Berlin Wall

country – or need reassurance that there are those who do).

Finally, you must show that you can express yourself intelligently – no small demand in a foreign language. Once you've made your case convincingly on the chosen subject – even if it differs from you host's or guest's – you've proved your mettle and may switch to a more comfortable topic, but make sure it's one you 're well versed in. Safe topics include sport (especially football), travel, your profession, current events (especially depressing ones) and beer – or things you like about Germany.

The typical German line of questioning became so tiresome and predictable for a friend that he made up a list of frequently asked questions (*häufig gestellte Fragen*, although most Germans use the initials FAQ) and presented it whenever he was introduced to a German.

As in most countries, there are topics that should be avoided in conversation with Germans. These include the following.

Second World War & Hitler

'Don't mention the war', as the saying goes – and it goes without saying that this is a taboo topic. Most Germans feel that they've been brow-beaten enough over the Second World War (not to mention the First) and would like to move on. Now and then you'll meet a German who invites discussion about it, which is okay, but the subject shouldn't be raised by you. You should never use the words

Nazi or Hitler or make a Nazi salute to insult a German, as it's not only extremely rude but also against the law. These words should never come up in conversation among expatriates where you could be overheard by Germans.

Money

Talking about your salary or asking a German his salary is considered uncouth and one of the worst blunders you could make (after talking about Hitler). You also shouldn't ask a German how much his or her car or apartment cost or discuss money matters as a way of establishing your guests' or hosts' status (except in Munich).

Immigrants

If you have any opinions about other immigrants in Germany, keep them to yourself. Sometimes Germans like discussing Turks, former Yugoslavians and other groups, but it's safer not to join in. People have strong feelings on the subject and you might easily offend someone (or equally be offended).

East Germany & the GDR

Although the Wall came down nearly 20 years ago, there are still lingering resentments on both sides that are too complex for most foreigners to grasp completely. A general synopsis is that the East Germans (*Ossis*) had high hopes when the Wall came down of a higher standard of living and social freedom. What they got was economic ruin and unemployment. The older generation had worked their entire lives under communist leadership and suddenly had little or no pension to show for it. Many people (mostly women) were promptly laid off with little prospect of finding another job. Partly for this reason, the birth rate in the former East German states has dropped to one of the lowest in the world. Before reunification everyone had jobs and homes provided by the state. Afterwards, they had to start making their own way.

Once the border opened up, the government offered subsidies to West German companies to build factories and create jobs in eastern Germany. After finding that it wasn't such a lucrative deal, many companies closed these factories and moved to cheaper countries, such as Poland and Slovakia. Many *Ossis* consider this a betrayal and condemn *Wessis* as cruel and greedy, while many *Wessis* resent having to pay 'solidarity' tax and denounce the *Ossis* as backward communists who wish to bleed the 'real' Germany dry with welfare and unemployment claims. East Germans may open up and tell you of the ridicule they've had to endure in moving to West Germany or their attempts to disguise their accent and origins to avoid discrimination, but it's best not to get involved if such a discussion arises.

Religion

Germans don't get worked up into a puritanical frenzy about religion, but it's definitely taboo to discuss it with strangers – or even with friends. Like most personal things, it should be kept private. Germans don't take kindly to proselytising.

Criticism of Germans

Germany has tried to make amends for the atrocities committed by Germans during the War and has become acutely self-critical in recent years. Germans are also unpleasantly aware that they have a reputation for being cold and unfriendly towards visitors – an image they're striving to change. There have even been state-funded and tourist

Pope Benedict XVI, born in Marktl am Inn, Bavaria

office campaigns (especially during the football World Cup) to encourage Germans to be polite to visitors. But self-critical as they may be, pointing out their failings isn't the best way to make yourself liked, therefore if you must vent your feelings you should reserve the German-bashing for exclusive expat gatherings.

Dress

Germans may dress casually in their own homes, but even when simply going to the supermarket they dress neatly. Trainers and sweatshirts are reserved for the gym, and you'll rarely see anyone dressed sloppily or men with their shirts off except in a park or on the beach. On the other hand, jeans are universally accepted, except at most nightclubs. In western Germany, many people like to wear 'designer brands' and carry flashy designer handbags, but in the former East Germany such ostentation would be tactless, considering the lower standard of living.

For all the complaining that expats do, it's interesting to note that 6.75m foreigners have lived in Germany for more than one year, and more than half as many for ten years or more.

EXPATRIATE COMMUNITY

Almost 9 per cent of Germany's population is foreign born, and a huge variety of nationalities are represented (including around 100,000 each of Britons and Americans), the largest group being Turkish. Immigrants live in all areas of Germany, but the states with the largest foreign populations are North Rhein-Westphalia, Bavaria, Baden-Württemberg, Hesse, and the city-states of Berlin, Bremen and Hamburg, while the eastern states have relatively few foreigners.

If you move to an area that's popular with other people of your nationality, the lack of cultural and language barriers makes socialising much easier. Many large cities have well established expat networks, and fitting into these is often straightforward. However, you should beware of becoming too dependent on expatriate society, which can be unstable (expats tend to come and go) and claustrophobic, particularly in small communities where little goes on and everyone knows everything about everyone else. Try to extend your contacts further afield and make an effort to meet the locals too – getting to know Germans will add variety and interest to your social life and open new doors to you.

Advantages

- You get to speak your own language.
- It's nice to vent your feelings of frustration related to culture shock with people who have been through the same thing.
- It's easier to fit in with people of your own nationality.
- You can get a lot of useful information from expats who have lived in Germany for a while.

Disadvantages

- Spending too much time with expats may encourage you to postpone, perhaps even indefinitely, your acceptance of German culture and your integration into German society.

- Time spent with other expats could be spent fitting into life with Germans.
- Many expatriate groups are little more than an excuse to complain about everything German – this may accentuate your own negative feelings towards Germany and won't help you overcome your culture shock or settle into your new home.
- The expats you meet aren't necessarily the type of person you'd mix with in your home country and you may find yourself socialising with people you don't actually like.

CONFRONTATION

Germans are often either passive-aggressive or confrontational, depending on the situation, and both types of behaviour can arouse aggression in foreigners. Germans will readily reproach you for any breach of accepted conduct and rarely apologise and almost never in a customer service situation. In fact, staff are trained not to say sorry to customers. The English word sorry is sometimes used, but usually in an accusatory tone, as if to say, 'It's your fault I bumped into you; why didn't you get out of my way?' If you say 'sorry' or 'excuse me' for something you aren't responsible for, you're considered a fool. In work situations, confrontation takes the form of (sometimes painfully) direct criticism. If you feel that the person is correct in their assessment of you, accept it and move on.

In the playground, German kids are expected to sort out their own squabbles – even if this involves fighting (as it often does). If this is unacceptable to you, you may have to face a confrontation with the offending child's parents.

If you're faced with any sort of confrontation, hold your ground (assuming you're sure you're in the right), but try not to raise your voice. When people refuse to wait their turn in a queue, they expect others not to say anything, but if you stand up for yourself in an assertive way, they normally back down. Even if things do get heated, Germans don't usually hold a grudge, and you may earn some respect – once the smoke has cleared.

DEALING WITH OFFICIALS

Living in Germany involves a lot of red tape, which means dealing with 'authority figures'. German officials tend to be at best businesslike and supercilious, at worst rude and insufferable. But corruption is rare.

To help your official dealings go smoothly, follow the tips below:

- Always use the polite (*Sie*) form of address.
- Always be civil, but not overly friendly and eager (it looks suspicious and weak).

- Always stay calm and never lose your temper.
- If you go in person, dress smartly, which will earn you respect.
- Don't expect officials to smile, as it isn't part of their job description.

Police

Contrary to popular belief, German police are normally approachable and not intimidating. They do their job briskly but can be reasoned with – up to a point. Normally, if the police stop you it's only to check your identity documentation, in which case you should be polite and courteous (on the other hand, they maybe brusque and officious). There's little point in being obstructive or arguing, which will only make things worse. If you think you've been stopped or fined illegally, make a complaint at a police station afterwards.

Civil Servants

Civil servants are unavoidable in Germany, as they hold the key to obtaining residence and work permits, paying taxes and managing many other aspects of daily life, therefore it's in your best interest to remain calm and civil when dealing with them. The last thing you want is for them to hold up your application or turn it down out of hand. Nothing annoys a civil servant more than being expected to speak English. Few of them speak good English, but even if they can, they may not do so on principle. You should always bring a German speaker with you if you cannot speak German.

Teachers

Teachers in German state schools are civil servants and their working hours are regulated, so that they arrive shortly before class begins and leave shortly after classes terminate, unless required to attend meetings or conferences. Teachers aren't required to stay behind after school to see you or help your child with his work, but may do so if asked. If you wish to see a teacher or the principal, you should phone for an appointment.

All classes are conducted in German, but some teachers speak English, although you should never assume this, therefore you may need to take an interpreter along with you if you don't speak German.

In addition to language difficulties, you may also face culture clashes, as German ideas on child rearing may not agree with your own and an overzealous teacher may try to circumvent you when making decisions regarding your child. This is most noticeable in nursery schools, some of which enforce toilet training irrespective of whether a child is ready for it or not and without notifying parents. When it comes to food, school meals may be freshly prepared with organic ingredients, but they aren't always balanced, often consisting of just noodles with meat sauce, followed by chocolate or other sweets, and children are often forced to eat what they don't like.

Where your child's welfare is concerned, you should be assertive and state your wishes clearly.

vineyards in autumn

plain & simple German?

5.
THE LANGUAGE BARRIER

The key to adapting to life in Germany and understanding the culture is to learn German, the second most widely-spoken language in Europe and the tenth in the world. Therefore, learning German should be at the head of your 'to do list' when coming to Germany (if not before). Everyone who has learned a foreign language knows that it isn't easy, especially at the beginning, and can relate horror stories of making embarrassing 'Freudian slips' with the language.

To help you avoid making such *faux pas*, this chapter contains tips on learning German and explanations of body and sign language (and their importance in communication), false friends, forms of address and greetings, and telephone and letter etiquette.

'I can understand German as well as the maniac that invented it, but I talk it best through an interpreter.'
Mark Twain
(American writer)

LEARNING GERMAN

Learning at least a few key German words and phrases can go a long way to making you feel more welcome and in control of your situation in Germany. People with no German skills can feel isolated and even paranoid when they don't understand what others around them are saying. In addition to making your transition to a German lifestyle smoother, learning the language has numerous other benefits.

In the western half of Germany, many people speak at least basic English, as they've learned it at school, whereas until 1990 people in the east learned Russian as a second language and weren't exposed to international music and television, therefore most of them speak very little or no English at all. However, as English becomes essential to businesspeople and travellers, more and more Germans are learning the language. This doesn't get you off the hook as far as learning German is concerned, however, as it's essential to communicate in German if you wish to lead a successful and enjoyable life in Germany.

The German alphabet has 30 letters: a to z (as in English) plus ä, ö, ü and ß. The letter ß is equivalent to ss, as in *Straße* (street), while the dots (*umlaut*) over an a, o or u indicate that a following e is 'missing', e.g. München (Munich) is sometimes written Muenchen. German is now printed in Roman fonts, similar to the typeface in this book. The German typeface know as Gothic (common forms are Fraktur and Schwabacher) was dropped in the '30s when studies found they were harder to read than Roman typefaces.

> **'It is easier for a cannibal to enter the Kingdom of Heaven through the eye of a rich man's needle that it is for any other foreigner to read the terrible German script.'**
>
> Mark Twain (American writer)

Why German is Essential

- Being able to speak German in an accident or emergency could save your or someone else's life.
- You'll greatly increase your chance of finding a job or starting a successful business.
- You'll be more self-reliant.
- You'll lessen your culture shock and feelings of alienation.
- You're more likely to get help or at least a positive response from the locals.
- It will help you to gain a better understanding of Germany and German culture.
- You'll increase your chance of making German friends.
- You'll meet people in your German class.

Compound Nouns

When you first see written German, you may be alarmed by the length of words. Germans simply like to string small words together – and are continually inventing words by doing so. The longest recorded word in the German language contains 79 letters: *Donaudampfschiffahrtselektrizitätenhauptbetriebswerkbauunterbeamtengesellschaft* (association for subordinate officials of the head office management of the Danube steamboat electrical service). However, even the longest words can fairly easily be broken down into their component parts.

Know Before You Go

Although your fluency in German should improve dramatically once you arrive in Germany there and are immersed in the language, it's well worth spending some time and effort before you go to establish the fundamentals of the language. Getting a head start of at least six months before your departure will help you absorb the basic grammar and vocabulary needed to make your arrival less stressful. German is a highly structured language with not only three genders (*der, die* and *das*) but also four cases; getting to grips with these requires time in peace and quiet – something you may not have in your first few weeks in Germany.

As Mark Twain so helpfully explained (he loved the German language): 'A dog is *der Hund*, a woman is *die Frau* and a horse is *das Pferd*. Now you put that dog in the genitive case and is he the same dog he was before? No, sir; he is *des Hundes*. Put him in the dative case and what is he? Why he is *dem Hund*. Now you snatch him into the accusative case and how is it with him? Why, he is *den Hunden*. But suppose he happens to be twins and you have to pluralise him –

what then? Why, they'll swat that twin dog around through the four cases until he'll think he's an entire international dog show all in his own person.'

Believing that you'll 'pick up' the language on arrival is a mistake, and waiting to learn German until you're in Germany will not only make the process more stressful, but will also tempt you to skip the accuracy in order to gain fluency as quickly as possible. Once you head down that road it's difficult to go back, and there are many expats who make basic errors after many years of living in Germany.

German is taught in many language schools around the world, therefore if you want or need a 'live' teacher you should have no trouble finding a suitable class. The Goethe Institute – the official German cultural representative abroad – offers language classes and opportunities to experience German culture in 142 institutes, in 81 countries around the world (UK offices are in London, Manchester and Glasgow); see 💻 www.Goethe.de.

For those who prefer to 'do it themselves' – and who have the self-discipline required – there are many self-help materials (books, CDs, DVDs, etc.) available via the internet or in bookshops such as Hugendubel. Language learning websites include 💻 www.deutsch-lernen.com, 💻 http:german.about.com and 💻 www.learn-german-online.net, and a popular online English-German/German-English dictionary is 💻 http://dict.leo.org.

Once in Germany

Upon arrival in Germany it's easy to be distracted from your German learning by logistical and other challenges, therefore it's essential to have a plan of attack to help you stay focussed. The first thing to do is to enrol in an 'integration course' (*Integrationskurs*), which may be suggested or even required if you're seeking permanent residence in Germany, depending on your country of origin and your German fluency. The course concentrates mainly on learning the language and it's subsidised by the state. When you apply for your residence permit, ask the immigration official if he can tell you where to find such a course or search the internet for *Integrationskurs*, which are offered by most language schools.

There are hundreds of language schools in Germany offering all types of courses at all levels, therefore it's just a matter of shopping around until you find the one that suits you and your pocket. If price isn't an issue, private tuition (around €30-55 per lesson) is usually the best option, as individual attention and a course tailored to your needs ensure faster progress. However, some people prefer learning in a group, which is cheaper and a great way to meet people.

You may wish to set up a language exchange, which involves finding a German wishing to learn English (there are many) and spending half the time speaking English and the other half German. It's another good way to make friends, but it's a rather unstructured way to learn a language and may work best as a supplement to a traditional course. You can advertise for a private teacher or language exchange on local bulletin boards (in libraries, universities and supermarkets) and newspapers, and through word of mouth at work or your partner's workplace.

> **'In prison, I studied German. Indeed, this seems to be the proper place for such study.'**
>
> Oscar Wilde
> (Irish playwright, novelist & poet)

Tips for Learning German

- Answer in German when Germans insist on showing off their English to you. They resist at first, but eventually get the message.
- Stay motivated – take every opportunity to practise.
- Accept that you'll make mistakes and persevere – everyone makes mistakes speaking foreign languages (and even in their own language) and your efforts will be appreciated nonetheless.
- Don't set impossible targets – give your brain time to absorb new material. People often reach a 'plateau' in their learning at about the intermediate level; it just takes time to get over it.
- Learn a set number of new words a week – and make sure to use them.
- Watch films and television and listen to the radio in German. This expands your passive vocabulary and helps you to learn idiomatic expressions. The more often you hear them, the more comfortable you'll feel using them.
- Read a book or watch a DVD in your language and then read or watch it again in German. Eventually you'll be able to understand it in German without the translation.

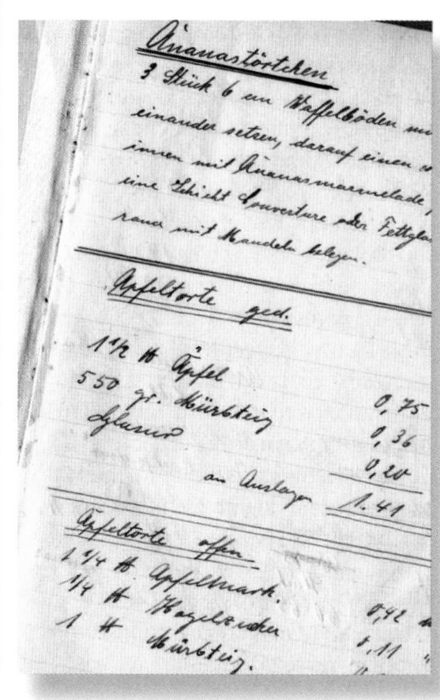

- Read children's books in German – although these aren't always simple to understand.
- Accept that you won't understand everything in conversation (you sometimes don't in your own language), but learn to pick out key words and phrases to get the gist of what is being said.
- When reading, don't waste time looking up every word. It's no fun and you may quickly lose motivation.
- Recognise and be satisfied with your progress, even if it's a slower than expected.
- If you're single, find a German partner.

Children

If your family relocates with you, they must also learn German. For children under ten, the transition to German school may not be too difficult, but it will go much more smoothly if your children begin learning German before departing for Germany. Children under ten may adapt within as little as three to six months, but older children usually have a harder time and may be unhappy throughout their first year. Learning German doesn't have to be dull; there are summer camps and outings on which they can learn German while at play.

Not only will they have learned the basics, but they will have more confidence in school if they can at least introduce themselves and produce a few other phrases. Besides, children are placed in classes according to their German knowledge, and may end up in a younger class until their German is of an acceptable standard. Some schools provide language 'bridging classes' for foreign children but you cannot rely on it, although it's one of the factors to consider when choosing a school for your child.

For safety reasons, all children should learn to say their telephone number and address in German as soon as possible.

You may decide to send your child to an international or bi-lingual school; the former allows them to avoid the language barrier altogether, while the latter is a good option if you wish to integrate your child into the German school system later on, and to ease them into the German language. Before making a decision, consider your child's character and adaptability and discuss the options with him.

Although Germany is home to people of many nationalities and cultures, it's no melting pot, and foreigners face stereotyping and prejudice. Whereas English-speaking kids may have a high status in some schools (English is considered 'cool'), other minorities may have more obstacles to overcome than the language.

OTHER LANGUAGES

Germany is a patchwork of regions and city states, where numerous languages and dialects intermingle with the official state language, High German (*Hochdeutsch*), and unless you're isolated within an expat bubble you're bound to encounter at least some of them. There are essentially three variations from *Hochdeutsch*: regional languages, foreign minority languages and dialects.

The only officially recognised regional language is Low German (*Niederdeutsch*), which is in fact a collection of languages spoken in northern rural areas (and in eastern parts of the Netherlands) by around 3m people. It's called 'Low' because of the low-lying land in that region and not because it's considered an inferior form of German. Some variants of Low German are associated with the Mennonite culture (e.g. *Plautdietsch*).

The essential difference between Low and High German is that Low German didn't undergo the 'consonant shift' that High German did and therefore sounds more like English, e.g. (examples are English followed by *Plautdietsch* followed by *Hochdeutsch*) p-ff (ship-*Schipp-Schiff*), p-pf (apple-*Aupel-Apfel*), t-ss (eat-*äte-essen*), t-tz (cat-*Kaat-Katze*), and k-ch (make-*maken-machen*).

The following minority languages are recognised and protected by the European Charter for Regional or Minority Languages (ECRML):

- **Danish** (*Dänisch*) – spoken by 50,000 people in northern Schleswig-Holstein, which borders Denmark;
- **Low Franconian** (*Niederfränkisch*) – spoken in the Rhine region and the area between the city of Cologne and the Dutch border. Limburgish is a dialect of Low Franconian.
- **North Frisian** (*Nordfriesisch*) – spoken by around 10,00 λ North Frisian (Nordfriesisch) – spoken by around 10,000 people in the region of North Frisia, in the state of Schleswig-Holstein;
- **Polish** (*Polnisch*) – spoken in the Ruhr area (*Ruhrgebiet*) of North Rhine-Westphalia but dying out;
- **Romani** – the language spoken by most gypsies in Germany;
- **Saterland Frisian** (*Saterfriesisch*) – the last remaining dialect of the language of eastern Frisia, spoken by 2,250 people in the region of Saterland, in Lower Saxony;
- **Sorbian** (*Sorbisch*) – a language originally brought to eastern Germany by Slavs that has two main variants: Upper Sorbian (*Obersorbisch*), spoken by 40,000 people in Saxony, and Lower Sorbian (*Niedersorbisch*), spoken by 10,000 people in Brandenburg;
- **Yeniche** (*Jenische*) – the language spoken by the Yeniche gypsies, said to be a mixture of Romani, Rotwelcsh (spoken by certain criminals, gypsies and travelling performers), Yiddish and various German dialects;

> **'Those who know nothing of foreign languages know nothing of their own.'**
>
> Johann Wolfgang von Goethe
> (German playwright, poet & novelist)

The Danish-, Sorbian- and Frisian-speaking regions are officially bi-lingual regions.

Turks make up the largest ethnic minority in Germany but, although the importance of their language is growing, Turkish (*Türkisch*) isn't officially recognised as a 'minority language'. Nevertheless, many banks and other businesses are now offering services in Turkish to increase business.

Regional and minority languages shouldn't present a huge problem when it comes to making yourself understood (most people also speak German) or understanding street signs and official documentation, which are in standard German. Conversing with the locals is another matter, however, and you may have difficulty understanding some of them.

Education in Bi-lingual Regions

Nearly all classes in state schools in Germany are taught in standard German, even in bi-lingual regions. However, minority languages may be taught as a subject. Students are expected to learn how to read and write *Hochdeutsch* even if their mother tongue is a regional language, minority language or dialect. For example, Swabians speak the Swabian dialect with their family and friends, but write letters in *Hochdeutsch*.

However, teachers naturally speak the local dialect and even when speaking German will have a regional accent.

Dialects & Accents

In addition to the above languages, between 50 and 250 dialects (depending on how the word dialect is defined) of German are spoken in Germany, and they're so varied that people from different regions of

Germany cannot understand each other unless they speak *Hochdeutsch*, which is why everyone learns *Hochdeutsch* in school. Add to these the countless regional accents and you'll realise that learning German is anything but a simple process.

If you live in rural Germany, you'll at least have to learn to understand the local accent or dialect, but in a cosmopolitan city you can usually get by with just *Hochdeutsch*. In Munich, for example, only 20 per cent of the inhabitants speak a Bavarian dialect (it's said that there are no more true *Münchner* left), but take a drive into the Bavarian Alps and you'll find that nearly everyone speaks in dialect.

You cannot be expected to understand every dialect and accent in Germany (neither do the Germans), but it's advisable to focus on at least understanding the dialect or accent of your region. If you don't understand what sounds like a dialect, you can politely ask the person to speak in *Hochdeutsch*.

It's generally reckoned that people from Hanover speak the clearest, least accented *Hochdeutsch*, whereas Hessian is universally hated (except in Hesse) and parodied in German comedy shows.

SLANG & SWEARING

Unless you're fluent in the language, it's best to avoid swearing and using slang. German has fewer swear words than English, and Germans sometimes swear in English (usually inappropriately), but you may be shocked at how common certain swearwords are in German conversation, some of them even appearing in children's TV programmes.

Slang can be one of the most difficult things to learn in any language, since it doesn't follow the normal 'rules'. Many language learners therefore use slang inappropriately, leading to some embarrassing faux pas. An entertaining and useful guide to German slang and swear words is *Scheisse: The Real German You Were Never Taught in School* (Plume).

BODY & SIGN LANGUAGE

German conversation isn't as animated as conversation in Italy, Spain or even France, and you don't see much gesticulating and body movement. Nevertheless, your posture and what you do (or don't do) with your body is important. For example, a 'laid-back' stance may seem disrespectful and smiling at strangers can make you appear insincere, superficial or just plain odd.

When you finish a presentation, talk or lesson, you may hear table-rapping instead of clapping if it was well received (common in academic settings).

Gestures

Gestures are sometimes useful and can be fun; here are a few you should recognise if not use:

- Instead of crossing your fingers to wish someone good luck, you drück die Daumen or squeeze your thumbs inside your fists. (Cross your fingers behind your back when telling a fib.)

- When gesturing to the waiter for another beer, remember that Germans begin counting with the thumb, so if you point your index finger you're likely to get two beers.
- Tapping the side of your head with your index finger means 'You're crazy'.
- Pointing with your index finger below your eye means, 'How stupid do you think I am?'.
- Never make the 'okay' sign – curling you index finger and thumb into a circle – which Germans consider very rude, or point your finger at your head, which is an insult.

Personal Space

Germans have a somewhat confusing concept of personal space. When speaking to people, you shouldn't crowd them and should keep them at arms' length. However, in banks, for example, where you particularly want people to keep a discreet distance, you often find them looming over your shoulder, hoping that you'll hurry up. If you don't keep close to the person in front in a queue, you might get a shove from behind – or someone will push in ahead of you.

Although Germans want their personal space to be respected, they often don't respect others. If someone bumps into you, they will rarely say '*Entschuldigung*' (excuse me), and on crowded buses and trains, Germans seem to be overcome by a sort of collective claustrophobia, often becoming pushy and rude.

FALSE FRIENDS

Dangerous Liaisons

Bub (rhymes with 'tube') = boy

Fahrt = drive or trip. (You'll often see the signs '*Einfahrt*' and '*Ausfahrt*', meaning entrance and exit.)

Dusche = shower

Schmuck = jewellery

Groß (pronounced like 'gross') = large, great

Präservativ = condom. You might get some odd looks if you ask if food contains *Präservativen*.

Both English and German belong to the same group of languages, i.e. Germanic, which means that English-speakers have a leg up when learning German (and vice versa), but you mustn't let that lull you into a false sense of security. Although many words look the same and some mean the same in both languages, there are many others that look familiar but mean something altogether different - called false friends (*falsche Freunde*). To help you avoid making linguistic blunders there's a list of common false friends in **Appendix D**.

Pseudo-English

Like the French, Germans cannot resist the temptation to adopt English words and expressions. To traditionalists this is annoying, as German usually has perfectly good words of its own with the same meaning, and English borrowings are usually used incorrectly. But, like it or not, German is becoming more anglicised every day and young people can barely put a sentence together without using at least one English word. Here's an example: *Du kannst deinen internet Provider switchen, du mußt ihn nur canceln.* (You can switch your internet provider simply by cancelling.)

Anglicising is especially prevalent in marketing, advertising, information technology and 'cool' slang, as in these recent borrowings:

- ***Beamer*** = projector (not an affectionate term for a BMW);
- ***Black Music*** = music that's typically considered a black genre, such as soul, R&B and hip hop;
- ***Body*** = a leotard or one-piece body suit, sometimes known as a 'onesie' in the US when referring to baby clothes;
- ***chatten*** = to chat;
- ***Handy*** = mobile (cell) phone – by far the most popular Anglicism.
- ***happy End*** = happy ending (and a brand of toilet paper);
- ***jobben*** = to do temporary work, such as a summer job;
- ***Mobbing*** = harassment in the workplace, hounding;
- ***Oldtimer*** = classic car;
- ***relaxen*** = to relax;
- ***shoppen*** = to shop;
- ***Slang*** = American accent, e.g. 'er spricht American Slang' (he speaks with an American accent);
- ***trendig*** = trendy.

> Almost any English verb can be made into a German verb simply by adding an ***n*** or ***en*** at the end, e.g. ***canceln, shoppen***, ***mailen***, ***stoppen***, ***partien***, ***stylen*** and even ***googlen***. To make the past participle (cancelled, shopped, etc.) put ***ge-*** at the front of the English past participle (or something like it), e.g. ***Ich habe*** (I have) ***gecancellt, geshoppt, gemailed, gestopped, gepartied, gestylt, gegooglet***. Verbs with a prefix have the ***ge*** in the middle: ***downgeloadet, forgewardet ...***

FORMS OF ADDRESS

Sie or Du?

German makes a clear distinction between the formal or polite word for 'you' (*Sie* – both singular and plural and always written with a capital S) and the informal du (singular)/*ihr* (plural). Knowing when to use which is difficult for English-speakers. The general rule is to use *Sie* with people you don't know, especially older people, and people you encounter in a professional environment, such as a shop or hospital, even if you meet them regularly, e.g. work colleagues. Such formality can feel strange to English-speakers, as it represents keeping your distance, but in Germany keeping your distance is a sign of respect.

Du is used with young people you meet in an informal situation such as at a bar or party, with children and in some companies with a young corporate culture, e.g. IT companies. If you're unsure, you should always use *Sie* and wait for the German to suggest using *du*. Switching from *Sie* to *du* can be a significant event, as it symbolises letting someone into your inner circle, and it may be celebrated over a drink.

If you normally speak English with your boss, don't forget to use *Sie* whenever you need to switch to German – even if you have a fairly close or informal relationship.

Siezen is to call someone *Sie* and *duzen* to call someone *du*. Use *Sie* when:

- addressing an official, e.g. a policeman, or civil servant;
- talking to a doctor, shopkeeper, salesperson or waiter;
- telephoning someone you don't know;
- addressing a neighbour;
- addressing someone in your workplace, school or university, irrespective of their position or 'rank';
- talking to someone obviously older than yourself;
- in any other case where you're unsure.

Surnames & Titles

In Germany it's typical to have one first name (*Vorname*), one last name (*Nachname*) and no middle name. If you have a middle name, it's referred to as a 'second first name' (*zweiter Vorname*). Most married women take their husbands' last name but occasionally they will hyphenate their name, using their maiden name first and their husband's surname second. Titles are important in Germany. For men and women there are two main titles: *Herr* for Mr and *Frau* for Mrs or Ms (whether married or not). The term for Miss (*Fräulein*) is now considered sexist and old fashioned, though it's occasionally heard in restaurants when a waitress is summoned (waiters are called '*Herr Ober*') and when young girls are addressed. Women are often politely addressed by strangers as 'the lady' (*die Dame*) or 'the young lady' (*die junge Dame*). If someone has a doctorate, they're referred to as *Frau Doktor* or *Herr Doktor* so and so; a male teacher with a PhD is addressed as *Herr Doktor Profesor*.

In 2007, the most popular baby names were Alexander and Maximilian for boys, and Marie and Sophie (*Sofie*) for girls.

GREETINGS

Shaking hands is important in Germany, where you should greet colleagues, business partners and friends with a handshake – accompanied by a subtle but important nod/bow of the head, particularly to a superior – and again on parting.

Handshaking Tips

- A handshake should be firm but not knuckle-breaking.
- When shaking hands, you shouldn't put your other hand in your pocket.
- Young people should wait for the older person to extend his hand first, and men should wait for women.
- Always stand to shake hands.

In some cities it's customary for friends to kiss twice, once on each cheek, or even three times when saying hello and goodbye. Hugging isn't common in Germany.

Children

Children should be addressed as ***du*** and given two kisses or a handshake (if they're teenagers). Your children should learn to address adults as ***Sie***, though they may use ***du*** with close family friends.

Informal greetings are '*hallo*'('hello' or 'hi') and '*grüß dich*' ('greetings'). More formal greetings are '*guten Morgen*' ('good morning'), '*guten Tag*' ('good afternoon'), '*guten Abend*' ('good evening') and '*gute Nacht*' ('good night' at bedtime). Informal goodbyes are '*tschüss*' or '*ciao*' ('bye'), '*bis bald*' ('see you soon') and '*bis später*' ('see you later'). Formal goodbyes are '*auf Wiedersehen* or *Wiedersehen*' (literally 'until we see each other again'), '*auf Wiederschauen*' or '*Wiederschauen*' (which mean more or less the same). When a German asks 'How are you?' (*Wie geht es Ihnen?*), it's meant as a literal question and it's rude not to answer. It irritates or confuses Germans if you ask them this every day – which English-speakers inevitably do – unless they're ill.

When a German enters a waiting room, shop or lift, he often greets those present with '*guten Tag*' or '*grüß Gott*' (in Bavaria) and says '*auf Wiedersehen/schauen*' upon leaving. It's polite to reply with similar greetings. When encountering someone around lunchtime, people often say '*Mahlzeit*', which literally means 'mealtime'. If you're in a restaurant or cafeteria, it's polite to say '*guten Appetit*' ('enjoy your meal'). The correct reply is '*danke, ebenfalls*' ('thank you, and the same to you').

TELEPHONE, LETTERS & EMAIL

Email is extremely popular in Germany, but telephone is the preferred means of communication for some people. Letters are also often used, especially in business, as the postal service is prompt and reliable: a domestic letter normally takes only one business day to arrive.

Telephone

Nearly everyone has a mobile phone in Germany (even old ladies), and there seems to be no such thing as mobile phone etiquette, as you hear them ringing constantly in restaurants and on public transport. People gabble away while queuing and, although it's illegal, while driving as well. Germans normally answer the phone with their last name and nothing else. It's considered rude to answer with a plain '*hallo*'.

Receptionists say the business name and their own last name before asking how they can be of service – for example '*Wilkommen bei BMW. Mein Name ist Schmidt. Wie kann ich Sie Helfen*?' You should address people you don't know as Sie, except children. When ringing off you say '*auf Wiederhören*' ('until we hear each other again').

Phonetic Alphabet

Spelling your name or trying to understand a German spelling his name over the telephone can be difficult – even if you know the German alphabet. Germans make it that much harder by using their own phonetic alphabet (below). If the caller hears you hesitate over his name, he will immediately 'translate' it into the phonetic alphabet. For example, Schmidt becomes Siegfried, Cäsar, Heinrich, Martha, Ida, Dora, Theodor. If you cannot remember it, keep a copy by your phone.

Phonetic Alphabet

A = Anton	N = Nordpol
B = Berta	O = Otto
C = Cäsar	P = Paula
D = Dora	Q = Quelle
E = Emil	R = Richard
F = Friedrich	S = Siegfried
G = Gustav	T = Theodor
H = Heinrich	U = Ulrich
I = Ida	W = Wilhelm
J = Julius	X = Xanthippe
K = Kaufmann	Y = Ypsilon
L = Ludwig	Z = Zeppelin
M = Martha	

Numbers

Another difficulty you may encounter is with numbers, as Germans (like the French) typically divide telephone numbers into pairs, and two-digit numbers are said backwards. For example, 47 is said 'seven and forty' (*siebenundvierzig*). So the number 563-7586 becomes *funf, dreiundsechsig, fünfundsiebzig, sechsundachtzig*. It helps to write the numbers as you hear them, leaving a space to the left of the second digit in each pair for the first.

The other thing that might trip you up is double or triple numbers. '00' is said as 'twice zero' (*zweimal Null*) and '555' as 'three times five' (*dreimal fünf*). In any case, make sure to repeat the number in German to check its accuracy.

Letters

Important communications such as cancelling a rental or service contract, quitting or applying for a job and filing a complaint must be in writing, therefore you should learn the essentials of letter writing.

Beginning

Formal letters start with *Sehr geehrte Frau* ... or *Sehr geehrter Herr* ... If you don't know the name of the person you're writing to, you should put *Sehr geehrte Damen und Herrn* (Dear Sir or Madam). Informal letters begin 'Dear': *Liebe Anne* or *Lieber Günther*. Always check you're using the correct ending: *er* (masculine) or *e* (feminine).

Addresses

Your name and address should be written (without a title) in the upper left-hand corner. The name and address of the recipient should be written below yours (see box). Note that when the street is named after a town or city it's written separately, e.g. *Rosenheimer Straße*, and *Straße* is often abbreviated to '*Str.*'.

In written correspondence, du and dich always have a capital D, whereas

German addresses are usually written as follows:

Private letters

Title (in the accusative case)	Herrn/Frau
Name of recipient	Helmut Schmidt
Street name and number	Hauptstraße 52
Postcode and town or city	12345 Berlin

Business letters

Name of company	Siemens AG
Title & name of recipient	Herrn Georg Schumann
Street name and number	Nymphenburger Straße 117
Postcode and town or city	80636 München

in texts (such as this one) they're all in lower case.

Date

The date should be written on the right and preceded by the name of the city and a comma. Usually, the day comes first (followed by a dot) then the month and then the year, e.g. *Hamburg, den 30. Oktober 2008* or simply *Hamburg, 30.10.2008*, but you may see dates written the other way round, e.g. *2008-10-30*.

> **Signing Off**
>
> **Formal letters** (the equivalent of 'Yours sincerely' or 'Yours faithfully'):
>
> - *Mit freundlichen Grüßen*
> - *Mit freundlichem Gruß*
> - *Es grüßt Sie*
> - *Mit besten Grüßen*
>
> **To someone you know well** (the equivalent of 'Kind regards'):
>
> - *Herzliche Grüße*
> - *Mit herzlichen Grüßen*
>
> **Informal letters to someone you're on du terms with:**
>
> - *Bis bald* (See you soon)
> - *Es grüßt echt herzlich* (Best wishes)
> - *Liebe Grüße* (Love)
> - *Alles liebe* (All my love)

Email

The convenience and immediacy of email often causes people to lower their formal guard, which can be a big mistake in German. The same rules of formality that apply to letters also apply to emails. Emails may be shorter and more to the point, but you

should use the *Sie* form of address, as appropriate, and sign on and off as shown above. There's nothing more offensive to a conservative business executive than to receive an email addressed '*Hallo Stefan!*'.

European Central Bank, Frankfurt am Main

6.
THE GERMANS AT WORK

It's important not to underestimate the differences in business culture and working practices between your home country and Germany. Being open to other ways of thinking and being aware of possible legal obstacles, commercial restrictions and cultural sensitivities is imperative if you're to be successful in the German business world.

'Sell a man a fish, he eats for a day, teach a man how to fish and you ruin a wonderful business opportunity.'

Karl Marx (German philosopher & revolutionary)

Some companies have learned the hard way about Germany's strict labour laws and workplace regulations, and the general German preference for quality over low prices, choice and service with a smile.

Others have adapted their corporate policies to the German mindset, without losing sight of their original mission.

A good illustration of this is Wal-Mart. When the American merchandising giant purchased the German chains Wertkauf and Interspar in 1997, it started by renovating all its newly acquired stores and introducing a wider range of brands than were found in most German chains, including many American imports. When it tried to implement the American customs of 'bagging' customer purchases and valet parking, however, Germans protested. Wal-Mart also massively underestimated the competitiveness of indigenous chains such as Aldi and Real and has recently been forced to sell out to Metro, a huge discount club.

Working in Germany usually involves a fairly steep learning curve for foreigners – professionally, linguistically and culturally. This chapter provides information on working for or with the Germans, setting up a business and business etiquette.

PERMITS & PAPERWORK

If you aren't an EU citizen, obtaining a work permit is complicated and getting permission to set up a business is difficult and expensive. Starting a business – even for a German – is no mean feat and can take up to a year. To secure a work permit as a non-EU citizen means finding someone willing and able (in accordance with the stipulations of the German Labour Office) to hire you in preference to an EU national.

FINDING A JOB

If you have qualifications or experience in a field or profession where demand matches or exceeds supply, you have at least a chance of finding a job in Germany. You should have a positive reason for living and working there (not merely that you're fed up with life in your home country), if not some necessity, such as your spouse having been transferred to Germany. Having a genuine interest in German culture or specific aspects of German society (not just the *Bundesliga*) can give you added credibility in your job search, as well as greatly enhancing your stay in the country.

Provided you have the necessary qualifications or experience, the easiest way to find a job quickly is through networking. Having a friend put in a good word for you could place your CV on the top of the pile, but it's your job to keep it there. Presenting a hard copy of your CV personally, as well as sending it electronically (sometimes preferred), and being polite and personable to reception staff (you never know what kind of influence secretaries have on their bosses) can help you make a good impression. Cold calls to the Human Resources department don't go down well, however. If you're invited for an interview, make sure that you're available – even if it's at an inconvenient time. The two best newspapers for jobseekers are the Süddeutsche Zeitung and the Frankurter Allgemeine. You should also check local newspapers and internet job listings on websites such as 💻 www.monster.de

Speaking German

It's essential to have at least a good working knowledge of German (preferably better) even if you plan to work in a multi-national organisation with connections with an English-speaking country. You may be able to get away with little German in certain scientific and academic areas, or in a high-demand sector such as IT, which is currently around 20,000 people short, but German fluency is always highly desirable. Most Germans study English at school, and enough are sufficiently competent to make a native command of English less of an advantage in the job market than relevant skills or experience.

Qualifications

Nearly every type of job from waiting on tables (no kidding!) upwards requires qualifications and a training programme lasting at least two or three years, with or without supervised on-the-job experience, or a formal apprenticeship. Expecting to start at the bottom with nothing but enthusiasm and work your way to the top is practically unheard of in Germany, and without the requisite qualifications and training you probably won't even make it through the door. Professional qualifications can be highly specific, making it difficult to change jobs unless you've taken a supplementary training course meeting the particular requirements of the new job.

Germany abides by the EU's general system for the recognition of diplomas and qualifications, which means that, if your field of work is regulated in Germany, you must have your home country's qualification formally recognised before you'll be allowed to work in that field. This applies not only to areas such as medicine and education, but also to professions such as an electrician, computer technician or even a builder.

Having a career (*Beruf*) is especially important to Germans – both men and women (unless they choose to be mothers). Changing fields of activity is regarded as a sign of a lack of seriousness. Not that long ago, it was standard practice to have your career engraved on your tombstone, and it's still listed on your marriage certificate. On a traditional CV, you should also list your parents' careers.

Discrimination

An anti-discrimination law (*Gleichbehandlungsgesetz*) makes it illegal to discriminate on the basis of race, ethnic origin, sex, religion, disability, age or sexual orientation. To prevent prejudice based on appearance, it's no longer required to add your photograph to applications. If you're certain that you aren't being treated fairly (and can provide evidence) you can take your employer (or a prospective employer) to court. In practice, of course, discrimination is very difficult to prove, especially during the screening process, when your application may simply be put at the bottom of the pile and 'forgotten'. See also Working Women below.

Employment Agencies

Government

The German Labour Office (Bundesagentur für Arbeit, more commonly known as the Arbeitsagentur and sometimes still referred to by its former name, the Arbeitsamt) publishes lists of jobs available throughout Germany and abroad on its website and provides vocational training and job-seeking guidance. It also administers various benefit programmes related to employment, compiles labour statistics and conducts market and labour research. However, most of its services are available only to the registered unemployed (who must, of course, be German residents). Others may access the database of jobs and use the Arbeitsagentur's computers and telephones for job-seeking purposes, but a word of caution: jobs posted on the Arbeitsagentur's database are rarely the pick of the crop. Desirable positions are usually filled by a company internally or advertised in newspapers.

If you become unemployed while living in Germany, the Arbeitsagentur can sign you up for vocational courses and arrange job interviews.

Private

In addition to the Arbeitsagentur, there are many private employment agencies, but these deal mainly in management jobs. In larger cities, there are branches of many international executive recruitment firms or 'head-hunters'. Temporary agencies are also active in Germany, where you can find Adecco, Kelly and Manpower, as well as German agencies. The practice of hiring temporary workers is growing in popularity as a convenient way of circumventing the restrictions (on employers) of permanent contracts, but a short-term position may lead to a permanent one.

Selection Process

You may ask a previous employer to write you a reference, although it's illegal for an employer to write a negative reference and what you think is a eulogy may conceal 'coded' messages to a future employer, telling him you should be avoided like the proverbial plague! However, if an employer writes you an obviously unfavourable reference, you have the right to challenge it

Your application to a German company should be thorough unless otherwise stated in the advertisement. Along with your CV and covering letter you should submit copies of any diplomas, degrees, certificates and letters of reference. Until recently, applicants were expected to include a (professionally taken) photograph as well as specifying their marital status and number of children, and this is still the case with some companies. Your application will be thoroughly checked for grammatical and spelling errors, and your referees and previous employers contacted.

Assuming your application passes muster, you're invited for interview. In many cases one interview is enough to secure a job, but if you aren't contacted within a week or two, it usually means you haven't been successful. If you're invited for a second interview, there's a good chance you'll get the job. If a company rejects your application, it's required by law to send it back to you. Some companies reimburse travel expenses.

Salary

It can be difficult to determine the salary you should receive in Germany, as salaries often aren't quoted in job advertisements and are kept strictly confidential, although many trades are

bound by collective agreements that regulate salaries, which will give you an idea of the minimum salary at least. Rest assured, however, that Germans are among the best-paid workers in Europe and receive generous benefits, such as up to six weeks' holiday and usually a Christmas bonus (known as a '13th month' payment) and sometimes a holiday bonus (generally an additional half month's salary or more) during the summer. If you're quoted an annual salary, you should therefore divide it by 13 or 13.5 (not 12) to determine what your monthly pay will be.

When assessing your German salary, however, you should also take into account the high cost of living in Germany, taxes and the various social insurance contributions, which total around 40 per cent of your gross pay (depending on your tax bracket and the amount you earn).

Manual labourers in western Germany earned an average of €2,669 gross pay per month in 2006, while their white-collar colleagues received €3,595 gross, excluding bonuses and overtime. Comparable workers in the east earned some 74 per cent of western pay levels.

Salary Payments

In order to receive payment you need a German bank account, as your salary is paid by bank transfer – usually at the end of the month. You receive a pay slip (*Verdienstabrechnung* or *Lohnabrechnung*) that itemises your salary plus any bonuses, commissions or overtime rates, your remaining annual holiday days (*Resturlaub*) and tax, social security, and other deductions (both your share and your employer's).

CONTRACTS

The standard employment contract is referred to as an 'unlimited' contract (*unbefristeter Vertrag*), meaning that it's for an indefinite period. It usually includes a probationary period (*Probezeit*) of six months, depending on the job or industry, before the contract becomes binding on both parties. After the *Probezeit* it's very difficult for an employer to fire someone.

A 'limited' employment contract (*befristeter Vertrag*) is for a fixed term, usually 6 to 24 months. Limited contracts are used when a company needs a temporary substitute, e.g. when a key employee is on maternity leave, or to complete a project. Companies are also becoming more cautious and avoid Germany's strict labour laws by hiring people who can be more easily and cheaply dismissed.

Collective Agreements

Collective agreements (*Tarifverträge*), approved annually between management and unions, exist for just about every profession and job in Germany. They specify working conditions as well as salary scales.

STARTING OR BUYING A BUSINESS

Starting or buying a business involves jumping through a number of hoops, each of which must be successfully negotiated before you tackle the next. Make sure that you've done extensive research into the paperwork involved or, preferably, hire a lawyer or other specialist to help you – the cost of whose services can be partly reclaimed (see **Grants** below). Filing incorrectly can lead to your application being denied or your business being excessively taxed. Illegal traders are always caught eventually, made to pay huge fines and in some cases banned from setting up another business in Germany.

First, you must obtain a residence permit (see **Chapter 3**). If you're a non-EEA citizen coming to start a business in Germany, you usually need to invest a minimum of €1m and create at least ten jobs. If you're unable to meet these conditions, exceptions are sometimes made, depending on how viable your business idea is and whether or not it will compete with a German-owned business.

Loans

An investment loan (known as *Startgeld* – 'start money') of up to €50,000, backed by a guarantee from the European Investment Fund, is available to those starting a business, small and medium-sized enterprises and self-employed professionals.

Immigrants are eligible for the loan but must show that their business has excellent prospects. The loan periods are ten years with a two-year 'grace' period or five years with a one-year grace period. After the grace period, the loan must be repaid in six-monthly instalments. Other loans, such as the Entrepreneur Loan (*Unternehmerkredit*) for sums of up to €10m, are available under other terms and conditions. For further information about investment loans, contact the Kreditanstalt für Wiederaufbau (www.kfw-mittelstandsbank.de – in German only).

Getting a loan from a private German bank is next to impossible unless you have significant collateral or a large amount of capital. Banks are also even less inclined to approve loans to foreigners than to Germans.

Grants

Three types of grant for the reimbursement of consultancy fees are available to business founders:

- **Before start-up** – 50 per cent of consultancy fees up to €1,500;
- **After start-up** – for up to three years after start-up consultancy fees as above, or up to €3,000 if the consultancy relates to different aspects of the business and occurs at different times;
- **After the first three years** – 40 per cent of consultancy fees up to €1,500.

you have the flexibility to move premises if your business grows (or shrinks); and you can offset the rent against tax.

The main disadvantage of leasing is that it's difficult to terminate a lease before the term expires unless you sell the lease on. Even then, the lessee must be approved by the lessor and you need to pay the lessor a cancellation fee. Another possible drawback, if your company prospers and you don't wish to move, is that the lessor may raise the rent upon renewal of the contract – and as a commercial lessee you have no legal protection against rent increases.

The main difference between leasing and renting (see below) is that a lessee buys a lease, for which he must make an initial payment and which includes fixtures and fittings, in addition to paying rent.

Conditions include that the branch is located in Germany, that the consultancy is undertaken by a professional business consultancy and that the application is made after the fees have been paid – and no later than three months after the end of the consultancy. Application can be made online at www.beratungsfoerderung.net.

The German Labour Office is also keen on helping unemployed people start businesses (thereby removing them from the unemployment statistics) and provides start-up grants to those officially registered as unemployed.

Premises

Most business premises (*Räume*) are leased or rented for tax reasons and because commercial property is extremely expensive.

Leasing

The advantages of leasing over buying a commercial property are: lower capital outlay; you're unaffected by property depreciation;

Renting

Renting has all the advantages of leasing (see above) plus the initial outlay is less, you have more rights and it's difficult to be evicted. The snag is that many business premises are available only on a lease basis.

Working from Home

If you're self-employed or have a small business, working from home may be a viable option. It requires paperwork (what doesn't in Germany?), but it has financial advantages, as you can deduct the cost of your home office from your taxes. There are certain requirements of course, and you must be able to prove that you use a room exclusively for business purposes. Your work must also be something that doesn't disturb the peace.

Self-employment

To become self-employed (*selbstständig*) or start a freelance business in Germany, you need to register with the appropriate trade or craft guild (*Handwerkskammer*) and the tax office (*Finanzamt*), where you receive a tax number (*Steuernummer*). You must also have the appropriate, recognised qualification (see **Qualifications** above). However, those with relevant experience may be able to set up in self-employment in certain fields, e.g. craft activities, retailing, catering and hotel-keeping, food and drink production, insurance broking, teaching, transport services and hairdressing.

Marketing

In Germany, established companies with a reputation for quality fare better than companies that offer cheap goods or short-term price reductions. Germans don't mind spending a bit more for something if they believe it will last and they often prefer to 'buy German' whenever practical. Therefore, to enter the German market it's necessary to prove your credibility by building up stable relationships with clients. Once you have a foot in the door with one major customer, you'll find it easier with the next. Nurture and cultivate business relationships as much as possible with regular phone calls and invitations to cafes and restaurants.

Advertising is – like most things – highly regulated in Germany and it's illegal to make false claims or compare a product or service with a competitor's. It's permitted to say that a product is number one or the best-selling, but you must be able to substantiate it with objective data – if you cannot your advertising can be taken off the airwaves or removed from publications by the government.

BLACK ECONOMY

Although there are those who work 'on the black' in Germany, the practice isn't universally accepted and it's very risky. You may be able to get away with doing the odd job *im Schwarz*, but you run the risk of expulsion and/or huge fines if you're caught. In restaurants and on building sites – the most common places for *Schwarzarbeit* – spot inspections are made, and long-term offenders are eventually caught. Despite their desire for privacy, Germans don't mind their own business, and new restaurant owners are often reported to the authorities by nosy neighbours or competitors (even if they haven't broken the law).

If you accept a short-term job, your boss should provide proof of your social security registration and you should receive a social security card in the post; otherwise you're working illegally.

WORKING WOMEN

On the surface, Germany appears to be a progressive country with regard to the role of women, but statistics paint a different picture. According to *In the Spotlight – Women in Germany 2006*, the most recent study on the subject of women in the workplace by the Federal Statistics Office (Statistische Bundesamt), two-thirds of executive positions are filled by men, who earn 30 per cent more than their female counterparts (of equal status).

In support of working women's protests, a women's group recently put forward a proposal to help close the gap in earnings between the sexes: lower taxes for women!

Women in business are often not taken seriously and treated merely as representatives of their male bosses. Many of the oldest, most respected companies in Germany are run by an 'old boy' network of men and have a low 'glass ceiling' for women, only 5 per cent of whom attain positions of responsibility and power. To get noticed, women must usually work twice as hard as their male colleagues, and to be successful in business, a woman – particularly a

foreign woman – must quickly establish her ability and position.

Working women who become pregnant or return to work after giving birth may perceive a change in their status at work, even though by law their jobs are protected for three years (i.e. they're entitled to return to the same position up to three years after the birth of a child). You may not be taken seriously, may be overlooked for promotion and may be asked questions such as, 'Where's your baby?' in a tone implying that you must have left it on a street corner somewhere – 'you *Rabenmutter*!' There will even be (male) colleagues who think the only reason you got the job to begin with was so that you could get parent benefit and job protection – which is why sexual discrimination starts at the job interview. And, although it's illegal to discriminate on the grounds of pregnancy, let alone on the grounds of presumed pregnancy (an applicant may not be asked about her childbearing plans or even whether she's pregnant before a job offer is made), it's virtually impossible to prove that discrimination has taken place.

Foreign women may have a slight advantage in the German business world in some respect, as they aren't expected to conform to the same social stereotypes; if they wish to leave their children 'at street corners', that's their problem. They may also seem less of a threat, as they may not be staying permanently.

BUSINESS ETIQUETTE

Generally speaking, German companies are more formal than most other European or American companies, placing a higher value on organisation, credibility and punctuality, and preferring the *Sie* form of address and the use of surnames. However, the entertainment, marketing and IT industries, as well as newer companies and younger employees, tend to prefer a more relaxed atmosphere. In any case, it's safer to err on the formal side and follow the lead of your German counterparts, as you're much less likely to offend someone by being too formal than by being too informal.

Appointments

Appointments are essential in Germany and should be made at least a week in advance.

Be punctual (which for some Germans means five to ten minutes early). If you're delayed or need to cancel, you should call. Preferred times for appointments are between 10am and 1pm and between 3pm and 5pm. It isn't popular to schedule appointments in the evening or on Friday afternoons. Germans have an average of six weeks' holiday a year and you should take that into account when planning meetings, especially in summer and during festival periods.

Business Cards

Business cards (*Visitenkarten*) are vital when doing business with Germans and you should always carry them with you. In addition to the usual information such as name and position, address, telephone and fax numbers and email address, you may list any degrees and professional titles you hold and the year your company was founded. If the card is in English, it isn't necessary to have it translated into German, although if you do a lot of business in Germany you may wish to have a translation on the back (or have special cards made). Your position in the company represents your level of responsibility and you should take care not to choose an inaccurate title in German.

Business Gifts

Giving business gift is more restrained in Germany than it is in many other

countries. Flashy gifts are considered inappropriate, especially between employees of different levels or to clients, who may consider them a bribe. Unless you're also friends with a colleague, giving personal items such as jewellery can cause embarrassment.

German companies don't normally give employees gifts at Christmas time, but if there's a special occasion to celebrate, someone (normally a secretary or receptionist) makes a collection to pay for a gift and everyone who contributes (usually around €5) signs a card. Everyone is invited to the presentation for a glass of wine or *Sekt* (sparkling wine) and some 'nibbles'.

Appropriate gifts may depend on the occasion. If you're celebrating someone's promotion, you might buy something useful for an office, whereas if a woman is going on maternity leave, baby clothes are an obvious choice. Some good all-purpose gifts are pens, gift certificates, picture frames, champagne, chocolates, flowers and book tokens. If you give wine, it should preferably be a top-quality imported red wine.

Business Lunches

If you're inviting someone to lunch, choose a smart but not extravagant restaurant; it's you (the one who makes the invitation) who should pay and you should insist. Lunch is the main meal of the day in Germany, when you may be served several courses, starting with a soup or salad and ending with a dessert. (To help you get through it all in the statutory hour, the starter and main course are often served together!)

It's acceptable to drink alcohol, but within reason (follow your guest's lead) – unless you're driving (see **Chapter 7**), when you should abstain. Business discussion should be limited to before and after the meal (if there's time), unless initiated by your host or guest.

Business (power) breakfasts are almost unknown in Germany and Germans rarely entertain business associates in their homes.

Dress

German business attire is practical and very conservative. Male managers usually wear dark suits, a white or light-coloured shirt and a tasteful tie, while women may wear dark suits, smart dresses or skirts (but not too short). Men normally keep their jackets on unless they're 'behind closed doors', and taking a jacket off during a meeting is considered impolite and isn't usually done even in hot weather.

Non-executive office staff often have more flexible dress codes, and some young companies allow employees to wear almost anything, including jeans, unless a client is visiting. If in doubt, check what your co-workers are wearing.

> **'Workers of the world unite; you have nothing to lose but your chains.'**
>
> Karl Marx (revolutionary)

Meetings

You should always meet the person at the correct level and it's considered unacceptable to use a low-ranking person to gain access to a superior. First meetings are intended for getting to know and evaluate each other, and above all to establish trust. Meetings are usually serious affairs and if Germans indulge in small talk (*belangloses Geplauder*) and levity, it will only be to appease US and UK partners; otherwise, jokes, laughter and even smiles are rare and considered inappropriate. Starting a speech or presentation with humorous anecdotes will go down like a lead balloon and you will be seen as flippant and lacking seriousness. Discretion is highly prized in business relationships and chemistry also plays a role – you should be able to relate to your opposite number.

Clarity is important and appreciated by Germans. If at any time you don't understand something or fear that your business partner has misinterpreted something, address it head-on. A presentation should be specific, factual, technical and realistic, with information backed up by facts, figures, tables and charts. You should know your topic inside out and prepare answers for probable and possible questions. If you're under-prepared, you won't be taken seriously.

Timekeeping

Germans are notoriously punctual and schedule-focussed. You should aim to be at least five minutes early for an important meeting and phone if you're delayed. Meeting deadlines, whether for delivery of goods and services or payment, is vital to retain trust and credibility with business partners.

Agenda

Germans tend to be organised and procedure-oriented and don't appreciate surprises. Therefore, meeting agendas are followed to the letter and any deviation is considered suspicious or a waste of time. If you have any amendments to make, you should have a very good reason and inform the chair in advance.

Language

Many Germans have at least intermediate proficiency in English, but it's impolite to assume that your German business partners can and will want to communicate in English, especially during key negotiations, when speaking in a second language would put them at a distinct disadvantage. If your German isn't up to scratch, bring along an interpreter.

Germans are tough negotiators and many see compromise as failure; they will expect 110 per cent but may just settle for 100 per cent.

Negotiating

When negotiating with Germans bear in mind the following:

- You need patience to negotiate with Germans, as they're methodical and thorough. Negotiations are slow and involve a detailed analysis of facts.
- Your negotiating team should include technical experts in addition to experienced executives. In Germany the metric system is used, therefore be sure to quote in kilos, metres, litres, centigrade, etc. – and prices in Euros!
- Expect your German counterpart to be very well prepared and ensure that you are also; Germans rely on objective facts, therefore you should

be prepared to provide comprehensive data to support any claims.

- Your counterpart may have to seek approval from a senior colleague before accepting an offer.
- Germans express disagreement openly. Too much tactfulness on your part might be seen as weakness or incompetence.
- Don't overplay your hand. Germans prefer straightforwardness and concreteness and are astute at picking up on someone who's bluffing. You should never promise something you cannot deliver.
- Germans are typically not risk-takers and always have contingency and fallback plans.
- Germans don't make concessions easily but are willing to look for common ground.
- Being confrontational and aggressive are counterproductive.
- Personal feelings and relationships aren't relevant to business negotiations, as they can compromise a deal.
- Contracts are final and once signed they leave no room for further negotiation. Failure to honour the terms and conditions of a signed contract can lead to legal action.
- Expect a celebratory drink or party upon closing a major deal.

> **'Customer needs have an unsettling way of not staying satisfied for very long.'**
>
> Karl Albrecht (founder of the Aldi supermarket chain)

Regional & Other Differences

Business etiquette may differ slightly from region to region, for socio-economic, political and cultural reasons. Northerners are considered more stolid and southerners more relaxed and open, for example.

But there are also contrasts in business style and methods, irrespective of region. Modern companies are often based on US models, using the latest technology and 'progressive' management styles, whereas long-established German companies may be conservative, having used the same business model successfully for years. You should take these differences into account and be flexible in your approach.

EMPLOYING PEOPLE

German workers enjoy extensive protection thanks to powerful labour unions and you must consider the implications carefully before taking on employees. Above all, can you trust them and do you think they will do a good job? Do you want them for the long term (they're nearly impossible to fire)? And are they worth the cost (see below)?

Contracts

When employing people in Germany it's essential to understand the difference between freelancers and contract employees. Freelancers (*freier Mitarbeiter*) are workers who take care of their own taxes and insurance and are a safer and cheaper option for an employer, as you don't need to pay health insurance and other contributions, and may use their services as required.

Contract employees (*Angestellte*) are the opposite of freelancers in that you're obliged to give them a set number of working hours, to pay insurance (health, unemployment and retirement) contributions, and holiday and sick pay (among other things), and it's difficult to terminate their contracts. Most contracts include a six-month probationary period (*Probezeit*), but after the six months are up, an employee automatically has a permanent contract (*unbefristeter Vertrag*) and can be dismissed only for serious breach of contract – and even then dismissal can lead to an expensive court case.

The other possibility is a temporary contract (*befristeter Vertrag*), which runs out after six months or a year and can be renewed. If after three years the employee still works for you, the contract may automatically become a permanent contract, but you'll know by then whether he's worth keeping.

Domestic Help

Hiring a cleaning lady or a nanny/babysitter is often done 'under the table' – especially with immigrants – in order to avoid red tape and (in the case of the person hired) taxes.

You should be careful of doing so, however, because if you're caught you may be fined. The other disadvantages of hiring illegally are that you cannot deduct the cost from your taxes and, if your hired help has an accident, he isn't insured and you could be held liable – which could be **very** expensive. When hiring domestic helpers, make sure you check their residence permits. There are stiff penalties for hiring illegal aliens.

Social Security

All German employees and foreign employees working for German companies must be enrolled in the German social security (*Sozialversicherung*) system. Social security provides disability, health, long-term care and unemployment benefits, work accident insurance and pensions.

Contributions are usually calculated as a percentage of gross income and are deducted by employers before salary payments are made. The cost of social security contributions is astronomical, totalling as much as 80 per cent of gross salary, split 50-50 between the employee and the employer.

Tax

As a business owner you must pay municipal trade tax (*Gewerbesteuer*) and value added tax (*Mehrwertsteuer*).

You must also deduct the income tax (*Einkommensteuer*), solidarity surcharge (*Solidaritätszuschlag*) and church tax (*Kirchensteuer*) from your employees' pay and send it to the tax office. If your business is incorporated, you may be subject to corporation tax (*Körperschaftsteuer*).

A 2007 KPMG study comparing European tax regimes showed that Germany ranked only 17th out of 22 countries for tax attractiveness (the UK ranked 12th). Some 45 per cent of interviewees felt that Germany's tax regime was unattractive and 25 per cent very unattractive, while only 25 per cent rated it as attractive.

TRADE UNIONS

Trade unions in Germany are highly organised and play an integral role in the 'social market economy'. The largest and most powerful union organisation is the Deutsche Gewerkschaftsbund (DGB), which is an umbrella group for Germany's eight industry trade unions with around 8.6m members. Normally, individual unions negotiate with the relevant employer organisations, and the resulting agreements apply to an entire industry rather than to individual companies or categories of employee.

Under German law, unions are allowed to organise on company premises, but 'closed shops' are banned. Civil servants (i.e. government employees) aren't permitted to strike in Germany, although they can be members of unions. Most private employees (including managers) have the right to strike and cannot be dismissed for striking, although, as usual in Germany, there are rules and regulations governing exactly how and when strikes must be announced and carried out.

Joining a Union

Employees cannot be required to join a union, but the benefits of membership include free access to legal services should you need to go to labour court, and job training programmes. Membership fees are tax-deductible.

If you're in a union, it's best not to advertise the fact to your boss, who isn't entitled to ask whether you're a union member.

WORKING HOURS

Working hours (*Arbeitsstunden*) in Germany vary according to your employer, your position, the industry in which you're employed and the regional or industry collective agreement, but most companies have a 38.5-hour week for full-time employees.

Office hours are normally between 8am and 6pm weekdays with a one-hour lunch break at either 12pm or 1pm. However, many companies operate on flexi-time, which means that employees can come in as early as 7am and stay as late as 9pm. Businesses with transatlantic partnerships often have later working hours to take account of the time difference.

In factories, work may start as early as 7 or 7.30am with quitting time at 3.30 or 4pm, depending on the length of the official lunch break. Most business premises are open from around 6.30 or 7am until 6 or 7pm Mondays to Fridays.

Breaks

Coffee or tea breaks (*Pausen*) are strictly scheduled in Germany and usually last 15 or 20 minutes. A break of 45 minutes to an hour for lunch is usual in most offices, where it isn't usual to eat at your desk (many companies have a canteen). Business lunches are usually taken between noon and 2pm and should last no more than an hour.

Holidays

Your annual holiday entitlement (*Urlaubsanspruch*) depends to some extent on your employer and the collective agreement (*Tarifvertrag*) that applies to your industry. Under German labour law, all employees working a five-day week receive a minimum holiday allowance of 20 working days (i.e. four weeks) per year, but in most industries a minimum of 25 days (or five weeks) is standard and the average amount of holiday actually taken is nearly 30 days. Part-time employees receive a pro rata holiday allowance based on the number of days they work a week. Employers cannot count German public holidays (see below) as annual holiday.

You should make holiday requests in writing at least two months in advance

Public Holidays

Date	Holiday
1st January	*New Year's Day (*Neujahr*)
6th January	Epiphany (*Heilige Drei Könige*) – only in Baden-Württemberg, Bavaria and Saxony-Anhalt
March or April	*Good Friday (*Karfreitag*), *Easter Sunday (*Ostersonntag*) & Easter Monday (*Ostermontag*)
1st May	*May Day or Labour Day (*Maifeiertag or Tag der Arbeit*)
May or June	*Ascension Day (*Christi Himmelfahrt*)
	*Whitsun or Pentecost Sunday & Monday (*Pfingsten/ Pfingstmontag*)
	Corpus Christi (*Fronleichnam*) – only in Baden-Württemberg, Bavaria, Hesse, North Rhine-Westphalia, Rhineland-Palatinate and Saarland
August	Assumption Day (*Mariä Himmelfahrt*) – only in Bavaria and Saarland
3rd October	*Day of German Unity (*Tag der Deutschen Einheit*)
31st October	Reformation Day (*Reformationstag*) – Protestant areas only
1st November	All Saints Day (*Allerheiligen*) – Catholic areas only
November	Day of Repentance (*Buß und Bettag*) – only in Saxony
25th December	*Christmas Day (*1. Weihnachtstag*)
26th December	*Boxing Day (2. *Weihnachtstag*)

(your company will supply a form). Most people take their holidays in summer, so you may have to compete with others to get time off. Parents with school-age children get priority during school holidays.

Christmas & Easter

The festive period in Germany is from 24th December to 6th January. The week preceding Easter Monday is also a peak holiday period and not a good time to do business.

Public Holidays

Public holidays (Feiertage) vary from state to state (Land) and sometimes from community to community within a given Land, depending on whether the predominant local religion is Catholic or Protestant.

The table above lists the public holidays in Germany. The days prefixed by an asterisk are national.

Local Holidays

As can be seen from the above list, Baden-Württemberg and Bavaria are the states with the most public holidays each year – usually 12 or 13 – and 24th and 31st December are often half-day holidays. But the place to live if you like holidays is the city of Augsburg (in Bavaria), which has its very own *Friedenfest* in August. In predominantly

Catholic areas, there may be semi-official holidays for Mardi Gras (*Karneval*) in February, such as *Weiberfastnacht* in Cologne and Dusseldorf, *Fasching* in Bavaria and Baden-Württemberg, and *Rosenmontag* in Bonn, Cologne and Dusseldorf.

Leave

There's no limit to the amount of sick leave you can take, though you're entitled to 'only' six weeks' paid leave for the same illness; thereafter, your health insurance (if you have one) pays you a reduced salary. Your doctor must give you a sick note (*Arbeitsunfähigkeitsbescheinigung* or *Krankmeldung*) for illnesses lasting three days or more, stating that you're unable to work.

In contrast to most other countries, where taking sick days is considered lazy and may even get you the sack, in Germany it's widely believed that if you're ill you should rest (usually for a week) and recover fully before returning to work – both to prevent a relapse and to avoid infecting others. Coming to work with a cold can make you very unpopular – the German attitude is 'keep your germs to yourself'. (Incidentally, a good way to get a few seats to yourself on public transport is to cough and sneeze.)

Most German companies allow days off for moving house, your own or a family marriage, the birth of a child, the death of a family member or close relative, and other major 'life events'. Grounds for compassionate leave (*Sonderurlaub*) are usually defined in collective agreements.

Parental Leave

Under the Mother Protection Law (*Mutterschutzgesetz*, abbreviated as *MuSchG*), mothers and mothers-to-be are entitled to paid maternity leave (*Mutterschutz*) for six weeks before and eight weeks after the birth of their child. Mothers and fathers are entitled to up to three years' partially paid parental leave (*Elternzeit*) to raise the child, with job protection, although it's uncommon for fathers to take this. If you choose to return to work before the three years are up while continuing to receive *Elternzeit* pay, you may work part-time for up to 30 hours a week and resume your original work contract after three years. You also have the right to cancel *Elternzeit* at any time before the three years are up and return to your old job, which means you forfeit your right to the extra work protection provided during *Elternzeit*.

The government pays the first 12-14 months of parental leave at 67 per cent of the person's average salary. If only one parent takes leave, he is paid for 12 months; if both parents take at least two months' leave, they're eligible for 14 months' benefit, divided between them. They may stay at home or work for up to 30 hours a week – either way they receive the same benefit. Immigrant parents are also eligible for this subsidy, provided they live and work in Germany legally.

If a public holiday falls on a weekend, there's no substitute weekday holiday for those who don't normally work weekends. If a holiday falls on a Tuesday or a Thursday, many workers (particularly civil servants) are allowed to take the preceding Monday or following Friday off. This is known as a 'window-day' (*Fenstertag*).

Chilehaus, Hamburg

ICE train

7.
ON THE MOVE

Most German cities and large towns have excellent and affordable public transport system and extensive networks of bike lanes, and there are first-rate nationwide bus, rail and airline services. But despite all this, Germany is a car culture. To help prepare you for the shock of driving in Germany, this chapter contains useful tips on driving etiquette and where to park, as well as a summary of the road rules and information on getting around on public transport.

Germans loathe speed cameras and have been know to pelt them with rocks, shoot at them and even set them on fire.

DRIVING

Germany has one of the highest rates of car ownership in Europe, with a total of over 46m registered cars. Germany also manufactures some of the world's most impressive high-performance cars (e.g. Audi, BMW, Mercedes and Porsche) and has a superb free motorway (*Autobahn*) network with no speed limits, which encourages the German propensity for high-speed driving. Irrespective of your motoring experience, you may find driving in Germany a taxing, and at times nail-biting, experience (unless you're Italian, Portuguese or Spanish ...).

If someone on the road annoys you, don't 'give them the finger' or you could be fined over €1,000. If you insult a police officer or other uniformed traffic official, the fine is €1,500. Until recently, the German police had an official list of offensive phrases and corresponding fines – presumably derived from long experience of being insulted.

Drivers

Like most things in Germany, driving is taken very seriously and you must undergo a stringent testing process to earn a driving licence. This ensures that motorists have a fairly high level of competence, and Germans generally follow the rules of the road (both written and unwritten – see below) and expect you to do the same.

Most serious crashes occur on 'ordinary' roads, outside built-up areas, rather than on the motorways (as one might think), and are caused by speeding or impatience. Many drivers are extremely aggressive: tailgating, honking their horns the second a light turns green, constantly changing lanes and often cutting in with no more than a few metres to spare. Some tell you to get out of 'their' lane by flashing their headlights at you, which is illegal. Not all aggressive drivers on the *Autobahn* are Germans, however: foreigners often come whizzing by at impossible speeds in Ferraris and Aston Martins, taking advantage of the almost unique German speed-limit-free roads.

German Roads

Most German cities are connected by the *Autobahn* network, which extends for 11,500km (7,132mi). Motorways are generally in good condition and there are rest stops at convenient intervals. Although there's no official speed limit on most parts of the network, there are official speed limits at junctions and in other dangerous areas and a 'recommended' speed limit everywhere. Although the recommended speed is 130kph (82mph), driving in excess of 160kph (100mph) is common and high-performance cars can (just) be seen racing by at well over 200kph (125mph).

There's also a well developed and maintained network of inter-state roads (*Bundesstrasse*). Unless a sign indicates otherwise, the speed limit is 50kph or 60kph (31 to 27mph) in cities and 100kph (62mph) in country areas. Not surprisingly, there are a lot of 'accidents' in Germany, where well over 5,000 people are killed annually on the roads and some 450,000 injured. If you wish to avoid becoming one of them, it's essential to study the rules below and to practise defensive driving.

'Winter' tyres (i.e. tyres with studs) are required for driving on snow-covered roads. If apprehended without them you must pay a fine and in the event of an accident you may lose your insurance cover.

Road Rules

The following rules apply to driving in Germany generally:

- The Germans drive on the right-hand side of the road.
- All motorists must carry a red warning triangle (*Warndreieck*) and an up-to-date first aid kit, which should be stored inside the car within reach of the driver's seat and not in the boot (trunk), as this could be damaged and jammed shut in an accident. If you have an accident or breakdown, the triangle must be placed at the edge of the road, at least 50m (160ft) behind the car on secondary roads, 100m (325ft) on major roads and 200m (650ft) on motorways.
- If you need to wear glasses or contact lenses when driving, this is noted on your German driving licence and you must always wear them and carry a spare pair.
- When motoring outside the country in which your car is registered, your vehicle must display either the new EU-style number plates, which incorporate a letter or letters showing the country of registration surrounded by the EU yellow stars, or have a nationality sticker affixed to the rear.
- The wearing of seatbelts is mandatory and includes passengers in rear seats where seat belts are fitted. Children up to the age of 12 and shorter than 150cm (59in) are permitted to ride in a vehicle only in an approved safety seat that's appropriate for their size. They may

not ride in the front seat if they can be accommodated in a back seat.

- All drivers must give way to police cars, ambulances and fire engines 'on call' (i.e. with flashing lights and wailing sirens) and trams and buses when they're leaving stops.
- Drive no faster than walking speed (*Schritttempo*) when passing a stationary tram or bus, particularly a school bus. Where passengers must cross a road to reach a pedestrian path, e.g. from a tram stop in the middle of the road, you must stop and give way to them. You may not pass a school bus when its red lights are flashing.
- On secondary roads without priority signs (a yellow diamond on a white background, used throughout most of continental Europe), you must give way to vehicles coming from your right. **Failure to observe this rule is the cause of many accidents**. The priority to the right rule usually also applies in car parks.
- When two vehicles meet on a narrow mountain road, the ascending vehicle has priority and the other must give way or reverse as necessary. On roads where passing is difficult or isn't permitted, slower traffic is required to pull over when possible to allow faster traffic to pass.

Motoring Fines

On-the-spot fines (*Strafzettel* or *Bußgeld*) of up to €35 can be imposed for traffic offences such as minor speeding, not being in possession of your driving licence or vehicle documents, failing to remove the ignition key when leaving a vehicle unattended, not using dipped headlights at night and parking infringements.

- Using your mobile phone (unless it's a hands-free model) when driving isn't permitted in Germany and can earn you a fine of €40.
- If you witness an accident, you must stop and give assistance.
- You must signal before overtaking and when moving back into an inside lane after overtaking.
- In a city or town you may not use your horn except when necessary to avoid a collision (a rule that's often ignored).
- You must stop for pedestrians waiting at a crossing if they show any intention of crossing the road. Pedestrian crossings that aren't at traffic lights are indicated by thick

white stripes on the road known as zebra stripes (*Zebrastreifen*). It's prohibited to overtake on or near zebra stripes or to park your car on them.

- Vehicles with a gross permitted weight of 7.5 tonnes or more are prohibited from public roads on Sundays and public holidays from midnight until 10pm (i.e. from midnight Saturday until 10pm Sunday evening) and at other times they must pay a toll (*Maut*).

The following regulations apply on German motorways:

- Vehicles with a maximum speed of less than 60kph (37mph), including bicycles and mopeds, are prohibited from using motorways, as are pedestrians.
- Overtaking on the right is prohibited. Slower vehicles must move to the right to allow faster traffic to pass. The left-hand lane is for overtaking only and as soon as you've completed your manoeuvre you must return to the right-hand lane.
- Stopping, parking, U-turns and reversing are prohibited, including on motorway (*Autobahn*) hard shoulders and entrance and exit roads (except in an emergency).
- In traffic jams, motorists must leave a gap between the left-hand lane and the adjacent lane for emergency vehicles. This is accomplished by traffic in the left-hand lane moving as far to the left as possible and traffic in the adjacent lane moving as far to the right as possible.
- It's illegal to run out of petrol (you can be fined for doing so) or use full beam (high beams), unless appropriate.

> Fines for exceeding the speed limit are between €15 and €425.

And, last but not least, here are some unwritten 'rules' you should be sure to observe:

- Never drive through a traffic light that's about to turn red.
- When a traffic light turns yellow preparatory to turning green, go immediately or the driver behind you will honk or possibly rear-end you.
- Always signal when turning or stopping and use your hard warning lights if you're causing a temporary obstruction.
- Don't leave your engine running when waiting, as you may be reported for causing pollution.

- Don't drive in the left lane of an *Autobahn* unless you're an experienced driver, your vehicle can reach at least 200kph (125mph) and you have nerves of steel.
- Don't drive below 120kph (75mph) on an *Autobahn*; take a scenic route instead.
- Don't overtake a car on the right on the *Autobahn* (except in slow-moving traffic).
- Remember that BMW and Mercedes drivers believe they have the right of way and many stop at nothing to get it – unless you're driving a Porsche.

Points System

Germany has a licence points system: you begin with zero points and with each violation you accrue a certain number of points on your licence (and fines), which has the following consequences:

> **Twelve points** – You receive a warning to pay attention to your driving habits
>
> **Fourteen points** – You must attend driving classes to retain your licence
>
> **Eighteen points** – You lose your licence

Points for minor violations are removed from your record after between two and five years, unless those violations resulted in an 'accident', in which case you must wait ten years.

- over 30mg/100ml blood along with signs of intoxication – 7 points on your licence, up to five years' imprisonment or a fine (whether you've caused an accident or not) and withdrawal of your licence;
- 50-110mg/100ml blood without apparent signs of intoxication – 4 points on your licence, a fine of up to €1,500 and withdrawal of your licence;
- over 110mg/100ml blood – as first bullet above.

If your licence is suspended (which it can also be for speeding) for up to three months, the police generously allow you to choose when it would be most convenient for you to be without a car. To regain your licence, you must pass physical and psychological tests at your own expense.

Finding Your Way

It's highly recommended that you study a map carefully (or use a satnav system) before hitting the road. You

don't want to be 'rear-ended' by some impatient driver because you've stopped or slowed down unexpectedly to check something. The German motoring club, ADAC, and Shell publish excellent maps of Germany, and local maps are readily available at kiosks, railway and petrol stations and tourist offices. You can also download route plans and city maps from the internet.

Motorcyclists & Pedestrians

Be wary of cyclists and moped riders. It isn't always easy to see them, particularly when they're hidden by the blind spots of a car or are riding at night without lights (illegal, but it happens). When overtaking cyclists or motorbikes, give them a wide berth.

By law there must be at least 150cm (60in) between your vehicle and a cyclist when you overtake. Be warned that motorcyclists often overtake on the inside and weave in and out of traffic.

German pedestrians usually wait for the green light to cross the road, but it's as well to be cautious.

Roundabouts

Roundabouts (traffic circles) aren't as popular in Germany as in some other countries, although they've become more common in recent years. Vehicles on a roundabout have priority and not those approaching it, who are faced with a give way sign (a white triangle with a red border). But, of course, traffic flows anti-clockwise around roundabouts and not clockwise as in countries where motorists drive on the left (e.g. the UK).

Traffic Jams

Although the country has an excellent road system, which includes some 226,500km (140,312mi) of main roads, it's notorious for its traffic jams (*Stau*), which can be encountered at any time. You might be disappointed when you set out on a trip with high expectations of racing along the motorways and find instead a giant car park, with traffic backed up for miles.

In addition to the expected congestion during rush hours, the roads are usually clogged on school and public holidays, when millions of Germans take to their cars. School holiday dates vary from state to state in an attempt to reduce road congestion, but it seems to have little effect.

Rush Hours

Rush hours are on weekdays from 7 to 9.30am and 4 to 6pm. Evenings are usually fairly quiet, although in major cities rush hour seems to last all day. On Fridays, especially at the start of holiday periods, rush hour begins as early as 1pm. On Saturdays, streets are congested by shoppers and the worst hours are 1 to 5pm.

Parking

After surviving the *Autobahn* and reaching your destination, you may find yourself with a new challenge: finding somewhere to park. In heavily populated residential areas and business districts, finding a parking space is a major problem and drivers must find often find a 'creative' solution – usually by mounting kerbs or parking sideways (the miniscule Smart car is very popular for this reason). In many larger cities, areas are reserved for resident parking during morning and afternoon rush hours. 'Park and ride' services are available in most cities.

Parking is prohibited:

- on or within 5m (16ft) of a pedestrian crossing or junction;
- within 10m (32ft) of 'Stop' and 'Give Way' signs and traffic signals, if parking would obstruct other motorists' view of the sign;
- within 15m (50ft) of a bus or tram stop;
- within 50m (160ft) of a railway level crossing outside a built-up area and within 5m of a pedestrian crossing in a built-up area;
- on a main road outside built-up areas;
- in front of entrances/exits;
- adjacent to a traffic island or roundabout;
- on taxi ranks and motorways;
- anywhere there's a 'No Parking' sign (a blue circle with a red border and a single red diagonal line).

Legal street parking is indicated by a blue sign with a white 'P', although wherever you park there must be at least 3m (10ft) between the middle of the street and your car. This may require that you park partly or completely on the pavement. Parking in some areas is subject to time limits, in which case you need a parking disc (*Parkscheibe*); you set the time you parked and leave the disc within view.

There are also a lot of covered car parks or garages (*Parkhäuser*) and on-street parking places where you must buy a ticket from a machine for a specific period.

Parking Illegally

Fines for parking illegally are usually between €5 and €25 and the ticket is left on your windscreen. If you're obstructing an exit, pedestrian crossing (crosswalk) or fire lane (like a bus lane, for fire engines), your vehicle may be towed away, in which case you must contact the police to get it back and pay a fee of around €200. Double parking isn't common in Germany, but if you cannot get out of a parking space because someone has double parked, it's no good calling the police, as they won't help you. You can either call a towing company, pay the fee and try to sue the owner of the other vehicle for the cost (which may be more trouble than it's worth) or simply wait for him to return.

Petrol Stations

Petrol stations (*Tankstellen*) in Germany are mostly self-service. Opening hours vary, but most stations are open from 7 or 8am until 10 or 11pm, although many are open 24 hours a day. Since supermarkets normally close early, petrol stations are handy for after-hours shopping, but you pay dearly for the convenience.

Petrol pumps which accept credit cards aren't common in Germany and after you've filled your tank you usually have to go to the cashier and give the number of your pump. Unless otherwise stated, garages accept payment in cash or by debit card. Most petrol stations also accept credit cards, although you shouldn't rely on paying by credit card in rural areas. If a garage is in an area with a high risk of robbery (especially after dark), you may be required to pay in advance; if you pay in cash, no change may be given, as all money is deposited directly into a safe (which the attendant is unable to open) to prevent robberies.

PUBLIC TRANSPORT

Public transport (*öffentlicher Verkehr or öV*) in Germany is reliable, clean, safe, comfortable and comprehensive, with excellent connections between different modes of transport, which include planes, trains, trams, buses and underground trains (subway). There are also river and lake ferries and cable-cars, although these usually cater more for tourists than residents. Inter-city services are provided largely by air and rail, and inter-city bus services are virtually non-existent.

City transport is easy to use, as only one ticket is required for all modes of transport within a city or region. Rural transport, by contrast, offers only infrequent services outside school starting and finishing times. Weekend services, particularly outside tourist areas, can be very limited.

> **Disabled Access**
>
> Access to public transport for the disabled and for people with pushchairs is limited and not to be relied on. At ticket windows you can get a brochure listing all stations with disabled access (barrierefrei). Be sure to check whether there's a lift at a railway or underground station, as some have only an escalator. Even so, lifts (and escalators) are sometimes out of order and you may have to phone for assistance. Buses normally have ramps and the bus driver will get out to help you board if necessary. Trams and taxis are rarely wheelchair accessible, although taxis for the disabled can be ordered by phone.

Planes

Travelling by plane in Germany is efficient and convenient. The three largest national airlines are Lufthansa (💻 www.lufthansa.com), Air Berlin (💻 www.airberlin.com) and Tui Fly (formerly Hapag Lloyd Fly/HLX, 💻 www.tuifly.com/en). Lufthansa has hubs at Frankfurt and Munich airports and, surprisingly, offers regular discounts on fares between German cities (sometimes cheaper than train fares). Even better value are the dozen or so 'no-frills' airlines, which include subsidiaries of Air Berlin and Lufthansa (e.g. Condor), German Airlines (💻 www.german-airlines.com), German Wings (💻 www.germanwings.com) and LTU (💻 www.ltu.de).

Major city airports are huge but well organised with signs and information desks to help you find your way, but the distances from car park to check-in to departure gate can be vast, and you should allow plenty of time to catch your plane. There are still some smoking areas in German airports; if you're a smoker, enjoy them while you can.

Rail

The different modes of rail transport in Germany are:

- *Eisenbahn* – main-line railways, connecting cities. The extensive railway network is run by Deutsche Bahn, which has made huge investments in recent years, particularly in high-speed lines allowing trains to travel at up to 320kph (200mph). Trains are reliable and, because most main stations are in the city centre, you often need no further transportation – which is why taking the train can be more convenient than air travel. Rail fares are based on the quality and speed of trains, in addition to the distance travelled, which means that money can be saved by choosing a slower train.
- *Strassenbahn* – trams (streetcars or trolleys), which operate in many cities. Using trams is a pleasant way to get to know a city but much slower than the U-Bahn, since they must negotiate road traffic. Trams marked with an 'N' run every half hour or hour throughout the night.
- *U-Bahn* – underground (subway) in Berlin, Hamburg, Munich and Nuremberg – the quickest way to get around, running approximately

every five minutes at peak times, otherwise every ten minutes. The *U-Bahn* usually stops soon after 1am.

- *S-Bahn* (short for *Stadtbahn*) – suburban ('light') railway found in many cities. The *S-Bahn* often runs underground in the city centre and above ground outside the city and can be distinguished by a circular green sign with a white 'S' in the centre. Stops are normally further apart than on the *U-Bahn* and trains less frequent – every 10 to 20 minutes is typical – but routes extend into the surrounding area. At a main station the *S-Bahn* often runs from underground platforms (*Bahn* or *Gleis*) separated from the main part of the station and accessible via an escalator or lift.

Trams and *U*- and *S-Bahnen* are integrated into city transport systems and can be used with a universal ticket that's also valid on buses.

Make sure that you validate your ticket before travelling on public transport; otherwise you're riding illegally and will have to pay a €40 fine if apprehended. Tickets bought from machines in trams and buses are automatically time-stamped by the machine.

Buses

Regional bus companies offer connections between urban areas, as well as services linking major towns to outlying villages. In most cases these operate in conjunction with regional train services and generally the bus station adjacent to the railway station. Many services cater particularly for schoolchildren, however, and therefore operate only during term time, from Mondays to Fridays (or Saturdays), and at the start and end of the school day. Travelling long distances by bus is uncommon.

Ride-sharing

One way to save money, either as a driver or a passenger, is through a ride-sharing service. Drivers register their destination, how many places they have free in their cars and their intended departure time at a *Mitfahrzentrale* (usually located near the main railway station), and potential passengers register their desired destination and pay a nominal fee. When the driver drops you at your destination, you also pay him a fee, which is regulated by the *Mitfahrzentrale*.

Taxis

Taxis in Germany are easily identified by their cream colour and the 'Taxi' sign on the roof. Many are quality makes such as Mercedes and Audi. Fares are shown on a meter inside the vehicle and usually consist of a minimum fare of €2 to €3 plus €1 to €2 per kilometre. Prices for long journeys can be negotiated in advance. Round up to the next euro for tip or add a little extra for good service. Rates for evenings and weekends are usually higher, although there are basic rates between towns that are fixed by the local authorities.

Taxis can be hailed on the street (an illuminated 'Taxi' sign indicates that a cab is available) or hired from an official taxi stand found at railway stations, airports and other designated areas, in which case you must take the first taxi in the queue (unless you need a larger vehicle). Taxis can be summoned to your home by telephone for €1.

As in many countries, some taxi drivers are foreigners with little clue where they're going (and possibly no GPS to rely on), so it's good to have at least a general idea of where you're headed before you get in.

ON FOOT

You must wait for a green light before crossing the road at a crossing with a pedestrian traffic light, irrespective of whether there's any traffic, and you can be fined €5 (or, if you're lucky, firmly chastised) for failing to do so. If you choose to cross on a red light, be very careful, as many

German drivers won't stop (they have the right of way and you're at fault for disobeying the rules) and if an accident results you'll be liable for any damage to a vehicle or its occupants – not to mention that you'll probably be seriously injured.

Cyclists are seldom more tolerant. Take care that you don't walk in a bike lane or a cyclist may run you down – and then stop to yell at you for getting in his way.

Gute Reise.

tram, Berlin

Oktoberfest, München

8.
THE GERMANS AT PLAY

When moving to a new country, you may feel like a fish out of water if you don't know the social norms. As Germans generally place a high importance on following rules, whether it be a dress code or table manners, you risk being left stranded. Knowing in advance of what to do and what not to do will make your transition to the German way of life all the smoother. This chapter gives an overview of social customs you're likely to encounter.

'The best education for a clever person is to be found in travel.'
Johann Wolfgang von Goethe (writer & poet)

DRESS CODE

There are few strict dress codes in Germany, although people usually dress neatly and are well groomed. They may not be fashion paragons, though in wealthier cities such as Munich, Stuttgart and Dusseldorf many wear well tailored and designer clothes, but wearing shorts and T-shirts (especially those with silly messages on them) will make you stand out as a foreigner – and an ignorant one. Sweatshirts and trainers are also a no-no unless you're jogging or playing some kind of sport. Germans, do however, often wear sandals with white (or grey) socks.

Young people are heavily influenced by American fashion and you often see little 'gangstas' or 'skaters' strutting about in dangerously low-riding jeans and back-to-front baseball caps.

At home, anything goes unless visitors are expected. Germans will happily slop around in tracksuits, housecoats and slippers – which is one reason they don't like to receive uninvited guests.

Places of Worship

Germany has many beautiful cathedrals and churches, and tourists flock to see them, often wearing shorts and T-shirts, to the chagrin of many, who see church as a holy place of worship. Signs are hung in churches reminding people to comport themselves respectfully. It isn't necessary to wear your Sunday best, but you should dress decently. Not that mosques and other holy places have a strict dress code (e.g. no shorts and uncovered arms).

Social Occasions

Germans dress smartly for social occasions – even just to go out to a beer garden or café. The more important the occasion, the better they will dress. For clubbing, the 'approved' apparel is skin-tight black clothes and, above all, smart shoes; jeans are a no-

no. For information on what to wear to weddings and funerals see **Formal Occasions** below.

Traditional clothing (*Tracht*) is still popular in some parts of Germany – particularly in Bavarian villages, where 'Sunday best' consists of dirndls (dresses with a close-fitting bodice, full skirt and apron) for women and lederhosen and a felt hat with a 10cm goat whisker plume for men. In the cities, especially Munich, you'll sometimes see older people wearing traditional clothing, and it's common among young people during festivals and in beer gardens in summer. If you go to the Oktoberfest, *Tracht* is 'required' and you'll feel out of place if you aren't wearing it.

Work

There's an unwritten sartorial hierarchy in many German companies, where top managers wear a two-piece suit and tie, middle management a jacket and tie and office staff smart-casual clothes. Some companies have very loose rules, allowing employees to wear jeans and polo shirts, provided they don't have direct contact with clients. Manual labourers often wear standard issue bright blue overalls, while in hot weather on a construction site anything (and almost everything) goes.

DINING

Germans like hearty meals, and most restaurants serve *gutbürgerliche Küche*, which means 'cuisine for fine, upstanding people' but equates to 'plain cooking' – usually involving pork (*Schwein*) and potatoes. German food is somewhat heavy and flavourless, and its spiciness spectrum ranges from mild to bland, with no seasoning except for salt and pepper. The only exception is *Currywurst*, a 'curried' sausage. Nevertheless, Germans take the quality of their food seriously, often eating organically produced food with no preservatives or colouring, and they restrict themselves largely to seasonal fruits and vegetables. Even fast food (you've guessed it – *Fastfood*) is generally of a high standard, consisting of *Bratwurst* with mustard, *Leberkäse* (meatloaf) or *Schnitzel* – all served in a bun with *Pommes* (chips). However, the Turkish döner kebab is also popular and a recent survey claimed that Germany's most popular restaurant was McDonald's (somewhere no German admits to going!).

> ***'Der Mensch ist, was er isst'***
> **(Man is what he eats).**
> Ludwig Fuerbach (German philosopher)

Meals

Breakfast

The essential ingredient in any German breakfast is bread, which comes in hundreds of varieties and should be freshly baked. The usual accompaniment is sliced cheese, sausage or ham, or cheese or meat spread instead of (or sometimes in addition to) butter, although some prefer jam or Nutella (a chocolate and hazelnut spread). Coffee is the most popular drink, and it's served reasonably strong. Working people, however, are often reduced to making a mad dash to the bakery – of which there are thousands – to grab a roll (*Brötchen, Semmel*), with either cheese or ham

(they usually aren't served together), croissant or a soft pretzel (*Breze*).

Breakfast at the weekend is usually a more extensive affair, involving plates of cold meat, rolls and spreads, and occasionally a glass two of *Sekt* (sparkling wine).

Lunch

Lunch is the main meal of the day and is normally eaten between 11.30am and 2pm. It usually begins with a small mixed salad topped with a yoghurt or vinaigrette dressing. Soup is another possible starter, made from whatever is in season, e.g. cream of asparagus soup during the *Spargelzeit* (asparagus season) – from mid-April to 24th June – which is officially the latest date you can harvest your asparagus (woe betide you if you're seen picking some up on 25th).

The main course is typically a pork or pasta dish (Italian food is popular), accompanied by a glass of wine or beer. There's seldom room for dessert, but if there is it may be apple strudel (*Apfelstrudel*) with vanilla sauce or ice cream, red fruit compote (*Rote Gruetze*) or sugared pancakes with raisins (*Kaiserschmarrn*), depending on the region.

Many people eat out in their lunch break, when the best deal is usually the 'daily special' (*Tageskarte*).

Brotzeit

Brotzeit – literally 'bread time' – is a between-meals snack that traditionally consists of bread with sliced cheese, ham, *Wurst, brawn* or smoked meat and radishes. It's also referred to as *Vesper*, *Pausenbrot* or *Znüni*, depending on the region.

Dinner

Dinner is usually eaten between 6 and 8pm and consists of either a light cooked meal or a cold meal similar to breakfast with cold meats, boiled eggs and cheese. Beer or wine is served before, during and after the meal. Coffee is sometimes served with dessert, if there is one.

Bread

Although bread is a requirement for breakfast (see above), it isn't an essential accompaniment to lunch or dinner as in some countries. If you're eating in a restaurant and want bread, you may have to ask for it; if a basket of assorted rolls and soft pretzels is already on the table, you usually pay around €1 for each one you eat.

Conversation

Germans don't talk much during meals, but if conversation is initiated it should cover light, neutral topics and you should avoid controversial subjects (see **Taboos** in **Chapter 4**). Don't be

surprised, however, if other diners pepper you with questions about your origins, why you came to Germany and what you like better about Germany than your native land (and vice versa). Tread carefully when answering: Germans typically ask these questions to reassure themselves that foreigners really do like Germany.

Cutlery

Formal Dining

When dining formally and faced with an array of cutlery on either side of your plate, you should start from the outside and work your way in. Dessert cutlery is placed above the plate. Your fork should always remain in your left hand while eating (Americans please note) and you should use your knife only for cutting. Germans eat everything with a knife and fork, including chicken wings, chips and other things you may think of as finger food. If in doubt, follow your host's (or guest's) lead. When you've finished eating, you should place your knife and fork diagonally across your plate, and lay your serviette neatly folded on top.

Informal Dining

The same rules apply as above, except you're given only one set of cutlery and retain it between courses.

Grace

Some households say grace before a meal, but you aren't obligated to do so and may just bow your head out of respect until it's finished. By the same token, if you're the one who initiates grace, don't expect others to join in if they aren't so inclined.

When to Start

It's polite to wait for everyone to be served before starting to eat and for the host to say '*guten Appetit*', to which the polite response is '*gleichfalls*'. In restaurants, however, it's common for dishes to arrive in an uncoordinated fashion (the reason given being that some take longer to prepare than others), in which case it's acceptable to begin immediately so that your food doesn't get cold. In fact, the other diners will normally save you from embarrassment by telling you to dig in. If you're the guest, make sure you say '*das schmeckt*' (it tastes good).

Noises

Coughing and trumpet-like nose blowing are common occurrences at the German table, even in restaurants. Burping and slurping are both considered ill-mannered, however, and such a noise escapes despite your best efforts you should say *Entschuldigung* quietly and act as if nothing has happened.

Seating

On formal occasions, men and women are alternated (a process known as *bunte Reihe machen* or 'making pretty rows') and the host sits at the end of the table. The guest of honour should sit to the left of the hostess if male, to the right of the host if female. The host will tell you where to sit on such occasions or there will be name cards to show you.

Table Manners

In a restaurant or at a formal private dinner, you should always have your hands on the table and never in your lap, but not put your elbows on the table, and your napkin should be in your lap. At informal dinners these rules are relaxed and you sometimes see people with their elbows and serviettes on the table. In any case, you should leave a clean plate, as taking more than you need is considered wasteful, and you shouldn't smoke (if smoking is permitted) until the meal is finished – after politely asking for permission. Using a toothpick is allowed provided it's done discreetly behind your hand.

DRINKING

Drinking (beer) is an integral part of life in Germany and is neither considered uncouth nor regarded merely as a means to getting drunk. Germans each consume an average of 115 litres of beer and 26 litres of wine per year. In Bavaria, beer is classified as food (*Lebensmittel*), which means that it attracts a low rate of value added tax and is often cheaper than soft drinks in restaurants.

The Prosit Song

In order to get the most out of your German beer-drinking experience (and it's one that's hard to avoid), you should learn the Bavarian drinking song:

Ein Prosit, ein Prosit der Gemütlichkeit, ein Prosit, ein Prosit der Gemütlichkeit ... eins, zwei, drei, g'suffa! (or, in Bavarian dialect, *oans, zwoa, drei, g'suffa!)*

'A toast, a toast to that cosy feeling, a toast, a toast to that cosy feeling … one, two, three, bung ho!'

One more time with feeling ...

German beer is world-renowned for its quality and flavour, being brewed in accordance with a centuries-old purity law (*Reinheitsgebot*), and causes a hangover only if consumed in (very) large quantities – or so they say. Drinking is even allowed in the street, although drinking 'responsibly' is expected and you'll rarely see a German falling down drunk – even at the Oktoberfest, where the drunkards are invariably tourists. Drinking ages are low – 16 for beer and wine and 18 for spirits – and rarely enforced, as it's the parents' responsibility to teach their children to drink in moderation.

Germany produces 40 types of beer (*Bier*) and an estimated 5,000 varieties, so why is it that at nearly every pub, restaurant and beer hall you have little or no choice of beer? The reason is that the powerful breweries mark out their 'territories' and draw up contracts with their pub-owner 'customers' (who must clearly mark their brewery affiliation outside their door) dictating how much beer they must buy per month and how many (if any) 'foreign' beers they're allowed to sell. Pub-goers are so used to this that they simply order 'a beer' without bothering to ask what kind is on offer. Each kind of beer is served in a particular type of glass, designed to bring out its full flavour and even at sporting events beer isn't served in a flimsy plastic beaker, but in the appropriate glass.

Toasting

Toasting is extremely popular in Germany (too popular for some), especially in beer halls and at beer festivals, where the band invokes it by playing the *Prosit* song every three minutes (a sneaky trick to make you consume more beer). Although toasting consists of nothing more complicated than clinking glasses (*anstoßen*) and wishing other people good health (you don't need to propose a toast to anyone), to toast like a native you must observe the proper etiquette, which Germans are only too happy to teach you. It's generally as follows:

- The first toast is made once everyone has received their first drink, and you shouldn't start drinking until you've said *Prost* (normally with beer) or *zum Wohl* (normally with wine) and clinked glasses with everyone within reach – one at a time.
- Be sure to look each individual in the eyes and not to clink across other clinkers, which is considered bad luck.
- In some regions you bang the beer mat once with your glass before drinking.
- If you cannot reach someone to clink, make eye contact and nod before drinking.
- Never toast with water.

CAFES, BARS & RESTAURANTS

> **Smoking**
>
> If you're a smoker, Germany is the place for you, as you can find cigarette machines all over town and you're still allowed to smoke in some public places – but not for long. A partial smoking ban is in the pipeline – to be introduced in all states by the end of 2008 – which will ban smoking in the workplace, schools, public buildings and on public transport. As ever in Germany, details will vary from state to state, but most states will allow large restaurants, bars and clubs to have a smoking area, provided it's well ventilated. Some establishments are circumventing the ban by creating private 'smokers' clubs', where only members are admitted.

Cafés

Main cities have a popular café culture, modelled on that of Spain and Italy, and every year at the first sign of spring café terraces are crowded. Many cafés provide outdoor heaters to accommodate guests who prefer to drink *al fresco* in the colder months. Cafés are meant more for people-watching rather than eating, and most provide only soups, salads and toasted sandwiches. However, there are also restaurant-cafés, which offer a full menu and cocktails. Other types of café are the *Café-Konditorei*, which specialises in fine cakes and pastries, and the *Eiscafé*, like an Italian *gelateria*, serving an assortment of Italian-style ice cream.

Germany has two coffee cultures: Italian and Starbuck's. The former consists of elegant cafés serving latte macchiatto, espresso and cappuccino to savour while you soak up the sun and people-watch, the latter of standardised establishments churning out XL frappaccinos 'to go' in paper cups where you can plug into a free internet connection, eat muffins and cookies and feel at home (if you're American, that is). It's usual to take your time over your coffee, and you won't be rushed to pay the bill. In fact, if you see a waiter you should nab him, as terrace service is notoriously slow.

Bars & Pubs

The smallest villages in Germany have at least one bar or pub, while large cities have hundreds. They vary greatly in quality and in the food they offer. Small pubs normally offer snacks (*Kleinigkeiten*) only and are open until midnight or 1am. Larger locales often have more comprehensive menus and stay open until 3am. Places that are open all night are often rather seedy and generally to be avoided. Bars serve draught (local) beer, bottles of imported beer, wine and *Sekt*, and cocktails. Irish pubs are popular and serve Guinness and cider as well as having live music.

Pub prices vary throughout Germany, but you can normally get a half litre (just under a pint) for between €2 and

€3.50 while cocktails usually cost €7 to €9. You normally run up a tab, the waiter or bartender marking each drink served on your beer mat, and pay when you've finished, rounding up to the next euro or two for a tip.

When looking for a table in a pub, you may see tables with a wooden sign on them (or the ashtray) that reads '*Stammtisch*'. These are reserved for regulars, who not only have their own table but also sometimes their own beer steins, stowed away in a private locker. A *Stammtisch* is like a private club of friends or co-workers who meet to let their hair down, and often get into heated debates. If you're invited to sit at one, it's a great honour.

Beer Gardens

Two things that most Germans love are sitting out in the fresh air and sun and drinking beer, which is why beer gardens are hugely popular in southern Germany (the sun isn't so warm in the north). Beer gardens aren't only for beer drinking, however, and the largest seat thousands of people and include playgrounds for children, making them ideal places for family outings. Hot and cold meals are usually available, as well as soft drinks. You may help yourself, or bring your own food, and sit at a table without a tablecloth; those with cloths are reserved for customers who want waiter service. There are often brass bands – unlike their British equivalent consisting of trumpets, French horns, trombones, tubas and sometimes woodwind instruments, such as saxophones and clarinets – playing traditional and (occasionally) modern music.

Dogs

Dogs are allowed almost everywhere in Germany, provided they're well behaved, and you'll see them in shops, restaurants (except upmarket establishments), on public transport and in church. If they aren't allowed, there's usually a friendly sign asking the dog to wait outside for its owner, with hooks provided for the leads.

Restaurants

In larger towns and cities, you can find restaurants serving cuisine from almost every country in the world. The most popular, apart from German, are Italian, Greek and Turkish. Asian restaurants are rather hit and miss, often serving poor quality meat. Thai and Indian restaurants can be good, but the food is usually much milder than the real thing. 'Mexican' restaurants are also popular, but they tend to serve American dishes such as burgers and barbecued chicken wings – Germans usually fail to distinguish between Mexican and American food, both of which are considered to be anything containing sweet corn.

When planning to eat at a restaurant in Germany, you should note the following:

- **Opening hours** – In the cities, most restaurants are open all day every day (noon to midnight on weekdays and noon to 1am at weekends), although family-run establishments have a day off (*Ruhetag*), usually Mondays or Tuesdays. In small towns, most restaurants are open in the evening only (e.g. 5pm to 1am), except perhaps at weekends.
- **Booking** – On Friday and Saturday nights after 8pm any restaurant worth eating at is full, therefore you should book, which can be done in person or by telephone. Note that if you're 15 minutes late on a busy night you may lose your booking.
- **Menu** – Restaurants offer appetisers (*Vorspeisen*), main courses (*Hauptgerichte*) and desserts (*Nachspeisen*). Food is prepared to order and doesn't usually arrive simultaneously for everyone, therefore it's acceptable to start when your food comes (otherwise it will get cold). Sharing starters and desserts is also accepted practice, but you should ask for an extra side plate and cutlery. Restaurants often provide simpler dishes or smaller portions for children, normally listed on the menu under something like '*Unsere kleinen Gäste*'.
- **Seating** – In a German restaurant (i.e. one serving German food), you normally choose your own table and seat yourself; in 'ethnic'

establishments, there may be a sign telling you to wait to be seated. In southern Germany it's acceptable to sit with strangers if a restaurant is full and you need only ask '*Ist da noch Frei*?' (Are these seats free?).

Lighting a cigarette (not that you allowed to smoke anywhere in public any more) with a candle is considered crass and is especially frowned upon in Bavaria, where folk tradition has it that if the flame goes out you kill a sailor.

- **Table settings** – Cutlery and serviettes are often already on the table (in beer steins or glasses) and you simply take what you need. In some restaurants, cutlery is brought just before or with your meal. If there's a basket of rolls and soft pretzels on the table, you usually have to pay around €1 for each one consumed.
- **Water & ice** – Tap water is never served automatically in Germany. If you'd like water, make sure to ask for *Leitungswasser* (tap water); otherwise you'll be served mineral water, which is usually the most expensive soft drink on the menu. Be warned, however, that this request might provoke eye-rolling. If you want ice in your drink, you'll need to ask for it, unless it's a cocktail – but some restaurants will be unable to supply it.
- **Service** – Service is often slow and/or brusque and customers are frequently made to feel unwelcome, although there's little to be gained by complaining. Attitudes are steadily improving as globalisation takes hold, however, and you might be pleasantly surprised.
- **The bill** – You aren't asked to pay or given the bill unless you ask for it, as it's considered rude to rush customers (and there's always the hope that you'll order something else). When you're ready to pay, you should attract your waiter's attention by waving or saying '*Entschuldigung*' and ask for '*die Rechnung, bitte*' or say '*zahlen, bitte*'.
- **Paying & tips** – The waiter brings the bill and, if each person or couple is paying separately, calculates how much they owe. (It's worth checking that this has been done accurately.) Payment is made directly to the waiter, who carries a large wallet, and you may

get a dirty look if you pay with a high-value note. Waiting is considered a profession or trade in Germany, where you won't find many students or other part-timers waiting on tables, and waiters are paid a reasonable wage, therefore they don't rely on tips; nevertheless, many people round their bill up to the next euro or five euros, unless the service has been poor. For adequate service a 5 per cent tip is the norm, and for good service 10 per cent is more than enough (you can tell that Germans aren't big tippers, as modest tips are usually gratefully received).

NIGHTLIFE

Metropolitan areas offer a vibrant nightlife with diverse clubs and bars, including nightclubs (mostly referred to as Discos), jazz clubs, cabarets and sex shows.

Nightclubs

In the major cities, clubs are often found in huge 'entertainment' complexes along with bars and fast food kiosks, open all night. There are sometimes combined tickets, which allow you to club-hop at no extra charge. The most popular clubs play techno, mainstream hits, and what Germans refer to as 'black music' (soul, R & B, hip hop, rap, etc.), but you can also find clubs playing jazz, heavy metal and various types of 'alternative' music.

Note the following when planning a night out in Germany:

- **Opening hours** – Clubs open between 10pm and midnight and usually remain open until 5am or until people start to leave.
- **Age** – Most nightclubs are for 18-year-olds and over, but checks aren't usually made, and if you look at least 18 you're usually allowed in. For younger teenagers there are teen clubs or 'teen nights' in regular clubs.
- **Dress** – Venues often have unwritten dress 'rules', and whether you're admitted or turned away depends largely on whether the bouncer on the door likes the look of you or not. If you're a woman and are smartly dressed (including tidy black shoes), you should have no problem getting in. As clubs want to have an equal ratio of men and women, men sometimes have a harder time – especially in Munich and Stuttgart, where the quality and condition of your shoes can make or break the situation; if they're scuffed or dirty, you might as well have stayed at home.

Cologne by night

Admission Charge

Most clubs charge between €5 and €10, depending on their 'exclusivity' and size and the night of the week; Fridays and Saturdays are usually more expensive.

- **Drinks** – Clubs serve all types of alcoholic and soft drinks but not hot drinks, and there's often a limited selection of cocktails. Everything is a bit more expensive than in a bar (German bars charge exorbitant prices). A favourite 'club' cocktail is Caipirinha (cachaça rum, lime and brown sugar) and a popular long drink is vodka with Red Bull. In most clubs you order drinks at the bar and pay as you go, rather than paying before you leave, as in a bar or pub.

FAMILY OCCASIONS

Birthdays

It's widely believed that the traditional children's birthday party, with a decorated cake and candles, derives from German custom. But a particular feature of a German child's birthday is that a wooden 'wreath' is sometimes placed on the table, with one candle for each year of the child's life (up to the age of 12) and a 'life candle' in the centre. The birthday girl or boy tries to blow out the candles in a single breath – and gets to make a wish if successful.

Adults are expected to throw their own birthday parties, either at home or in a restaurant, where they must pay for everyone's drinks. It's considered bad luck to wish people a happy birthday (*alles Gute zum Geburtstag*) or give them presents before the actual day.

Christenings

Christening ceremonies normally take place before the first birthday for Catholics and later for Protestants, who may wait until children are old enough to decide for themselves whether they wish to be christened. Families often have baptismal gowns that are passed down through the generations. Only family and close friends are invited to the ceremony and there's a party with coffee and cake afterwards. If you're invited it's appropriate to take a gift.

A godmother (*Patin*) and godfather (*Pate*) are chosen for the child. To be chosen is considered a great honour, as it means that you uphold Christian values and will assume guardianship if the child's parents die. Godparents should buy a baptismal candle, which is lit during the ceremony. There's also a financial obligation in being a godparent, as you're expected to give your godchild expensive gifts for every birthday, Christmas and Easter. These should be something permanent, such as jewellery or cuff links.

First Communions

Many children undergo a first communion (*Erstkommunion*) or confirmation (*Konfirmation*) ceremony and enjoy a huge celebration afterwards with family and close friends, who offer gifts. The age for first communion varies widely – anywhere between 6 and 12 – but the ceremony usually takes place on the Sunday after Easter (*Weißer Sonntag*) when a child is in the third class and aged 10 or 11. Protestant confirmation takes place at 14. Girls wear white lace dresses and gloves, and boys wear suits.

Advent

The Christmas holiday season is hugely important in Germany, where many Christmas traditions originated. The season officially starts with Advent (*Adventszeit*), which spans the four Sundays before Christmas and lasts until Epiphany on 6th January. At the start of Advent, families place a Christmas wreath of pine branches on the table with four red candles, lighting one each Sunday until Christmas. Children count the days until Christmas using an advent calendar, which has a door for each day in December (up to the 24th) concealing a piece of chocolate or other treat.

Herr Nikolaus

Saint Nicholas (Sankt Nikolaus) – known in the US as Santa Claus and in the UK as Father Christmas – makes his rounds in Germany in the evening of 5th December, filling children's shoes with small presents such as chocolates, oranges and nuts. In the Catholic tradition, Nikolaus appears at children's homes or schools, wearing a bishop's habit and mitre and carrying a golden book, in which he has kept a record of those who have been naughty and those who have been nice. In some regions he brings along a scary, devilish sidekick, Krampus or Knecht Ruprecht, who 'beats' the naughty children with a cane.

Christmas

Christmas (*Weihnachten*) is a time for families to get together. On Christmas Eve the festivities begin with the decorating of the tree with various ornaments and sometimes candles. The decorating may be done secretly to add to the excitement of the event for children, and at some point in the evening a little bell is rung to signify the arrival of the Christ-child (*Christkind*), when the tree and all the presents are 'magically' unveiled and then opened. Traditions vary greatly from family to family, but the Christmas feast often includes carp, pork or sausages and potatoes. Popular desserts are rice pudding, marzipan, Stollen (fruit-nut bread) and gingerbread biscuits (*Lebkuchen*). On 25th and 26th there's more feasting, when a goose may be eaten. Families also sing carols and play games.

New Year

New Year's Eve (*Silvesterabend*) is normally celebrated with friends in the form of a fondue party at home (with plenty of alcohol) or a night on the town. Most cities in Germany become a party zone and restaurants offer (pricey) five-course dinners and entertainment lasting well into the morning. Be sure to book several months in advance.

Germans like to exchange good luck charms to bring good fortune in the new year, such as horseshoes, ladybirds, chimney sweeps, pigs and four-leafed clovers filled with chocolate or marzipan. Tradition dictates that wearing new red underwear ensures a happy love life for the rest of the year. Another popular tradition is *Bleigiessen*, the pouring of molten lead into cold water to divine the future. Shops sell 'lead kits' (no longer containing real lead) around New Year's Day for this purpose.

Firework displays are common, but if you attend one be sure to find a safe viewing place, as in addition to the official displays there are usually impromptu (and haphazard) 'displays' by people who have bought their own fireworks (sold only between Christmas and New Year's Eve). It's also amusing to watch the normally orderly and conscientious Germans losing their manners as they guzzle champagne from the bottle and ditch their environmental awareness as they smash the bottle on the street. The next morning the country looks like a war zone!

Epiphany

Epiphany or Twelfth Night (*Epiphanie* or *Dreikönigstag*) on 6th January is a holiday in Catholic parts of Germany (mainly the south) and commemorates the day on which the three wise men (or kings), bearing their well known gifts, first laid eyes on the baby Jesus. It also marks the end of the Christmas 'season', when the Christmas tree is 'plundered', meaning that all the edible decorations on it are eaten and it's taken down. Groups of *Sternsinger* (literally 'star singers') go from house to house singing songs, reading poetry and collecting for charity (e.g. UNICEF). On each door they write 'C+M+B+' – which stands for the names of the three kings (Caspar, Melchior and Balthasar) – or the Latin phrase for 'Christ bless this house' (*Christus mansionem benedicat*) and the year.

Weddings

German weddings are usually all-day affairs involving singing, dancing, games and tricks – and a few peculiarly German traditions.

> **Polterabend**
>
> The betrothed couple normally throw an informal party – the *Polterabend* (literally, 'noisy evening') – during the week before the wedding, inviting neighbours, friends and colleagues, who aren't necessarily invited to the wedding itself. Guests bring old plates and cups made of porcelain or stoneware (no glass) and, as they arrive, smash them on the ground; the bride- and groom-to-be then sweep up the mess, which symbolises togetherness even in tough times.

Invitations

Wedding invitations are usually professionally printed and sent by the couple themselves. You should respond in person, via telephone, email or letter directly to the couple (rather than to the parents), within a week. You may be given the names, addresses and room rates of nearby hotels, but it's up to you to arrange accommodation if required.

Gifts

To the ever-practical Germans, an appropriate wedding present is almost always cash, but they've developed creative ways to give it, such as origami butterflies made of €20 notes. The amount you give or spend on a gift depends on how close your relationship is, but it should be no less than around €30 per person. Wedding lists (gift registries) are rare, but if you'd like to buy something rather than give money it's best to choose a household item from a department store, where it will be professionally wrapped.

Dress

For church ceremonies, family and close friends usually dress to the nines, often spending hundreds of euros on an outfit, while other guests dress formally or semi-formally. For the official marriage ceremony at the *Stadesamt* (see below) smart casual is acceptable.

> **Wedding Rings**
>
> The bride and groom wear identical plain, gold wedding bands on the ring finger of their right hand and there's usually no engagement ring.

Key Players

There are seldom bridesmaids or flower girls at a German wedding, and the bride and groom often walk down the aisle together, unaccompanied. The bride's father leads the speeches at the reception, and the witnesses (*Trauzeuge*) sign the certificate. The male witness (similar to a best man) is in charge of 'kidnapping' the bride (see below) and the female witness (similar to a maid of honour) helps out at the reception but has no other duties. Traditionally, the father of the bride paid for her wedding, but nowadays both sets of parents split the cost or the couple pay.

Procedure

German couples often have two wedding ceremonies: the official one, conducted by a justice of the peace at the *Standesamt*, and a church blessing. A legal requirement, the official ceremony normally takes place before the blessing and is a simple affair, lasting under 20 minutes, often accompanied by

rather corny organ music. The official ceremony normally takes place before the church ceremony and is necessary to be married in Germany.

The church ceremony, in contrast, is usually a drawn-out affair – it often goes on for one and a half hours – and includes a sermon, vows and songs. The bride and groom may arrive together bearing candles trimmed with flowers and ribbons, which they place on the altar beside their 'unity candle' (*Traukerze*). Afterwards, the *Traukerze* is taken away by the couple, who light it on every wedding anniversary thereafter.

Wedding Paper

Someone is usually detailed to compile a 'wedding newspaper' (Hochzeitszeitung), which is an amusing collection of old and recent pictures of the bride and groom, anecdotes from friends, cartoons, etc. The newspaper is offered for sale at the reception, the proceeds going to the newlyweds.

When the bride and groom leave, guests may throw rice at them and the number of grains that stick in the bride's hair is (supposedly) the number of children she will have. The bride hands out white ribbons for guests to tie on their cars, and they drive through the town or village in a procession, honking their horns (other drivers sometimes honk back to wish the couple good luck). The bride and groom's car is covered with flowers.

Reception

The reception is usually held at a restaurant and begins with coffee and cake followed by a formal dinner, drinking and dancing. The bride wears her wedding dress the whole night and won't remove her veil until she has had the first dance – typically a waltz – with her husband, after which she dances with her father and the groom with his mother, while the bride's mother dances with the groom's father. During the reception, there are speeches and silly games such as scavenger hunts (collecting a number of everyday items, such as pencils and paper clips, from houses in the neighbourhood), to encourage everyone to mix. The festivities usually go on until late.

At some point during the reception, the bride is 'kidnapped' by the male witness (or another designated man), who carries her off, accompanied by onlookers, to a nearby restaurant or bar. There they sit and drink until the groom arrives with the other guests, whereupon several hours of drinking, games and music ensue. Eventually everyone goes back to the reception. Traditionally, the groom goes from bar to bar to find his bride and pay for everyone's drinks along the way. (This is apparently because most villages had two restaurants, so whenever there was a wedding one was full and the other deserted; the 'kidnapping' was a way of sharing the business.) Nowadays, the kidnapping usually takes place in the bar of the same restaurant.

FUNERALS

When people die in Germany, they're either buried or cremated, but it isn't permitted to scatter the ashes or to keep them in an urn. People often have a simple gravestone or none at all. The family is expected to tend the grave but when the lease on the burial plot expires (usually after 25 years or so) it's re-used.

Services occur at a chapel on the cemetery grounds or at a church (there are no private cemeteries). The casket is normally closed and mourners may throw earth and flowers into the grave. Some services include balloons, music and videos of the deceased, but a traditional solemn ceremony is usual. Afterwards, you may be invited to a restaurant by the surviving relatives. A contribution of €20 (in an envelope) is usual.

As in most countries, people wear black or dark clothes (nothing ostentatious) to funerals.

CLUBS

One of the best ways to meet people and integrate into German culture is to join a club (*Verein*), which include everything from municipal services (e.g. fire-fighting) to sports and social activities, such as games (e.g. chess and bridge), art, music, sports, theatre, cinema and field trips. In addition to an array of German clubs, there are numerous expatriate organisations, including ambassador clubs (which champion humanitarian causes and number over 1,000 in Germany), international women's and men's clubs, business clubs and Rotary clubs.

Your town hall or library will have information about local clubs and your local embassy or consulate may also keep a list of expatriate clubs.

POPULAR CULTURE

Festivals & Fairs

Despite their reputation for being dour, the Germans are fun-loving people, which is illustrated in their vibrant traditions, particularly that of the festival (*Fest*). Every city, town and village in Germany has its festivals, centring on religious, historical or social (i.e. drinking) traditions – or all of the above – and sometimes there are many festivals going on simultaneously in different quarters of a city. Festivals involve parades, loud music, fireworks, displays by artisans and craftspeople, and lots of eating and drinking; they may be billed as 'street festivals' (*Strassenfeste*), craft fairs, or wine or beer festivals (*Weinfeste/Bierfeste*). You don't need to be invited and can simply join in; it's a good opportunity to meet people as everyone lets their hair down. There's little crime, except for occasional pick-pocketing at larger events. Germany's largest and most important festivals are as follows (from January to December):

Festivals in villages and towns are usually organised by the volunteer fire brigade or the local Burschenverein ('bachelors' club').

- **Carnival (*Karneval* or Fasching)** – a Catholic festival normally beginning on Epiphany and culminating on Mardi Gras or Shrove Tuesday (*Faschingsdienstag*). Karneval is most popular in the Rhineland, where the party really gets going on *Weiberfastnacht* (women's carnival) on the Thursday before Ash Wednesday, with women running around cutting off men's ties. From Saturday to Tuesday parades take place in many towns, the most important of which are on

Rose Monday (*Rosenmontag*), when most of the town shuts down and hundreds of thousands of people join in. The main festivities are in Cologne, Dusseldorf and Mainz, where things can get quite out of hand with revellers in costume, drinking and trying to catch prizes thrown from floats. Political satire is an especially popular theme.

- **Starkbierfest** – The period between Ash Wednesday and Easter is normally a time to reflect and to fast in Christians communities, but the idea of not eating for a month was a bit too much for the Bavarian monks, who came up with an officially sanctioned fasting loophole: *Starkbier*, which they referred to as 'liquid bread'. Legend has it that a delegation of Bavarian monks was sent with barrels of the strong (9 per cent), dark beer for the Pope's approval, but unfortunately the delicate brew didn't survive the long journey, therefore when the Pope tried it the taste was so dismal that he instantly sanctioned its use during Lent, thinking that no one in his right mind would want to drink it anyway. Drink it the monks did, in copious quantities, and the tradition continues on to this day in beer halls in Catholic communities as the *Starkbierfest*.

  The most famous *Starkbierfest* is hosted by the Munich beer maker Paulaner at its 'Paulaner am Nockherber' restaurant and beer garden. It begins with a satirical comedy show, attended by leading German politicians, but politics soon give way to strong-man contests and, needless to say, beer guzzling.

- **Walpurgis Night & May Day** (***Maifest***) – Pre-Christian and Christian traditions meet to celebrate the victory of spring over winter, starting on 30th April, when pagans believed that witches would have a final party on the highest peak of the Harz mountains, the Brocken. In Christian times the occasion was named after the Catholic Saint, Walpurga – hence *Walpurgisnacht* (Walpurga's Night) – who was thought to be able to drive out evil spirits. The festival became immortalised in Goethe's *Faust*, but nowadays it's mostly an excuse to throw a party – albeit one with a Halloween-like flavour. Some towns even hold 'witch-burnings', using a wooden witch. Many towns also host May Day festivals on 1st May, with maypole dancing and – you've guessed it – drinking.

- **The Love Parade** – Claiming to be the largest music event in the world, attracting around 1.2m people, this annual one-day summer festival now takes place in the industrial Ruhr area, including Bochum, Dortmund, Duisburg, Essen and Gelsenkirchen. The theme is peace, love, harmony and tolerance, but the music is deafening techno. There's talk of making it a weekend event in future.
- **Oktoberfest** – The world's largest party takes place in September/ October in Munich over 16 days, during which 6.5m visitors down over 6m litres of beer. Surprisingly, the *Oktoberfest* has its origin in a wedding party – that of Crown Prince Ludwig to Princess Theresa von Sachsen-Hildburghausen at Theresienwiese (Theresa's Meadow) in 1810 – it didn't develop into a beer festival until 1896. Today, the 'meadow' is cemented over and accommodates 14 beer tents and an amusement park. The festival originally included horseracing, and horses (now otherwise confined to an agricultural sideshow) still play a major part on opening day, when representatives of all the Munich breweries parade through the Theresienwiese in elaborately decorated carriages drawn by magnificent Clydesdale horses.

  The first keg is ceremoniously tapped (an act known as *O'zapft*) by Munich's *Bürgermeister* (mayor), who tests the quality of the brew – which, it goes without saying, is superlative – before the drinking can begin. Oktoberfest beer is served by the litre (*Maß*) and has a higher alcohol content than ordinary beer (up to 7 per cent).

beer stein

  The *Oktoberfest* – or *Wiesn*, as the locals call it – is nevertheless as much a family festival as a drinking orgy, the families focusing on the amusement park area. Every Tuesday is a 'Family Day' (from noon to 6pm), when the price of rides, shows and confectionery is reduced.

- ***Christkindlmärkte*** – Almost every city in Germany (Nuremburg is one of the most celebrated) boasts a Christmas market – normally beginning on the Saturday before Advent and lasting until midday on Christmas Eve – and each has a unique tradition and atmosphere. Common to most, however, are the scent of *Lebkuchen* (gingerbread biscuits), *Maroni* (roasted chestnuts) and *Glühwein* (mulled wine), live entertainment, life-size nativity scenes and children's activities, as well stalls offering everything from handcrafted glass, ceramic and wooden ornaments in traditional and modern designs to kitchen utensils, pottery and candles.

> **Wagner Festspiele**
>
> The *Festspiele* in Bayreuth, Bavaria in August is a world-famous opera festival celebrating the work of Richard Wagner and has been organised by Wagner's descendents ever since his death in 1883. Demand for tickets is huge and it can take years to get hold of one. If you cannot get a ticket, don't despair as you may be spared a fate worse than death; in the words of Paul de Saint-Victor (French author): 'The music of Wagner imposes mental torture that only algebra has a right to inflict.'

- **The Passion Play** – Performed every ten years in Oberammergau, Bavaria almost continuously since 1634, when the villagers made a promise to God to perform a play in return for their release from the grip of bubonic plague (depicting the life and death of Jesus). Lasting seven hours, including a much-needed interval, and including 2,000 performers, it's presented several times over a five-month period and attracts a total of around 500,000 spectators. The next Passion Play will be in 2010.

Trade Fairs

Famous annual trade fairs and shows in Germany include the Frankfurt Book Fair in October (the world's premier book fair), the CeBIT computer industry trade fair in Hanover in March and the BUGA Garden Show from April to October (held at a different location each year).

Gambling

Licensed casinos are often found in spa resorts (such as Baden-Baden – so good they named it twice), where formal attire is required in the evening. Typical games include roulette, blackjack, poker, craps and slot machines. Most gambling outside of casinos is illegal, except for lotteries, horseracing and slot machines limited to small payouts, which you normally find only in seedy pubs. State and national lotteries are popular and draws are televised live on Saturdays and Wednesdays.

Street Life

Germans love to be outdoors and when the weather is fine the streets are invariably busy. People-watching from street-side cafes is a popular pastime, and on Sundays, when nearly everything is closed, Germans go window-shopping.

Gardening & Parks

Being outside and 'at one with nature' is what Germans love best, and it follows that Germans are keen gardeners, with even the tiniest of plots crammed with plants and shrubs. Those with more space have immaculately mown lawns, apple trees and vegetable gardens. City dwellers hang geraniums from balconies or rent an allotment on the outskirts of the city and spend their weekends gardening or lying in the sun. Most allotments include a hut or shed for tools – with room for the obligatory beer refrigerator.

soccer fan

German cities have beautiful parks that are kept as neat as a pin and are often full of sunbathers, musicians, picnickers, dog-walkers ... and beer drinkers.

Spectator Sports

Football

Football or soccer (*Fussball*) is Germany's unofficial national sport, with literally thousands of amateur football clubs, and Germany is one of the most successful nations in the world at both club and international levels. Germany has won the World Cup three times (in 1954, 1974 and 1990 – only Brazil and Italy have won it more often) and was runner-up in 1966, 1982, 1986 and 2002; it has also won the European Championship three times – in 1972, 1980 and 1996. Germany hosted the World Cup in 2006, when it came third. During European and World Cup competitions, Germany is therefore almost always in the running – and the government takes full advantage of the distraction by passing unpopular legislation.

The national team is, however, going through what is euphemistically described as a transition phase, suffering (like many other countries) from the fact that a large number of foreigners play in its domestic leagues, which hinders the progress of home-grown talent. Many top German footballers also play abroad – mostly in Italy – but increasingly in the UK.

The federal football league (*Bundesliga*) is the premier domestic competition, comprising 18 teams, among which the top dogs in recent years have included Bayern Munich, Borussia Dortmund, Bayer Leverkusen, Hamburg SV, Werder Bremen, FC Köln, FC Kaiserslauten and VfB Stuttgart. Bayern Munich (who play at the Allianz Arena in Munich) is Germany's most successful club side and the current champions.

Bayern Munich boast four European Cups, two Intercontinental Cups and one UEFA Cup and are 13-times DFB cup winners and 21-times German champions.

The average attendance at *Bundesliga* matches is around 25,000. The most popular German players are Michael Ballack (the most popular idol among youngsters, although he now plies his trade with English club, Chelsea), Oliver Kahn, Miroslay Klose, Jens Lehmann and Lukas Podolski.

The football season runs from August to May with a break between Christmas and February, and most matches are played on Saturday afternoons (although they're also played on Fridays and Sundays). German cup (*DFB*) matches are usually played during the week, as are European competition matches. Tickets can usually be purchased at grounds on the day of matches or from ticket offices, and cost from around €15 for standing places (*Stehplätze*) and from €20 for seats. Tickets for big matches and internationals cost at least €50 – if you can get hold of one.

Almost every village or town has a football club, and there are local leagues throughout Germany. Though not quite as extreme as Italian or Spanish fans, German fans are as 'dedicated' as their counterparts in most other countries and there is some hooliganism, especially when English clubs or the England team come to town.

Other Sports

American football: Germany's American football league has 12 teams, divided between north and south conferences, which compete for the German Bowl.

Basketball: A popular sport in Germany, where the top teams participate in the European Clubs Championship, professional basketball has a strong following with 18 teams competing.

Boxing: Although he has lost his last few fights, Germans still haven't completely lost hope that their heavyweight champion, Kosovo-Albanian Luan Krasniqi, will seize the WBO title. Krasniqi has won an Olympic bronze medal and the European Heavyweight and Intercontinental titles.

Golf: The three major annual golf tournaments held in Germany are the BMW International Open, the Deutschebank Players Championship of Europe and the Mercedes-Benz Championship (previously known as the Linde German Masters). The Golf World Championship was held in Germany (Berlin) in 2000 for the first time.

Motor sports: The German Formula One Grand Prix is normally held in August at Hockenheim (near Heidelberg), while the Belgian Grand Prix, just across the border at Spa-Francorchamps, is usually dominated by German spectators.

Tennis: Germany stages a number of professional tournaments annually, among them the BMW Tennis Open in Munich (April/May), the German Open in Hamburg (May) and the Mercedes Cup in Stuttgart (July). Germany also has a Federal Tennis League in which top German and foreign players compete.

THE ARTS

> **Arts Spending**
>
> In a recent comparison of government spending on the arts in 11 wealthy countries, Germany was ranked second (after Finland) with €77 per capita – well ahead of the UK at €21 and the US at a measly €5.

Germany's tradition of investment in the arts dates from the period when each state had a royal patron. As a result, modern Germany has no single 'cultural capital'. Funding is mostly provided by state governments and municipalities and is spread fairly evenly. Almost every town boasts a theatre – over 150 are permanently staffed – an opera house and several museums. Germany's recent economic difficulties are beginning to take their toll, however, and generous state subsidies aren't expected to continue much longer.

Booking

Tickets can be purchased in the following ways:

- **Online** – Most large museums, theatres and cinemas have websites on which you can book, but usually with no English-language option, where you can pay with a credit card or by bank transfer. For an extra fee you can have your tickets delivered; otherwise you need to pick them up before the show at the box office (Abendkasse), after showing your identification and possibly the card you used to pay for them.
- **By telephone** – Calling the box office is a good idea if you want advice on where to sit. Payment methods are the same as for online booking and you can have tickets sent or pick them up.
- **From cash machines** – At most major railway stations there are cash machines which double as service terminals, not only listing tourist information and cultural events, but also allowing you to book tickets using a debit or credit card. Tickets are usually printed immediately.
- **In person** – If you feel more comfortable doing your booking face-to-face, you can obtain tickets for most concerts and shows at the local tourist office, a ticket counter in an underground station or department store, or, of course, at the box office of the venue.

Cinema Booking

Popular films and English-language screenings often sell out quickly, therefore it's worth booking, but you may have to pick up your ticket at the box office no later than 30 minutes before the film starts – or it will be resold. At most cinemas, you're assigned a particular seat and cannot sit anywhere you like.

Cinema, Concerts & Theatre

Disabled Access

Large theatres and cinema complexes usually have disabled access, but most small cinemas and theatres don't.

Food & Drink

It's prohibited to take food into theatres, but food is offered during the interval – at exorbitant prices. For long shows (e.g. Wagner operas) there's a lengthy meal break; you order your meal before the first half and it's waiting for you when you get to the restaurant.

You aren't permitted to take your own food and drink into cinemas (though some people sneak it in), but can buy popcorn (sweet or salted but not buttered), nachos with cheese, hot dogs and the usual sweets (all good healthy grub). In addition to soft drinks, a variety of bottled beers is sold and sometimes even wine, *Sekt* and *Schnaps*.

Germany has numerous annual film festivals, the most famous of which are the Berlinale (Berlin), the Fantasy Film Festival (Munich), the International Film Festival (Mannheim/Heidelberg) and the International Short-film Festival (Oberhausen).

Late Arrival

If you arrive late for a theatre or concert performance, you must wait for the interval or at least the end of the first piece or act before being admitted. Late entrance into a cinema is allowed but is met with disapproval.

Noise

Theatre- and cinema-goers are usually quiet during the show but may chat through trailers and commercials. Mobile phones usually go off once at least once per show, despite repeated requests to turn them off, and the person responsible is loudly chastised.

Homework

If you're going to the opera with German friends or colleagues, you should read up on the plot and the meaning of each song beforehand, as they will almost certainly do. It's considered gauche not to.

Museums & Art Galleries

For historical reasons (see **The Arts** above) and because Germans are passionate collectors, Germany has a staggering number of museums (over 3,000), covering a wide range of topics from science and technology, ancient sculpture and modern art to chamber pots. No single museum is considered 'the best' but some of Germany's most famous museums include:

Bauhaus Museum, Berlin – the Bauhaus architectural movement (1919-1933)

Bayerisches National Museum – Bavarian art and culture

Deutsches Museum, Munich – science and technology

Egyptian Museum, Berlin

German Historical Museum, Berlin

Gutenberg Museum, Mainz – writing and printing

Oberhaus Museum, Passau – Medieval art and culture

Pergamon Museum, Berlin – Classical art and architecture

Pinakotheken, Alte, Neue and Moderne, Munich – painting from medieval times to the present day

Römisch-Germanisch Museum, Cologne – Roman and Germanic history and art

Museum Night

Museum addicts should take advantage of the annual *Lange Nacht der Museen* ('Long Night of Museums') offered by most cities, when you buy a ticket for around €15 and have unlimited access to virtually every museum in the city and to public transport or shuttle buses running between them. In addition to their permanent exhibitions, the museums organise shows with live music and even 'champagne' parties that last until 2 or 3am.

Audio tours: At major museums, 'audio tours' are available in multiple languages. These normally consist of headsets with controls that allow you to hear the description corresponding to a particular display. You can start, stop and replay the recording as you wish. 'Audio tours' are usually free, but you must pay a deposit and surrender an identity document.

Cafés & shops: Only large museums have cafés and shops, in both of which the choice is often limited, although most children's museums have good gift shops. Smaller museums usually sell only catalogues and postcards.

Curators & security: German museum curators and security staff aren't very approachable and don't allow you to get too close to the exhibits, bring in large bags or backpacks, or use mobile phones.

Disabled access: As most museums are housed in historic houses or castles, many aren't wheelchair accessible therefore it's important to check before visiting. Some of the grandest museums have been refurbished and lifts added, although you may have to ask to use one.

Displays: Large museums have attractive displays with multi-lingual labels, and science museums tend to have interactive displays, but small museums often have dusty old relics with descriptions only in German.

Entrance fees: Most museums charge an entrance fee of between €2 and €9. Discounts are available for students, children and sometimes senior citizens. Many museums have free-entry days (e.g. Sundays). Season tickets and discount passes are often available, and many cities offer tourist tickets that include public transport and discounts at major museums.

Noise: German museums are quiet, and people making a noise are reprimanded.

Opening hours: Opening times vary considerably, but large museums are usually open from 10am to 6pm. Most museums are closed on Mondays and many have extended hours on one day a week (usually Thursdays). Almost all museums are open on public holidays. Last admission is usually 30 minutes before closing time.

Tübingen, Baden-Württemberg

eigene Remstal-
Kürbis
Hokkaido
Muskat-
kürbis
Butternuss
Roter Zentner
Halloween
Zierkürbis
Türken-Turban
Sweet Dumpling
Spaghetti-Kürbis

9. RETAIL THERAPY

Germany offers a wide choice of shopping experiences, from sophisticated boutiques, world-renowned department stores and hypermarkets, to local farmer's markets and grocers offering regional specialities. However, Germany's shopping 'culture' may be very different from what you're accustomed to – particularly if you're coming from the US. It can be a pleasant experience if you modify your expectations and follow the 'rules', which are explained in this chapter.

Germans love to shop. In fact, you might say it's a national pastime.

CUSTOMER SERVICE

Germany is still somewhat behind the times with regard to customer service and you can come away from your first shopping experience with the feeling that shop owners and staff aren't very interested in selling their products. In many shops and department stores you're expected to fend for yourself, which is fine if you know exactly what you want, but if you're looking for any special attention or general advice you may be greeted with an icy stare and a muttered 'that's not my department'. Some clerks go as far as sending you to competitors to get you out of their hair. If staff are talking amongst themselves, they may not even look up and acknowledge your presence until they've finished their conversation (even if it's a personal one); if you're so bold as to interrupt them, you're likely to receive even more brusque service than usual. Entering a shop shortly before closing time is also sure to make you unpopular with the staff.

That said, the quality of service varies from store to store (and from shop assistant to shop assistant), and many larger shops are trying to improve their service. If you receive poor service or have a complaint, you should ask to see the manager (see **Complaints** below).

Greetings

In small shops you should greet staff (and other customers) with a *guten Tag* or *grüß Gott* (in the south) and *auf Wiedersehen* or *auf Wiederschauen* when you leave.

OPENING HOURS

German shops are highly regulated, and strict labour laws protect the rights of staff (like all other workers), which translates into limited opening hours. Shop hours are decided at state level and therefore vary from state to state, but also from shop to shop. Generally speaking, supermarkets are open from 8am to 8pm Mondays to Saturdays and clothing and department stores from 9.30 or 10am to 8pm Mondays to Saturdays. Most states now allow shops to stay open until 10pm (or even later) on Fridays and Saturdays and to open on some Sundays (see below). Bavaria is the exception: all shops (except bakeries) must close on Sundays and by 8pm on Fridays and Saturdays.

In small towns, shops are often family-owned and close at around 6pm, as well as usually closing for one day a week (*Ruhetag*), on annual family holidays and during local festivals.

Sundays & Public Holidays

Sunday is still considered a day of rest in Germany (whether you want to rest or not) and shops are generally closed, with a few exceptions:

- Every state apart from Bavaria allows shop owners to choose four to six Sundays or public holidays on which to open each year. These are usually during the Christmas shopping season.
- Most shops in airports, petrol stations and railway stations are often open on Sundays, sometimes for 24 hours.
- Bakeries may open for a few hours on Sunday mornings (usually no later than 11am) to cater to the German passion for fresh bread.
- Sunday trading is also permitted if a bakery or small food shop serves 'fast food' (*Imbiss*), in which case it qualifies as a restaurant.

QUEUING

Perhaps the most exasperating part of life in Germany is waiting to be served, when the rule of thumb seems to be whoever is pushiest gets served first. 'Queuing' brings out the same sort of aggression in Germans as driving, everyone feeling that they should have priority. If there's the slightest hesitation on your part in joining a queue or closing the gap between yourself and the person in front, you're considered fair game by queue jumpers. The answer is to be assertive – smiling and being polite will definitely lose you your place – and say '*Ich bin der Nächste*' while moving smartly forward.

In banks and post offices where there are several windows or counters (or machines), there's no such thing as

the snaking 'one-queue-fits-all' system that commonly operates in the UK (which would spoil all the 'fun'). You simply choose one machine and wait in front of it, hoping not to find yourself behind the person who has lost his pension book or card. When you reach the head of the queue, you may think it polite to keep a discreet distance from the person being served, but such discretion is likely to cost you your place. For this reason, you shouldn't be surprised if the person behind you encroaches on your 'personal space' when you're performing a transaction.

Small supermarkets often have only one cash register open at a time, therefore waiting can be interminable – and the impatience levels stratospheric. Don't be surprised if the person behind you plays bumper cars with his trolley if you don't keep close up to the person in front, even though this makes not the slightest difference to his waiting time. Placing a separating bar behind your purchases is also a must, as is bagging them at lightning speed before the next customer pushes you out into the car park.

When it comes to public transport, there's no semblance of order. Those waiting to get on often don't even let people off first. If you're slow – whether elderly, disabled or encumbered by bags or a pushchair – the unwritten rule is that you let everyone else go first, though it isn't unknown for people to be run over by pushchairs or hit with a cane.

SALES & BARGAIN SHOPPING

Until just a few years ago, sales were permitted only twice a year, in summer and in winter – to help shops to restock for the new season. Nowadays, shop owners are permitted to hold sales at any time, although the tradition of the *Winterschlussverkauf* and *Sommerschlussverkauf* persists, and the largest and best sales are usually those held at the end of January and July.

The discount retail chain Aldi has an almost mystic reputation with Germans, who are convinced that its own brands are really top brands in disguise.

Germans are avid bargain-hunters, and at sale times they're ready to pounce as soon as the shops open to get the best deals. This is especially true of the weekly discounts offered at Aldi stores, where shoppers often come close to blows over a cheap grill or a flannel shirt. Sales aside, there are plenty of low-cost retail outlets and discount food shops are especially common and include the Aldi, Lidl, Norma, Penny Markt and Plus chains. Electronics superstores such as Saturn Hansa and Media Markt offer many bargains, while inexpensive clothing chains include C&A (Dutch) and H&M (Swedish).

Flea markets are common and are advertised at town halls, in local newspapers and via leaflets. You can also find them on the internet under *Flohmärkte* (💻 www.flohmarkt.de). Second-hand shops are listed in the Yellow Pages under the English name.

TYPES OF SHOP

There's a constant battle in the German psyche between the desire to retain traditional ways of buying and the lust for bargains. Although hypermarkets are cropping up on the outskirts of cities, most German shops are still compartmentalised, specialised and don't conform to a one-stop shopping system. On the one hand this has the disadvantage of making people visit several different shops to fulfil their needs, while on the other hand is the advantage that small shops tend to have more knowledgeable staff and, for city dwellers, are more conveniently located.

Some of the more common specialist shops are described below:

- ***Bürofachgeschäft*** – provides goods for the office and for arts and crafts and school projects. It also sells legal contracts for all purposes; for example, if you want to let an apartment, you can buy a standard lease that includes all the typical clauses to which you need only add the address, names and price – particularly handy if you don't speak German well or know the relevant regulations;
- ***Drogerie*** – sells toiletries, cosmetics, cleaning products, organic food, baby food, snacks, wine and Sekt and mild vitamins – strong vitamins and medicines are available only from a chemist's (Apotheke) – and provides a photo-developing service;
- ***Eisenwarenhandlung*** – a hardware store which also sells top-of-the-range housewares and provides locksmith's and watch battery-changing services and, believe it or not, cookery classes with 'star' chefs. An Eisenwarenhandlung usually has a huge stock distributed over several floors.
- ***Feinkost-Supermarkt*** – little gourmet food shops, where you can find unusual and local items and quality wines. There are ethnic Feinkost shops in every city

run by migrants from China, Greece, India, Italy, Turkey, Vietnam, the former Yugoslavia and other countries.

- ***Getränkemarkt*** – a 'drinks market' offering a wide selection of drinks (including alcohol) in crates, which you can have delivered. You must pay a deposit on the crate and the bottles, which is refunded when you return them.
- ***Kiosk*** – selling newspapers, magazines, telephone cards, public transport tickets, lottery tickets, ice cream, drinks, sweets, chewing gum, cigarettes and cigars. Kiosks also stock a few baked goods, but it's better to go to a bakery.
- ***Reformhaus*** – a health food shop, supplying herbal remedies, teas, organic foods and products for certain dietary needs, such as gluten-, sugar- or lactose-free food.

It's advisable to do as much of your shopping as possible in local shops, which gives you the chance to practise your German and become part of the local community, giving you a sense of belonging.

Markets

Food Markets

Food markets in Germany are generally outdoors – sometimes in temporary 'tents', sometimes (especially the well established markets) in more permanent buildings. Small farmer's markets (*Bauernmärkte*) are held in village church squares once a week and sell fresh fruit, vegetables, meat and cheese from local farms. They sometimes turn into a mini-festival, with music and fast food (such as bratwurst and chips), with an adjoining flea market.

The largest food markets, such as the Viktualienmarkt in Munich and the Winterfeldtplatz market in Berlin, have hundreds of stalls selling local and imported goods, including fine wines, fish, honey, spices, flowers and plants. Goods are pricey but usually of top quality and, of course, fresh, and the vendors are knowledgeable (and may even be friendly!).

Markets aren't normally self-service and you shouldn't touch the goods, but you can ask to try something before buying, which is usually no problem. If you make regular trips to a market and the stallholders get to know you, they might throw in a few extras – and they often have a stash of lollipops for children.

> **Bring a Bag**
>
> Supermarkets charge for bags for financial as well as environmental reasons, therefore you should remember to bring your own. Strong cloth bags are available at most shops for around €1, while plastic bags cost between €0.10 and €0.60.

FOOD & DRINK

Food quality is important in Germany, where many people may go to the supermarket daily to get fresh produce. The Germans haven't developed a taste for much foreign food, except Italian (although the large population of Turks is beginning to change that), so it's usually necessary to visit a *Feinkost-Supermarkt* (see above) or a hypermarket to find foreign specialities. Some supermarkets offer a small selection of British and

American goods, such as chutney, shortbread, peanut butter and (extremely expensive) maple syrup, as well as some spicy Asian sauces and condiments.

The best foods to be found in a German supermarket are the breads, cheeses and sausages (*Wurst*), which are all of excellent quality and available in a huge variety. Good seasonal produce includes apples, plums, pears, berries (e.g. blueberries, blackberries, raspberries and strawberries), porcino mushrooms (*Steinpilze*) and white asparagus (*Spargel*).

Fresh produce is sold by the kilo and normally weighed and priced by the cashier, but in some supermarkets you weigh it yourself and the scale automatically prints a price label. If you forget to weigh when you're required to you won't be popular at the checkout.

Meat

Pork is the meat of choice in Germany; it's eaten almost daily and in countless varieties, which can make living in Germany difficult for vegetarians and Muslims – and for the squeamish. Germany is the home of blood sausage (*Blutwurst*), and no part of a pig is wasted: some butcher's shops (*Metzgereien*) proudly display tongues, livers, feet, heads and other body 'parts'. Other meats such as poultry (mostly

Expect the Wurst

Es ist mir Wurst – Literally 'It's sausage to me', meaning 'It doesn't matter to me' or 'I don't care'.

Alles hat ein Ende, nur die Wurst hat zwei – 'Everything has an end, only sausages have two' (i.e. all good things must come to an end – except *Wurst*).

Rache ist Blutwurst – 'Revenge is blood sausage' (roughly equivalent to the English saying 'Revenge is a dish best eaten cold').

Sie spielt die beleidigte Leberwurst – 'She's playing the insulted liver sausage', meaning 'She's throwing a tantrum' (only used of women, as German men don't do such things).

Sich durchs Leben wursteln – Literally 'to sausage oneself through life', meaning 'to muddle through'.

Jemanden die Wurst vor der Nase halten – 'To hold a sausage in front of somebody's nose', meaning 'to tempt someone'.

Jeder will seine Wurst haben – 'Everyone wants his share'.

Es geht um die Wurst – 'The sausage is now at stake', meaning 'It's do or die'.

Wurstschnappen – A popular game at children's birthday parties which involves eating a sausage hanging from a string as fast as you can with your hands behind your back.

turkey) and beef are available, but aren't always of high quality, and pork is often added to minced beef. Many supermarkets have a meat counter, which is similar to a butcher's shop but usually with a smaller selection.

Butchers normally specialise in one kind of meat, such as pork, poultry, beef or game, and will prepare it exactly to your specification, including boning, filleting, mincing or slicing. German butchers take great pride in their work and are happy to give advice on quantities, storage and even cooking.

Germans don't only love eating *Wurst*; they also use the word in many everyday expressions, a few of which are listed above:

Milk

Germany is the world's sixth largest producer of milk (*Milch*) with an annual output of 28.5m tonnes and is increasing exports to fill the market gap caused by Asian milk shortages, resulting in inflated prices. Germany has a long history of quality dairy production in monasteries, which is still carried on today. If this creates an image of monks in flowing habits herding cows into abbatial courtyards, squatting on three-legged stools and gently squeezing the milk into battered pails, think again. Monasteries have secularised and become huge dairy product (and beer) factories that ship their products throughout Germany and the world – though you can still find the monk-produced kind if you visit a local monastery. In Bavaria, all milk (and lots of other dairy products and beer) sold in shops and supermarkets (even in Aldi) is 'monastery produced' – and proudly labelled with a picture of the monastery, e.g. Weihenstephan or Andechser.

Metric/Imperial Conversion

Weight

Imperial	Metric	Metric	Imperial
1 UK pint	0.57 litre	1 litre	1.75 UK pints
1 US pint	0.47 litre	1 litre	2.13 US pints
1 UK gallon	4.54 litre	1 litre	0.22 UK gallon
1 US gallon	3.78 litres	1 litre	0.26 US gallon

Capacity

Imperial	Metric	Metric	Imperial
1 UK pint	0.57 litre	1 litre	1.75 UK pints
1 US pint	0.47 litre	1 litre	2.13 US pints
1 UK gallon	4.54 litres	1 litre	0.22 UK gallon
1 US gallon	3.78 litres	1 litre	0.26 US gallon

Note: An American 'cup' = around 250ml or 0.25 litre.

Supermarkets sell both fresh (*frisch*) and sterilised milk (*UHT-Milch, H-Milch*, often marked simply as *haltbar* – storable), which can be bought in bulk and stored for some time without refrigeration. There's no fat-free or skimmed (skim) milk, and milk with under 1 per cent fat (*Magermilch* – 'slim' milk) is only available sterilised. Most Germans prefer full-fat or whole milk (*Vollmilch*) or milk with 1.5 per cent fat (*fettarme Milch* – low-fat milk). You can also buy *crème fraîche* and whipping cream at any supermarket.

Organic Food

'Health food' has become a German obsession, evidenced by sales of organic food, which were worth €4.5bn in 2006 (a 16 per cent increase over the previous year). Around 4.5 per cent of German farms are chemical-free and nearly one-third of all organic food sold in the EU is bought from German supermarkets. Organic food can also be found in health food shops (*Reformhäuser*) and some *Drogerien* (see **Types of Shop** above). Baby food is available almost exclusively organic. Over 30,000 organic products are available, identifiable by a green '*Bio*' logo; it's even possible to buy 'organic' gummy bears (similar to British wine gums), without gelatine (strictly, vegetarian rather than organic), and some Christmas markets sell organic *Glühwein*.

Wine

Germany officially has 13 wine-producing areas but around 87 per cent of the grapes grown are white. German wine doesn't have the reputation of French or Italian wines and doesn't

appeal to everyone, especially as much of it is sweet. This doesn't, however, mean that there aren't some high-quality German wines. Wine quality is clearly labelled with its quality, *Tafelwein* (table wine) being the lowest (best used for cooking) and *Landwein* (country wine) the next - the equivalent of French *vin de pays*. *Qualitätswein* is of higher quality, followed by *Qualitätswein bestimmter Anbaugebiete* (QbA) and, the best quality, *Prädikatswein* (renamed from *Qualitätswein mit Prädikat/QmP*), which is wine of distinction.

Most German wines are made from the Riesling grape, which tends to produce a sweet wine. If you prefer a drier wine, look for the word *trocken* (dry) or *halbtrocken* (semi-dry) on the label. German sparkling wine is called

Sekt, which Germans love to drink at impromptu celebrations whenever the opportunity arises - it's also served for breakfast – though not every day. Like German food it doesn't travel well and is rarely seen outside German-speaking countries.

Foreign wines are also popular, especially Italian, and most supermarkets offer wines from around the world. Many Germans appreciate good wine and have a well stocked cellar.

The Germans are exceedingly fond of Rhine wines; they are put up in tall, slender bottles, and are considered a pleasant beverage. One tells them from vinegar by the label.

Mark Twain (American writer)

Quality designations

The best quality German wines are further classified by quality (*Prädikat*) according to their must weight (density), sugar content and grape juice; the level required is dependent on grape variety and region and is defined in terms of the Oechsle scale. The *Prädikat* system has its origin at Schloss Johannisberg in Rheingau, where the first *Spätlese* was produced in 1775, where wines received different colour seals based on their must weight. The different *Prädikat* designations used are as follows, in order of increasing sugar levels in the must (and therefore quality):

- ***Kabinett*** ('caninet') – fully ripened light wines from the main harvest, typically semi-sweet with crisp acidity, but can be dry if designated so.
- ***Spätlese*** – ('late harvest') – typically semi-sweet, often sweeter and fruitier than *Kabinett*, but can be a relatively full-bodied dry wine if designated so. Although *Spätlese* means late harvest, it isn't as sweet as a dessert wine.
- ***Auslese*** ('select harvest') – made from selected very ripe grapes, typically semi-sweet or sweet, sometimes with some noble rot character. Sometimes *Auslese* is also made into a powerful dry wine, but the designation *Auslese trocken* has been discouraged after the introduction of *Grosses Gewächs* (great growths, adopted in 2001 by Germany's best growers). *Auslese* covers the widest range of wine styles and can be a dessert wine.
- ***Beerenauslese*** ('select berry harvest') – made from individually selected overripe grapes often affected by noble rot, making rich sweet dessert wine.
- ***Eiswein*** (ice wine) – made from grapes that have been naturally frozen on the vine, making a very concentrated wine. They must reach at least the same level of sugar content in the must as a *Beerenauslese*. The most classic *Eiswein* style is to use only grapes that aren't affected by noble rot. Until the '80s, the *Eiswein* designation was used in conjunction with another *Prädikat* (which indicated the ripeness level of the grapes before they had frozen), but it's now considered a *Prädikat* of its own.

- ***Trockenbeerenauslese*** ('select dry berry harvest' or 'dry berry selection') – made from selected overripe shrivelled grapes often affected by noble rot, making extremely rich sweet wines.

Beer

Germany's beer is generally considered to be the best in the world (although the Belgians and Czechs may disagree) and there are countless varieties of it. Even the cheapest German beer must be made in accordance with the *Reinheitsgebot* – the 'purity law' making it illegal to use chemicals or preservatives – and is more than drinkable.

German beer is freshest and best on tap (*vom Fass*) from a bar or pub, but it can also be bought in kegs, glass or plastic bottles (and occasionally) cans at supermarkets, petrol stations and *Getränkemärkte* (see **Types of Shop** above). After draught beer, the best tasting beer is usually from glass bottles, which carry a deposit (*Pfand*) of around €0.08. Plastic bottles and cans carry a €0.15-0.25 deposit. Beer is inexpensive in Germany and often costs less than non-alcoholic drinks.

All drinks that come in cans or bottles carry a deposit (*Pfand*) unless they're marked PET (polyethylene terephthalate). The amount varies from €0.08-0.50. Drinks bought at discount chain supermarkets such as Aldi or Penny Market always carry a €0.25 Pfand. Bottles and cans can be returned to any supermarket or Getränkemarkt that sells the same brand. Major supermarkets have a machine for returned bottles; after swallowing your bottles it issues a receipt that you present at the check-out to receive your refund. Discount shop assistants collect your returned bottles at the check-out and deduct the refund from your bill.

CLOTHES

It's a common misconception that all Germans are fat, while in fact clothing sizes in most shops only go up to size 44 (UK size 18 or US 16 or 'large'). If you need larger sizes, your choices are limited, especially if you're young, as 'outsize' styles tend to be aimed at the older population. The only hope for larger young women is the discount clothing store C&A, which now has an XL clothing line for 'young people'.

As in most countries, different manufacturers 'interpret' sizes in different ways and it's common to find that the size you need varies slightly from brand to brand and from shop to shop. Men's shirts are classed by overall size, e.g. small or medium, rather than the collar size.

Shoes

It's quite difficult to find good-quality shoes for under €100. Women with large feet may have a problem as few shops stock shoes above size 40 (UK 6) and it's almost unheard of to find women's shoes in a size 42 (UK 8) or above. German shoes also tend to be made wider and shorter than British and American shoes. Shops selling Italian and Swiss footwear provide a wider range of sizes, but at higher prices.

Children's Clothes

Children's clothes are easy to find and fairly cheap but there isn't much variety, and you may find a number of children at a *Kindergarten* wearing the same things. Pseudo-American styles (which Germans think are in all the rage in the US, such as baseball caps with the New York Yankees logo in the wrong colours, worn backwards) are popular in Germany, and clothes (especially shirts) are often emblazoned with ridiculous or incomprehensible 'English' words or phrases. Casual dress is the norm for children (i.e. jeans and T-shirts) unless it's a special occasion – but even casual clothes should have a 'designer' label. Finding attractive clothes for boys can be difficult as German shops cater much more to girls. Infants' clothes

Continental to UK/US Size Comparison

Women's Clothes

Continental	34	36	38	40	42	44	46	48	50	52
UK	8	10	12	14	16	18	20	22	24	26
US	6	8	10	12	14	16	18	20	22	24

Men's Shirts

Continental	36	37	38	39	40	41	42	43	44	46
UK/US	14	14	15	15	16	16	17	17	18	-

Shoes (Women's and Men's)

Continental	35	36	37	37	38	39	40	41	42	42	43	44
UK	2	3	3	4	4	5	6	7	7	8	9	9
US	4	5	5	6	6	7	8	9	9	10	10	11

aren't usually practical for nappy (diaper) changing, e.g. they don't have poppers (snaps). Surprisingly, cheaper shops such as C&A and Woolworth often provide a wider selection than more expensive stores. Another popular store for children's clothes is the Swedish clothing chain, H&M.

Alterations

Large department stores provide an alteration service for a small fee, while expensive boutiques may include it in the price. Another possibility is to go to a tailor (*Schneider*), although they usually charge more. Greek tailors have the best reputation.

MAIL-ORDER SHOPPING

Shopping from home is popular in Germany, as it's convenient and efficient. Whether you order by phone, internet or post, delivery is usually made within 24 hours for smaller items, unless otherwise stated, e.g. in the case of out-of-stock items or furniture.

Internet

Internet shopping has taken off in a big way in Germany, where every department store, hypermarket, chain supermarket and Drogerie offers online ordering with rapid service (usually within 24 hours). There's a delivery charge of around €5 and normally a minimum order of €15. (So as not to detract too much from their core business, however, they often run in-store offers that aren't available online.) Drogerie websites offer a photo developing service online: you send your digital images via the internet and receive printed photos by post.

Booking travel and holidays via the internet is also popular and you can find travel websites galore, such as Expedia (💻 www.expedia.de), Travelocity (💻 www.travelocity.de) and Opodo (💻 www.opodo.de). Amazon and eBay also have German websites, and there are a number of German eBay spin-offs, such as 💻 www.second-hand.it – German website, Italian domain name – and 💻 www.lila-laune-shop.de. The German Amazon website (💻 www.amazon.de) has a large selection of English books and delivery is free within Germany.

Surprisingly, Germans aren't particularly worried about internet fraud and have no qualms about giving their credit card or bank details online.

Catalogues

There are long-established and reputable catalogues in Germany, the most famous being Neckermann, Otto and Quelle, which dominate the market. They frequently insert flyers in magazines and newspapers

which you can use to request a free catalogue, which include everything from clothes and furniture to electronics and appliances.

Delivery & Disposal

You can have furniture and appliances delivered (although there's usually a charge) and installation may be included in the price, depending on where you buy them. The delivery company is obliged to take away the packaging and may also dispose of your old appliance.

> **Stiftung Warentest**
>
> Germans don't like to leave things to chance and before buying a new product they often check the latest consumer reports (*Stiftung Warentest* – published by a non-profit organisation). You can check the reports at www.test.de or in the associated monthly magazines, *Test* and *FINANZtest*. Products that performed well proudly display their score on the packaging.

RETURNING GOODS

Consumer rights are strictly regulated in Germany and however much shopkeepers might protest, you're entitled to return faulty or unsuitable goods provided you have a receipt and return them within the time limit indicated. If you're returning something that isn't faulty (e.g. because you don't like it), it must usually be in the original packaging and in pristine condition. However, if you buy something in a sale, you cannot normally return it unless it's faulty.

Refunds

Some shops give cash refunds, but they aren't required to by law and may wish to issue you with a credit note or voucher instead. A store's refund policy should be printed on receipts or posted by the checkout. Refunds for credit or debit card purchases are made electronically.

Guarantees

All electronic items and appliances are guaranteed for two years under EU law, during which period you're entitled to free repair but not an automatic replacement or refund. Bear in mind that the item will often need to be sent to a service centre for testing – which is frustrating if it's something you use frequently, such as a washing machine. If it's irreparable, you'll (eventually) be given a replacement or a refund.

Complaints

Consumer rights are protected by the Verbraucherzentrale – the consumer association advice bureau – and if you have a serious complaint it should be made to the office in your state (listed on www.verbraucherzentrale.de/en/index.php). The Verbraucherzentrale is a state-funded, non-profit organisation whose purpose is to seek to improve consumer awareness of environmental and health concerns, prosecute law-breakers, and inform the media of consumer issues. It can advise you on your legal position and rights regarding loans and mortgages, investment, insurance, health services, transport and energy, as well as shopping. Further information can be found on their website (in German only).

Lorch, Rhine Valley, Hesse

10.

ODDS & ENDS

A country's culture is influenced by various factors and reflected in myriad ways. Among the principal influences are its climate, geography and religion, which are considered in this chapter along with various cultural manifestations, including crime, the national anthem and flag, government and international relations, pets, tipping and toilets.

'What does not destroy me, makes me stronger.'
Friedrich Nietzsche (philosopher)

CLIMATE

Germany is situated in the temperate zone between the Atlantic Ocean and eastern Europe and therefore has a moderate climate, with warm summers and cool winters; extremes of temperature are rare. In winter, average temperatures in the north are slightly higher than in the more mountainous south and, although summers are humid, air-conditioning isn't common. Winters are damp and may therefore seem more bone chilling to those from drier climates; ice is often a hazard, particularly when driving. In the north, storms sweeping across the Arctic Circle bring gales to coastal regions, although winter temperatures are moderated by the warm Gulf Stream and average a degree or two above freezing.

Centres of high pressure to the east of Germany can bring periods of cold, bright winter weather. The weather in the south is influenced by the Alps, which usually make winters long and cold, with regular snow. High in the Bavarian Alps, annual rainfall can be as high as 200cm (79in) in comparison with 60 to 80cm (24 to 31in) in the rest of the country, where summers are typically wet.

Changes in atmospheric pressure from winds passing over the Alps cause the *Föhn*, a warm, dry wind from the south which can raise the temperature dramatically in a short time and melt alpine snow. The *Föhn* also clears the air, allowing the Alps to be seen from great distances. When people in southern Germany are feeling a little 'under the weather', they often blame the *Föhn*.

Extreme Weather

Germany isn't usually subject to catastrophic meteorological phenomena such as tornadoes or cyclones, although in 2007 hurricane Cyril swept through the land, with winds as high as 190kph (118mph) causing a number of deaths and extensive damage to property, including Berlin's railway station. Most of the deaths occurred on motorways, when vehicles were blown off course. In spring and autumn there's a danger of flooding, even in some of the minor river valleys, when heavy rain combines with melting snow from the mountains to swell rivers.

CRIME

According to the Bundeskriminalamt's 'Police Crime Statistics Report' for 2006, there were around 76 crimes per 1,000 inhabitants, the lowest rate since 2000. The southern *Länder* – Baden-Württemberg, Bavaria, Hesse and Thuringia – typically have the lowest crime rate of between 54 and 73. Not surprisingly, those with the highest rates are the city-states of Berlin, Bremen and Hamburg, with between 135 and 146, while the second-highest rates (between 86 and 141) are in the north-eastern states of Brandenburg, Mecklenburg-Western Pomerania and Saxony-Anhalt. The city with the lowest crime rate is Munich at 88, while Frankfurt has the highest at 163. There's little crime in small towns.

Germany's position in central Europe makes it attractive to those involved in organised crime, most notably drug trafficking, but the police presence is quite high and avoiding crime is largely a matter of common sense. For example, you should avoid major railway stations and dark streets and parks at night, and keep clear of Neo-Nazi demonstrations. There are pickpockets in tourist areas, where it's wise to conceal your wallet and valuables and keep a firm grip on your handbag. Although the rates of murder, rape, robbery and theft have fallen in recent years, the number of assaults has increased.

In 2007, Munich was voted the world's most agreeable city to live in by *Monocle* magazine, partly due to the city's low crime rate.

FLAG & ANTHEM

The strictures imposed by the occupying forces after the Second World War forbidding 'outward displays of patriotism' became so ingrained in German culture that there's little anthem singing and flag waving even today (except at the World Cup). But this is gradually changing as Germany tries to establish a more positive image, both at home and abroad.

Anthem

The German national anthem – known simply as 'The German Song' (*das Deutschlandlied*) – was established in 1922 during the Weimar Republic, and is based on a melody written by Joseph Haydn (1732-1809) in 1797 with words by August Heinrich Hoffmann von Fallersleben (1798-1874). During the Nazi era only the first verse was used, beginning *Deutschland, Deutschland über alles* (Germany, Germany above all), but after the Second World War the Allies banned the anthem due to its association with Nazism. The third stanza was officially re-instated in 1952 as the national anthem and is the source of the national motto: *Einigkeit und Recht und Freiheit* (unity, justice

National Anthem

German	English
Einigkeit und Recht und Freiheit	Unity and justice and freedom
Für das deutsche Vaterland!	For the German fatherland!
Danach lasst uns alle streben	For these let us all strive
Brüderlich mit Herz und Hand!	Brotherly with heart and hand!
Einigkeit und Recht und Freiheit	Unity and justice and freedom
Sind des Glückes Unterpfand;	Are the pledge of fortune;
Blüh' im Glanze dieses Glückes,	Flourish in this fortune's blessing,
Blühe, deutsches Vaterland.	Flourish, German fatherland.

and freedom). Sadly, many Germans don't know the words of their national anthem, which are reproduced below.

Flag

The current German flag, recognised since 1919 and re-instated after the Second World War, consists of three horizontal stripes: black (at the top), red and gold (at the bottom) – the colours possibly having been copied from the flag of the Holy Roman Empire. When hung in a federal government building, the flag has a black eagle in the centre. The German Democratic Republic (GDR) or East Germany added a coat of arms depicting a hammer, compass and grain in the centre, but this was dropped after reunification. Since Germany's hosting of the World Cup in 2006, the flag has made something of a comeback, and you'll often see it hanging outside apartments and from car antennae – and even in the form of beach towels.

GEOGRAPHY

Germany is the third-largest country in western Europe (after France and Spain), covering an area of around 357,000km² (140,000mi²) and stretching 840km (520mi) from north to south and 620km (385mi) east to west. Germany's geography has played a pivotal role in its history. Situated in the centre of the continent, it shares borders with nine countries: Poland and the Czech Republic to the east; Switzerland and Austria to the south; France, Luxembourg, Belgium and the Netherlands to the west; and Denmark to the north. Land boundaries total 3,621km (2,250mi), while the coastline (which is entirely in the north, bordering the North and

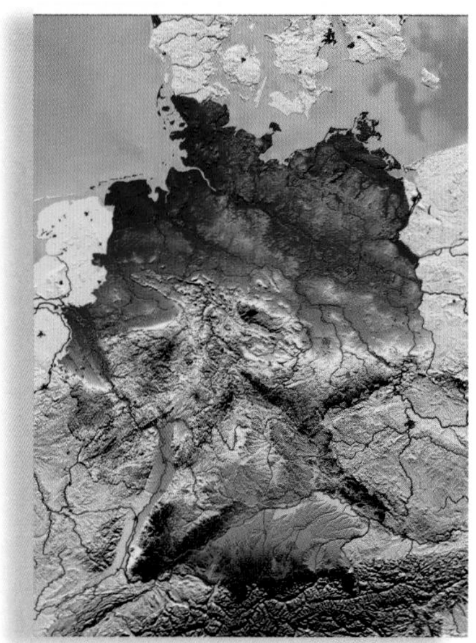

Baltic Seas) extends for 2,389km (1,484mi).

Geographically, there are three major regions in Germany. In the south, the terrain is mountainous, with the Bavarian Alps and the foothills of the Swiss Alpine mountain range.

The Central German Uplands consist of forested mountains and plateaux, which are part of the same formation as the Massif Central in France and continue east into Poland. The north of the country is part of the North European Lowlands, comprising marshes and mud flats extending to the coast and into Denmark. The Zugspitze in the Bavarian Alps (2,962m/9,718ft) is the country's highest point, while the lowest point is sea level along the coast in the north.

Germany has many rivers, including the massive and spectacular Rhine, which forms part of its border with France, and the 'Danube' (*Donau* in German – the English name isn't used by any of the countries the river flows through), which flows southwards to Austria and then on to Hungary.

A physical map of Germany is shown on page 6 and a map showing the 16 states and state capitals is included in **Appendix F**.

GOVERNMENT

The Federal Republic of Germany was established in 1949, but included only the western states. Delegates were sent from each state to form a parliament and the parliamentary council drafted the constitution (*Grundgesetz*), which was approved by the states. The eastern states were included in the republic after reunification in 1990 and the capital moved from Bonn to Berlin.

Parliament

German's parliament is bicameral, i.e. it has two houses: the upper house (*Bundesrat*) and the lower house (*Bundestag*). The *Bundesrat* is made up of three to six delegates from each state – depending on the population of the state – appointed by the state cabinets and led by a minister president. It has the right of veto over legislation passed by the *Bundestag* and must approve legislation affecting the states.

Members of the *Bundestag* are elected by a system combining proportional representation for political parties with the direct election of candidates within districts. Each voter has two votes, one for individual candidates running within the legislative district, the winner gaining a seat in the *Bundestag*; the other for the political party and all its state representatives (*Landesliste*), which determines the total number of seats each party receives in the *Bundestag*. There are two seats for each voting district in Germany, making a total of 656 unless the results of the party vote differ from those of the individual elections, in which case additional seats may be added to reflect the correct proportional outcome. (Don't worry if you don't understand this – Einstein wouldn't have either!)

The *Bundestag* makes and changes federal laws, makes constitutional amendments, debates government policy, approves the federal budget, ratifies treaties concerning Germany's external interests and elects the prime minister, called the chancellor (*Kanzler*).

'It seems to me that the fact that I am a woman is a bigger issue than the fact that I'm from the East. For me it isn't really important. I've only ever known myself as a woman.'
Angela Merkel
(first female Chancellor of Germany)

Chancellor & President

The chancellor is the head of the federal government, exercising executive power, and can be unseated only if the *Bundestag* passes a vote of no confidence and elects a new chancellor by an absolute majority at the same time. The president is head of state and is elected by a federal assembly (*Bundesversammlung*) made up of the entire *Bundestag* and an equal number of state delegates. The president can appoint and dismiss ministers, judges, civil servants and officers. Horst Köhler is Germany's current president and Angela Merkel is the current chancellor (2009).

POLITICAL PARTIES

A party needs to gain 5 per cent of the vote to be represented in the *Bundestag*, where there are currently six political parties represented:

Christian Democratic Party (CDU) – a centre-right party founded by Konrad Adenauer after the Second World War. CDU members include former chancellor Helmut Kohl and current chancellor Angela Merkel.

Social Democratic Party (SPD) – centre-left and Germany's oldest party, with working class roots but which has developed into a party of professional and white-collar workers. Former chancellor Gerhard Schröder belongs to the SPD.

Christian Social Union (CSU) – centre-right. This Catholic-influenced party is the Bavarian equivalent of the CDU, with which it forms a coalition. Edmund Stoiber, previous candidate for chancellor and the current minister president of Bavaria, belongs to the CSU.

Free Democratic Party (FDP) – a smallish centrist party with politically progressive but economically conservative policies. It generally forms coalitions with either the CDU or the SPD, depending on which way the wind is blowing. Although small, it can tip the balance of power.

The Left (*Die Linke*, previously WASG) – the former Party of Democratic Socialism (PDS), which ruled East Germany before it was integrated into the German Federal Republic in 1990. It's a small party that mostly represents East Germans and normally isn't welcomed into coalitions. In 2005, it formed an alliance with the western Electoral

Alternative for Labour and Social Justice (WASG) party, which supports same-sex marriage and advocates better treatment for immigrants. The Left did surprisingly well in the 2005 election, gaining 8.7 per cent of the vote and more than doubling the support it achieved in the 2002 election.

The Greens – an ecological and antinuclear party, which has formed a coalition with Alliance 90, an amalgamation of the three non-communist parties of the former East Germany. The Greens/Alliance 90 formed a coalition with the SPD to help them retain Schröder as chancellor.

The political system is designed to make it difficult for one party to have enough power to rule alone; even the strongest party usually needs to form a coalition with other parties in order to gain a majority of seats in the *Bundestag*, which often results in strange bedfellows.

A case in point was the 2005 election, which produced no clear winner. The CDU/CSU, led by Angela Merkel, were expected to win but received only 1 per cent more votes and four more seats than their great rivals, the SPD. Normally the CDU would have formed a coalition with the FDP, but it didn't do well enough to provide the necessary additional seats. However, the CDU didn't want anything to do with the Left (the former communist party) which did alarmingly well, therefore in the end the only option was for the two great adversaries to form a grand coalition.

THE EUROPEAN UNION

Germany plays a leading role in the European Union and has done since

its inception: in 1951 West Germany was a founding member of the European Coal and Steel Industry, which developed into the European Economic Community (EEC) in 1957 and the modern-day European Union (EU) following the Maastricht Treaty in 1993. Germany is at the forefront of moves toward more unified EU policies, especially in the areas of defence and security, and is consistently the highest financial contributor to the poorer members.

The German government supports the creation of an EU constitution and the incorporation of new members, much to the chagrin of many German people, who feel they have enough of a financial burden dealing with the reunified East Germany. The former chancellor Gerhard Schröder made himself loved by some and hated by others when he announced to Turkish leaders that he would do everything in his power to see Turkey integrated into the EU.

Germany's painful awareness of its past and of its lingering negative image may be the reason for its acquiescent and obliging manner in the EU. It wishes to show the Europe and the world that it will do everything to promote peace, unity and prosperity in Europe, and to prevent the growth of aggressive nationalism. Germany doesn't rock the European boat any more.

INTERNATIONAL RELATIONS

Until the immigration laws were tightened in 1993, Germany accepted around 80 per cent of all those seeking asylum in the EU.

Germany is the world's third-largest economic power, its largest exporter and its second-largest importer. In addition to being a member of the EU, the United Nations and NATO, it's among the Group of Eight (G8), an international forum representing 65 per cent of the world's economic power, and the Group of Four (G4), a political alliance with India, Japan and Brazil to support each other's bid for a permanent seat on the UN Security Council. Germany has strong political and economic ties with France (its largest trading partner) and Russia. Since the end of the Second World War, Germany has attempted to stay out of conflicts, participating merely in a peace-keeping capacity. Two exceptions were made by chancellor Schröder, who sent troops to Kosovo and Afghanistan as part of NATO operations. According to Germany's constitution, the country may only wage war in self-defence.

Relations with the USA

The US and Germany are economically and socially interdependent; almost 9 per cent of German exports are US-bound, 6.6 per cent of imports are from the US, some 43m Americans claim German ancestry, and Ramstein airbase near Kaiserslautern is the largest US military community outside the US. Since the end of the war, relations between the two countries have been peaceful and supportive.

This relationship was temporarily tarnished when chancellor Schröder denied US President Bush's request to send troops to Iraq in 2003, which set off a wave of anti-Americanism in Germany. Since then, political relations have improved, partly thanks to the 2005 election of a more pro-Republican chancellor, Angela Merkel, who lost no time in inviting president Bush to a barbeque (even though the concept is unfamiliar to most Germans). Although the two leaders seemed to remain friends, the German people's approval of US policies dropped considerably during the Bush administration from 78 per cent in 2000 to 37 per cent in 2006.

Studies have shown that at the beginning of the Iraq conflict, the German media showed five times as many negative images of US involvement than any other European country – as if Germans enjoyed having the moral high ground (and being proved right).

PETS

Dogs are the Germans' favourite pets, and it's a popular social 'sport' to show off expensive pedigree dogs – dachshunds, German shepherds and poodles being among the favourite breeds – and dogs accompany their owners almost everywhere. Most dogs are well trained and don't run up to strangers or beg, and may even snub you if you try to pet them. In any case, it's polite to ask the owner first before approaching a dog, as some people consider it an invasion of their private space or property. Owners are supposed to clean up after their dogs in public places – and, true to form, most do. There's strict legislation regarding what are called 'fighting dogs' (*Kampfhunde*), such as pitbulls, some of which are banned entirely, while others must be muzzled in public. Other popular pets are cats, rabbits, gerbils, hamsters, birds and fish.

Although pets are generally welcome in public places, landlords often refuse potential tenants with pets (except fish), and neighbours are likely to complain if a pet is noisy.

Religion is considered a private matter to Germans and the proselytising of groups such as Jehovah's Witnesses and Mormons isn't appreciated, and is even feared. Scientology is considered a business venture and therefore doesn't qualify as a religion in Germany.

RELIGION

The main religion in Germany is Christianity, with the north predominantly Protestant and the south Catholic – a legacy of the religious division at the time of the Reformation (see **Chapter 2**).

Regensburg cathedral

The next largest religious group is Greek Orthodox, followed by Islam, practised mainly by Turkish 'guest workers' and their descendents.

According to the constitution, all citizens have freedom of religion and no discrimination on religious grounds is allowed. However, the influx of non-Christians (mainly Muslims) since the '60s has caused Germans to reassess their value system and introduce legislation aimed at fostering Christian values, which have traditionally been held sacred. In most schools, children are required to take a course on religion, where Christianity and its values are the focus. The option of Ethics, which was introduced in order to placate the former East German states after reunification, has become a catchall subject for other religious groups and atheists. This has created a noticeable division in schools between Christians and non-Christians.

Before the Holocaust, around 600,000 Jews lived in Germany. As part of its reparation for the Holocaust, Germany has relaxed its immigration restrictions for non-EU Jews, who, provided they can show ties to the German Jewish community (or can find one willing to accept them) can immigrate from anywhere at any time, irrespective of their age or occupation, and may work in Germany, although they aren't automatically entitled to welfare benefits. This has caused an influx of Jews, especially from former Soviet states. Berlin boasts the fastest-growing Jewish community in the world, although there are still only around 200,000 Jews in Germany (0.25 per cent of the population).

There has also been much discussion about offering courses on Islam for Muslim students, but it's difficult to integrate the different types (e.g. Sunni, Alevite, Shi'a) into one class that satisfies all Muslims. Another hot topic is whether female Muslim teachers and students should be allowed to wear headscarves to class. There are few mosques in Germany, where most Muslims practise at home or meet in unused buildings to worship. Some cities have plans to build mosques to support the Muslim community, but these often arouse opposition from non-Muslim residents.

Germany imposes a church tax on those who register themselves as Christians or Jews – it's proposed that Muslims should also have to pay – which is perhaps the reason that around 30 per cent of Germans profess to have no religion. Only 30 per cent of the former East German population is registered as having no religion.

TIME

Germany is on Central European Time (CET), which is Greenwich Mean Time (GMT) plus one hour in winter and plus two hours in summer. The change to summer time occurs on the last Sunday in March at 2am and to winter time on the last Sunday in October at 3am.

The time in selected major cities when it's noon (in winter) in Germany is shown below:

Times are nearly always written and spoken using the 24-hour system in Germany, e.g. 1am is written *0100* and 1pm *1300*. Noon is *12 Uhr* and midnight is *24 Uhr* or *Null Uhr*, while 7pm is normally expressed as *neunzehn Uhr* (1900) but occasionally *sieben Uhr Abends* (seven o'clock in the evening). Note that when Germans say 'half eight' (*Halb acht*) they mean 7.30, not 8.30, and '*Viertel vor acht*' means a quarter to eight and '*Viertel nach acht*', or

Time Difference

Berlin	London	Jo'burg	Sydney	Auckland	Los Angeles	New York
noon	11am	1pm	10pm	Midnight	3am	6am

simply '*Viertel acht*', means a quarter past eight.

TIPPING

There's no hard and fast rule for tipping in Germany. Restaurants include a service charge, but you're also expected to give a tip of between 5 and 10 per cent. To save taking a calculator with you every time you go out to eat, if the total is €10 or under, just round up to the next euro; if the bill is between €10 and €50, round up to the next €5. If the service was inadequate, however, you shouldn't tip at all. The same principle applies to taxi fares.

When your waiter brings the bill, tell him the total you wish to pay, and you'll be given the appropriate change; there's no need to go to the cash register. When paying by credit card, you should give your tip in cash to the waiter to ensure that he gets it, and not the establishment. Tips are almost never left on the table. You should leave a few euros for hotel chambermaids and give a 10 per cent tip to a hairdresser – provided you don't end up looking like *Struwwelpeter* (shaggy or slovenly Peter, translated by Mark Twain).

TOILETS

Public toilets are few and far between in Germany, and although some towns and villages still provide free (and clean) public toilets (which may be closed at night and on weekends), they have largely disappeared. The solution is to pop into a bar, restaurant or department store. Every establishment serving food and drink with seating available for customers is required to provide a free toilet, although they don't like people using their facilities without buying anything and some may demand a fee. The men's is usually marked Herren/Männer and the ladies' Damen/Frauen – or there may be a graphic of a man or a woman.

Large establishments usually have toilet attendants, who keep a plate of coins near them to encourage you to 'tip' €0.20-50 – it isn't really a tip and should be accepted as a fee for using a clean toilet. Usually you tip on leaving, although some attendants have taken to demanding €0.50 before you enter.

At motorway rest stops, railway stations, city streets and other public places, there are pay toilets (many operated by Sanifair) where you usually pay €0.50 to use the facilities. On motorways, entry is via a coin-operated turnstile, where you receive a coupon which can be redeemed in the refreshment shop. Toilets are high-tech, automated and hygienic, and are cleaned automatically after each use. In street cubicles, the WC may fold into the wall after you're finished and the whole unit thoroughly steam-cleaned and auto-disinfected, including the walls and floors. There may be a time limit to do your business, e.g. 5 minutes, therefore your advised to leave quickly to avoid being cleansed!

You may come across so-called super-loos in cities, which are air-conditioned with soft lighting and relaxing music, a soothing video projection (e.g. showing swirling underwater bubbles) and 'targets' on the urinals to help male customers direct their aim. They may also be equipped with a disabled lift, a unisex baby changing area and 24-hour reception. All for €0.50.

Carnival masks, Schömberg, Black Forest

Nebelhorn, Allgäu Alps

APPENDICES

APPENDIX A: EMBASSIES & CONSULATES

In Germany

Listed below are the contact details for the embassies and high commissions of selected English-speaking countries in Germany. A full list of embassies and consulates in Germany is available on 💻 www.embassiesabroad.com/embassies-in/Germany.

Australia: Wallstrasse 76-79, 10179 Berlin (☎ 880 0880), 💻 www.germany.embassy.gov.au).

Canada: Leipziger Platz 17, 10117 Berlin (☎ 203120, 💻 www.dfait-maeci.gc.ca/canada-europa/germany).

Ireland: Friedrichstrasse 200, 10117 Berlin (☎ 220720).

New Zealand: Friedrichstrasse 60, 10117 Berlin (☎ 206210).

South Africa: Tiergartenstrasse 18, 10785 Berlin (☎ 220730, 💻 www.suedafrika.org/de/home.php).

UK: Wilhelmstrasse 70/71, 10117 Berlin (☎ 204570, 💻 www britisch ebotschaft.de/en).

USA: Neustädtische Kirchstrasse 4–5, 10117 Berlin (☎ 238 5174, 💻 http://germany.usembassy.gov).

Security measures are stringent at embassies and consulates (especially US consulates) and it's advisable to bring as little as possible with you. Bottles and electronic gadgets (including mobile phones) aren't usually allowed and bags will be thoroughly searched.

Abroad

Listed below are the contact details for German embassies in selected English-speaking countries. A full list is available at 🖳 www.konsulate.de.

Australia: 119 Empire Circuit, Yarralumla, Canberra, ACT 2600 (☏ 6270 1911, 🖳 www.germanembassy.org.au/en/home/index.html).

Canada: 1 Waverly Street, Ottawa, ON K2P 0T8 (☏ 613-232 1101, 🖳 www.ottawa.diplo.de/Vertretung/ottawa/en/Startseite.html).

Ireland: 31 Trimleston Avenue, Bootersown, Blackrock, Co. Dublin (☏ 01-2693011, 🖳 www.dublin.diplo.de/Vertretung/dublin/en/Startseite.html).

New Zealand: 90-92 Hobson Street, Thorndon, Wellington (☏ 04-473 6063, 🖳 www.wellington.diplo.de/Vertretung/wellington/en/Startseite.html).

South Africa: 180 Blackwood Street, Arcadia, Pretoria 0083 (☏ 012-427 8900, 🖳 www.pretoria.diplo.de/Vertretung/pretoria/en/Startseite.html).

UK: 23 Belgrave Square, London SW1X 8PZ (☏ 020-7824 1300, 🖳 www.london.diplo.de/Vertretung/london/en/Startseite.html).

USA: 4645 Reservoir Road, NW, Washington, DC-20007-1998 (☏ 202-298 4000, 🖳 www.germany-info.org).

The business hours of embassies vary and they close on their own country's holidays as well as on German public holidays. Always telephone to confirm opening hours before visiting.

APPENDIX B: FURTHER READING

Magazines for Expats

Accents Magazine – magazine for English-speaking expats in Baden-Württemberg (💻 http://accents-magazine.de).

Exberliner – magazine for English-speaking expats in Berlin (💻 www.exberliner.com).

Munich Found – magazine for English-speaking expats in Munich (💻 www.munichfound.de).

New in the City – magazine for recently arrived expats living in Berlin, Frankfurt, Hamburg or Munich (💻 www.newinthecity.de).

Rhine Magazine – magazine for English-speaking expats living in Bonn, Cologne, Dusseldorf and the Rhine region (💻 www.rhinemagazine.de).

Books

Culture

Elections, Mass Politics and Social Change in Modern Germany: New Perspectives, Larry Eugene Jones (Cambridge University Press)

The German Way, Hyde Flippo (McGraw-Hill)

Politics & Culture in Modern Germany, Gordon Craig (UWP)

Prost! The Story of German Beer, Horst D. Dornbusch (Siris Books)

Recasting East Germany, Chris Flockton & Eva Kolinsky (Frank Cass)

The Regions of Germany: A Reference Guide to History and Culture, Dieter K. Buse (Greenwood Press)

These Strange German Ways, Susan Stern (Atlantik-Brücke)

Understanding Contemporary Germany, Stuart P. Parkes (Routeledge)

Xenophobe's Guide to the Germans, Stefan Zeidenitz & Ben Barkov (Oval Books)

History

A Concise History of Germany, Mary Fulbrook (CUP)

After the Wall, Marc Fisher (Simon & Schuster)

A History of Modern Germany 1800-2000, Martin Kitchen (Blackwell Publishing)

Berlin: The Downfall 1945, Anthony Beaver (Penguin Books)

Defeat in the West, Milton Shulman (Cassell Military)

Germany: A New History, Hagen Schulze (Harvard University Press)

Germany in the Twentieth Century, David Childs (Batsford)

Germany Inc., Werner Meyer-Larsen (John Wiley)

Germany Since 1945, Pol O'Dochartaigh (Palgrave Macmillan)

Germany: The Third Reich 1933-45, Geoff Layton (Hodder Murray)

Journey to the White Rose in Germany, Ruth Bernadette Melon (Dog Ear Publishing)

Modern Germany: Society, Economy and Politics in the 20th Century, V.R. Berghahn (Cambridge University Press)

The Origins of Modern Germany, Geoffrey Barraclough (WW Norton & Company)

Party Politics in Germany: A Comparative Politics Approach, Charles Lees (Palgrave Macmillan)

The Rise and Fall of the Third Reich, William L. Shirer (Fawcett Crest)

Language

Berlitz Kid's German Picture Dictionary (Berlitz)

Collins Easy Learn German Series: Vocabulary, Grammar, Verbs, Words, Dictionary (Collins)

Essential German Grammar, Guy Stern & Everett F. Bleiler (Dover)

German: Lonely Planet Phrasebook, Gunther Muhl (Lonely Planet)

German with Ease, A. Chevel & others (Assimil)

Langenscheidt's Pocket Menu Reader Germany (Langenscheidt)

Langenscheidt's Universal Dictionary: German (Langenscheidt)

Mastering German Vocabulary, Gabriele Forst & others (B & T)

Oxford-Duden German Dictionary, O. Thyen & others (Oxford)

Teach Yourself German, Paul Coggle & Heiner Schenke (Mcgraw-Hill)

Ultimate German Beginner-Intermediate (Living Language)

Webster's New World Dictionary: German-English; English-German, Peter Terrel, Horst Kopleck (Webster's)

Living & Working in Germany

Doing Business with Germany, Jonathan Reuvid (GMB Publishing)

Living and Working in Germany, edited by Pamela Wilson (Survival Books)

Management and Organization in Germany, Thomas Armbruster (Ashgate Publishing)

Understanding American and German Business Cultures, Patrick Schmidt (Meridian World Press)

Universities in Germany, Werner Becker & Others (Prestel Verlag)

People

America in the Eyes of the Germans: An Essay on Anti-Americanism, Dan Diner & Alison Brown (Markus Wiener)

Being Jewish in the New Germany, Jeffrey M. Peck (Rutgers University Press)

The Germans, Norbert Elias (Columbia University)

The Germans: When Lies Were Decreed As Truth ... and a Nation Allowed Itself to be Deceived, Harry Conway (Shengold)

Germany and the Germans, John Ardagh (Penguin)

Germans or Foreigners: Attitudes Towards Ethnic Minorities in Post-Reunification Germany, Richard Alba (Palgrave Macmillan)

Germany Profiled, Barry Turner (Palgrave Macmillan)

Jews in Germany, Nachum T. Gidal (Konemann)

Tourist Guides

AA Explorer Germany (AA Publishing)

Baedeker's Germany (Baedeker)

Berlin, Gordon McLachlan (Odyssey)

Daytrips Germany: 60 One Day Adventures by Rail or by Car in Bavaria, the Rhineland, the North and the East, Earl Steinbeck (Hastings House)

Fodor's Berlin's 25 Best with Map, Christopher Rice & Melanie Rice (Fodor's)

Fodor's Germany (Fodor's)

Frommer's Germany, Darwin Porter & Danforth Prince (Frommers)

Frommer's Germany's Best-Loved Driving Tours, British Auto Association (Frommer's)

Frommer's Munich and the Bavarian Alps, Darwin Porter & Danforth Prince (Frommers)

Germany at its Best, Robert S. Kane (Passport)

Germany, Joanna Egert-Romanowskiej & Malgorzata Omilanowska (Eyewitness Travel Guides)

Germany for Dummies, Donald Olson (For Dummies)

Germany Pocket Adventures, Henk Bekker (Hunter Publishing)

Insight Guide: Germany (Langenscheidt)

Karen Brown's Germany's Exceptional Places to Stay & Itineries, Karen

Brown (Karen Brown Guides)

Let's Go Germany (St. Martin's Press)

Lonely Planet: Germany, Andrea Schulte-Peevers & Others (Lonely Planet)

Michelin Green Guide to Germany, Amy S. Eckert & Owen Cannon (Michelin)

Michelin Guide Deutschland (Michelin)

Michelin Red Hotel and Restaurant Guide: Germany (Michelin)

Moon Metro Berlin (Avalon Travel Publishing)

Munich and Bavaria, Andrea Schulte-Peevers, Jeremy Gray and Catherine

Le Nevez (Lonely Planet Regional Guides)

Rick Steve's Germany & Austria, Rick Steves (Avalon Travel Publishing)

The Rough Guide to Berlin, Jack Holland & John Gawthrop (Rough Guides)

The Rough Guide to Germany, Gordon McLachlan (Rough Guides)

Miscellaneous

The Beer Drinker's Guide to Munich, Larry Hawthorne (Freizeit Publishers)

Culinary Voyage Through Germany, Hannelore Kohl (Abbeville)

Customs and Etiquette in Germany, Waltraud Coles & Uwe Koriek (Bravo)

Festivals of the World: Germany, Richard Lord (Gareth Stevens)

Garden Lover's Guide to Germany, Charles Quest Ritson (Princeton)

Germany by Bike, Nadine Slavinski (Mountaineers books)

Germany: in Pictures, Jeffrey Zuehlke (Lerner Publishing)

Germany in Transit: Nation and Migration, 1955-2005, Deniz Gürktürk (University of Cambridge Press)

Germany Today: A Student's Dictionary, Charlie Jeffrey & Ruth Whittle (Arnold)

Germany's Romantic Road, Gordon McLachlan (Cicerone)

Germany: Unraveling an Enigma, Greg Nees (Intercultural Press)

Hitler's Sites: A City by City Guidebook, Steven Lehrer (Mcfarland & Company)

The Longing for Myth in Germany: Religion and Aesthetic Culture from

Romanticism to Nietzsche, George Williamson (University of Chicago Press)

A Traveller's History of Germany, Robert Cole (Interlink)

A Traveller's Wine Guide to Germany, Kerry Brady Stewart (Interlink)

Twelve Years: An American Boyhood in East Germany, Joel Agee (University of Chicago Press)

Walking in the Bavarian Alps, Paddy Dillon (Cicerone)

Walking in the Black Forest, Fleur & Colin Speakman (Cicerone)

The Wines of Germany, Stephen Brook (Mitchell Beazley)

APPENDIX C: USEFUL WEBSITES

The following list contains some of the many websites dedicated to Germany:

Culture

Film (🖳 www.film.de). The latest news from the world of the cinema in Germany and abroad.

German Arts Council/Deutscher Kulturrat e.V (🖳 www.kulturrat.de).

Kultur Portal Deutschland (🖳 www.kulturportal-deutschland.de). A portal which provides access to an array of German cultural information.

Museums in Germany (🖳 http://webmuseen.de).

Tickets & Concerts (🖳 www.eventim.de).

Education

Campus (🖳 www.campus.de). Information for foreigners thinking of studying in Germany.

German Academic Exchange Service/DAAD (🖳 www.daad.de).

Goethe Institut Inter Nationes (🖳 www.goethe.de).

Privatschulberatung (🖳 www.privatschulberatung.de). Information about private schools in Germany.

Government

Bund (🖳 www.bund.de). The main German government website, providing information, in English, on visa requirements, living, education and working in Germany.

Federal Government/Die Bundesregierung (🖳 www.bundesregierung.de/Webs/Breg/EN/Homepage/home.html). Federal govenment website in English, French and German.

Federal Insurance Agency/Bundesversicherungsanstalt für Angestellte (🖳 www.bfa.de).

German Embassy in Washington (🖳 www.germany.info/relaunch/index.html).

German Federal Labour Office/Bundesagentur für Arbeit (🖳 www.arbeitsagentur.de).

German President/Bundespräsident (🖳 www.bundespraesident.de/en).

Living & Working

American Chamber of Commerce (🖳 www.amcham.de).

Association of German Chambers of Industry & Commerce/Deutscher Industrie-und Handelstag (🖳 www.diht.de).

Berlin Mietspiegel (🖳 www.stadtentwicklung.berlin.de/wohnen/mietspiegel). Information on rents in Berlin.

British Chamber of Commerce in Germany (🖳 www.bccg.de).

Central Placements Agency/ZAV (🖳 www.arbeitsamt.de/ZAV).

Deutschebildungsserver (🖳 www.bildungsserver.de). Everything about German education.

German-British Chamber of Industry & Commerce (🖳 www.germanbritishchamber.co.uk).

Institute for Foreign Relations/Institut für Auslands-beziehungen e.V. (🖳 www.ifa.de).

Jobs (🖳 www.jobs.de; 🖳 www.monster.de; 🖳 www.job-world.de). A selection of Germany's leading employment websites.

National Association of German Business Consultants/Bundesverband Deutscher Unternehmensberater (🖳 www.bdu.de.).

National Chamber of Tax Consultants/Bundessteuerberaterkammer (🖳 www.bstbk.de).

Wohnen (🖳 www.immobilienscout24.de) Lots of links related to accommodation.

Wowi (🖳 www.wowi.de). This is a website intended for landlords and investors in rental property but contains lots of interest to tenants, particularly clear and straightforward coverage of recent changes in the law.

Media

Deutsche Welle (🖳 www.dw-world.de). Website of the German equivalent of the BBC World Service.

Der Spiegel (🖳 www.Spiegel.de/international/germany).

Frankfurter Allgemeine Zeitung (💻 www.faz.de). The online version of one of Germany's most respected newspapers.

Frankfurter Rundschau (💻 www.frankfurterrundschau.de). The online version of Germany's principal left-leaning liberal newspaper, the equivalent of The Guardian in the UK.

Süddeutsche Zeitung (💻 www.sueddeutsche.de). The online version of Germany's top broadsheet newspaper.

Die Welt (💻 www.welt.de/www.welt.de.english-news). One of Germany's leading newspapers (the website is available in English, French and German). It also publishes a compact edition entitled Welt Kompakt, a cut-down version of the main broadsheet with a fresher look targeted at a younger audience.

Miscellaneous

Allgemeiner Deutscher Automobilclub/ADAC (💻 www.adac.de).

Berlin (💻 www.berlin.de). The website of the German capital, containing copious information about all aspects of life in the city.

Billiger Telefonieren (💻 www.billiger-telfonieren.de). Compares telephone tariffs.

British Council (💻 www.british council.de).

Deutschebibliothek (💻 www.ddb.de). Website of the German National Library.

Focus Money (💻 www.focus-money.de). Financial information.

Germany Info (💻 www.germany-info.org). Comprehensive information about many aspects of Germany in English.

German Sports Federation/Deutscher Sportbund (💻 www.dsb.de).

Munich (💻 www.munich.de). Information on Munich.

Paperball (💻 www.paperball.fireball.de). Search engine which covers the German press.

Shopping24 (💻 www.shopping24.de). Web shopping portal for everything from flights to flowers.

Sport (💻 www.sport.de). Portal to comprehensive sports coverage but with the emphasis on football and Formula 1 motor racing.

Verivox (💻 www.verivox.de). Energy tariff comparison website.

The Voyage (💻 www.the-voyage.com). Comprehensive information on German-British youth exchanges.

Weihnachten Info (www.weihnachten-info.de). Information about Germany's Christmas markets.

Travel

Deutsche Bahn (www.db.de). German railway website.

Ebookers (www.ebookers.de). Last-minute travel and hotel bookings.

Expedia (www.expedia.de). Tickets online.

Flugplan (www.flugplan.de). Flight timetables to just about everywhere.

Germanwings (www.germanwings.de). Budget airline.

Lufthansa (www.Lufthansa.de). Germany's national airline.

Travel Overland (www.travel-overland.de). Travel tickets.

Meersburg, Lake Constance (Bodensee)

APPENDIX D: USEFUL WORDS & PHRASES

The following lists provide words and phrases you may need during your first few days in Germany. They are, of course, no substitute for learning the language, which you should make one of your priorities. All verbs are provided in the polite German form, which is the correct form to use when addressing a stranger.

Asking for Help

Do you speak English?	*Sprechen Sie Deutsch?*
I don't speak German	*Ich spreche kein Deutsch*
Please speak slowly	*Bitte sprechen Sie langsam*
I don't understand	*Ich verstehe nicht*
I need ...	*Ich brauche ...*
I want ...	*Ich will ...*

Communications

Telephone & Internet

landline	*Festnetz*
mobile phone	*Handy* (popular) *or Mobiltelefon*
no answer	*kein Antwort*
engaged/busy	*besetzt*
internet	*Internet*
email	*E-mail, Mail*
broadband connection	*Breitband Verbindung*
internet café/wifi spot	*Internet Café/Wifi Spot*

Post

post office	*Postamt*
postcard/letter/parcel	*Postkarte/Brief/Paket*
stamps	*Briefmarke*
How much does it cost to send a letter to Europe/North America/Australia?	*Wie viel kostet es, einen Brief nachEuropa/Nordamerika/Australien zu senden?*

Media

newspaper/magazine	*Zeitung/Zeitschrift*
Do you sell English-language media?	*Verkaufen Sie Englisch-sprachige Median?*

Courtesy

yes	*ja*
no	*nein*
excuse me	*entschuldigen Sie*
sorry	*sorry (*popular*), es tut mir leid*
I don't know	*Ich weiss es nicht*
I don't mind	*Es ist mir egal*
please	*bitte**
thank you (very much)	*danke (schön/vielen dank)*
you're welcome	*bitte(schön) or gerne*

* *bitte* has three meanings: please, you're welcome, and 'here you are' (when handing someone something).

Days & Months

All days and months are capitalised in German.

Monday	*Montag*
Tuesday	*Dienstag*
Wednesday	*Mittwoch*
Thursday	*Donnerstag*
Friday	*Freitag*
Saturday	*Samstag*
Sunday	*Sonntag*

January	*Januar*
February	*Februar*
March	*März*
April	*April*
May	*Mai*
June	*Juni*
July	*Juli*
August	*August*
September	*Septembe*r
October	*Oktobe*r
November	*November*
December	*Dezember*

Driving

car insurance	*Autoversicherung*
driving licence	*Führerschein*
hire/rental car	*Mietauto*
How far is it to ...?	*Wie weit ist es zum/zur ...?*
Can I park here?	*Kann ich hier parken?*
unleaded petrol (gas)/diesel	*bleifrei Benzin/Diesel*
Fill the tank up, please	*Volltanken, bitte*
I need €20/30/40 of petrol (gas)	*Ich brauche für zwanzig/dreißig/ vierzig Euro Benzin.*
air/water/oil	*Luft/Wasser/Öl*
car wash	*Autowaschanlage*
My car has broken down	*Mein Auto hat eine Panne*
I've run out of petrol (gas)	*Ich habe kein Benzin mehr*
The tyre is flat	*Ich habe einen platten Reifen*
I need a tow truck	*Ich brauche einen Abschleppwagen*

Emergency

Emergency	*Notfall*
Fire	*Feuer*
Help	*Hilfe*
Police	*Polizei*
Stop	*Halt*
Stop, thief	*Halt, Diebe*
Watch out	*Pass auf* or *Vorsicht*

Finding your Way

Where is ...?	*Wo ist ...?*
Where is the nearest ...?	*Wo ist der/die nächste ...?*
How do I get to ...?	*Wie komme ich auf ...?*
Can I walk there?	*Kann ich da zu Fuß hingehen?*
How far is ....?	*Wie weit ist ...?*
I'm lost	*Ich habe mich verirrt*
map	*Straßenkarte/Landkarte* or *Stadtplan*
left/right/straight ahead	*links/rechts/gerade aus*
opposite/next to/near	*gegenüber/gleich neben/nahe*
airport	*Flughafen*
bus/plane/taxi/train	*Bus/Flugzeug/Taxi/Zug*
bus stop	*Bus Haltestelle*
taxi rank	*Taxistand*
train/bus station	*Zug/Bus Bahnhof*

When does the ... arrive/leave?	*Wann kommt der ... Wann fährt der ...?*
one-way/return	*einfach/hin und zurück*
bank/embassy/consulate	*Bank/Botschaft/Konsulat*

Greetings

Hello	*Hallo*
Goodbye	*Auf Wiedersehen*
Good morning	*Guten Morgen*
Good afternoon	*Guten Tag*
Good Evening	*Guten Abend*
Good night	*Gute Nacht*

Health & Medical Emergencies

I feel ill (dizzy)	*Ich fühle mich krank/schlect (schwindelig)*
I need a doctor/ambulance	*Ich brauche ein Arzt/Krankenwagen*
doctor/nurse/dentist	*Arzt/Krankenschwester/Zahnarzt*
surgeon/specialist	*Chirurg/Spezialist*
hospital/healthcentre	*Krankenhaus/Poliklinik*
A&E (emergency room)	*Notaufnahme*
chemist's/optician's	*Apotheke/Optiker*
prescription	*Rezept*

In a Bar or Restaurant

Waiter (male/female)	*Herr Ober/Fräulein*
menu	*Speisekarte*
bill	*Rechnung*
well done/medium/rare (for meat)	*durch gebraten/Medium/englisch*
vegetarian	*vegetarisch*
meat/fish	*Fleisch/Fisch*

Numbers

1	*eins*	18	*achtzehn*
2	*zwei*	19	*neunzehn*
3	*drei*	20	*zwanzig*
4	*vier*	30	*dreißig*
5	*fünf*	40	*vierzig*
6	*sechs*	50	*fünfzig*
7	*sieben*	60	*sechzig*
8	*acht*	70	*siebzig*
9	*neun*	80	*achtzig*
10	*zehn*	90	*neunzig*
11	*elf*	100	*hundert*
12	*zwölf*	200	*zweihundert*
13	*dreizehn*	500	*fünfhundert*
14	*vierzehn*	1,000	*tausend*
15	*fünfzehn*	million	*Million*
16	*sechszehn*	billion	*Milliarde*
17	*siebzehn*	trillion	*Billion*

Paying

How much is it?	*Wie viel ist es?*
The bill, please	*Die Rechnung, bitte*
Do you take credit cards?	*Akzeptieren Sie Kreditkarten?*

Socialising

Pleased to meet you	*Es freut mich Sie kennenzulernen*
My name is ...	*Mein Name ist ... or Ich heisse ...*
This is my husband/wife/son/ daughter/colleague/friend	*Das ist mein Mann/Frau/Sohn/ Tochter/Kollege*
How are you?	*Wie geht es Ihnen?*
Very well, thank you	*Sehr gut, danke*

Shopping

What time do you open/close?	*Wie sind Ihre Öffnungszeiten?*
Who's the last person (in the queue)?	*Wer ist der letze in die Reihe?*
I'm just looking (browsing)	*Ich möchte nur schauen*
I'm looking for ...	*Ich suche ...*
Can I try it on?	*Kann ich das anprobieren?*
I need size ...	*Ich brauche Größe ...*
bigger/smaller/longer/shorter	*grösser/kleiner/kürzer*
a bag, please	*eine Tasche/Tüte, bitte*
How much is this?	*Wie viel ist es?*

APPENDIX E: MAP OF GERMAN STATES

The Federal Republic of Germany consists of 16 states (*Länder*), listed below. Three states are so called city states (*Stadtsstaaten*): Berlin, Bremen and Hamburg. The cities of Berlin and Hamburg are states in their own right, while the state of Bremen consists of two cities, Bremen and Bremerhaven. The remaining 13 states are termed area states (*Flächenländer*).

Baden-Württemberg
Bavaria
Berlin
Brandenburg
Bremen
Hamburg
Hesse
Mecklenburg Vorpommern
Lower Saxony
Northrhine-Westphalia
Rhineland Palatinate
Saarland
Saxony
Saxony-Anhalt
Schleswig-Holstein
Thuringia

SCHLESWIG-
HOLSTEIN
HAMBURG
MECKLENBURG
VORPOMMERN
BREMEN
LOWER SAXONY
BERLIN
BRANDENBURG
SAXONY-
ANHALT
NORTHRHINE-
WESTPHALIA
SAXONY
THURINGIA
HESSE
RHINELAND
PALATINATE
SAARLAND
BAVARIA
BADEN-
WÜRTTEMBERG

German shepherd dogs

INDEX

A

B

C

G

H

I

J/K/L

M

N

O

P

Q/R

S

T

U

W

Survival Books

Essential reading for anyone planning to live, work, retire or buy a home abroad

Survival Books was established in 1987 and by the mid-'90s was the leading publisher of books for people planning to live, work, buy property or retire abroad.

From the outset, our philosophy has been to provide the most comprehensive and up-to-date information available. Our titles routinely contain up to twice as much information as other books and are updated frequently. All our books contain colour photographs and some are printed in two colours or full colour throughout. They also contain original cartoons, illustrations and maps.

Survival Books are written by people with first-hand experience of the countries and the people they describe, and therefore provide invaluable insights that cannot be obtained from official publications or websites, and information that is more reliable and objective than that provided by the majority of unofficial sites.

Survival Books are designed to be easy – and interesting – to read. They contain a comprehensive list of contents and index and extensive appendices, including useful addresses, further reading, useful websites and glossaries to help you obtain additional information as well as metric conversion tables and other useful reference material.

Our primary goal is to provide you with the essential information necessary for a trouble-free life or property purchase and to save you time, trouble and money.

We believe our books are the best – they are certainly the best-selling. But don't take our word for it – read what reviewers and readers have said about Survival Books at the front of this book.

Buying a Home Series

Buying a home abroad is not only a major financial transaction but also a potentially life-changing experience; it's therefore essential to get it right. Our Buying a Home guides are required reading for anyone planning to purchase property abroad and are packed with vital information to guide you through the property jungle and help you avoid disasters that can turn a dream home into a nightmare.

The purpose of our Buying a Home guides is to enable you to choose the most favourable location and the most appropriate property for your requirements, and to reduce your risk of making an expensive mistake by making informed decisions and calculated judgements rather than uneducated and hopeful guesses. Most importantly, they will help you save money and will repay your investment many times over.

Buying a Home guides are the most comprehensive and up-to-date source of information available about buying property abroad – whether you're seeking a detached house or an apartment, a holiday or a permanent home (or an investment property), these books will prove invaluable.

For a full list of our current titles, visit our website at www.survivalbooks.net

Living and Working Series

Our Living and Working guides are essential reading for anyone planning to spend a period abroad – whether it's an extended holiday or permanent migration – and are packed with priceless information designed to help you avoid costly mistakes and save both time and money.

Living and Working guides are the most comprehensive and up-to-date source of practical information available about everyday life abroad. They aren't, however, simply a catalogue of dry facts and figures, but are written in a highly readable style – entertaining, practical and occasionally humorous.

Our aim is to provide you with the comprehensive practical information necessary for a trouble-free life. You may have visited a country as a tourist, but living and working there is a different matter altogether; adjusting to a new environment and culture and making a home in any foreign country can be a traumatic and stressful experience. You need to adapt to new customs and traditions, discover the local way of doing things (such as finding a home, paying bills and obtaining insurance) and learn all over again how to overcome the everyday obstacles of life.

All these subjects and many, many more are covered in depth in our Living and Working guides – don't leave home without them.

The Expats' Best Friend!

Other Survival Books

The Best Places to Buy a Home in France/Spain: Unique guides to where to buy property in Spain and France, containing detailed regional profiles and market reports.

Buying, Selling and Letting Property: The best source of information about buying, selling and letting property in the UK.

Earning Money From Your French Home: Income from property in France, including short- and long-term letting.

Investing in Property Abroad: Everything you need to know and more about buying property abroad for investment and pleasure.

Life in the UK - Test & Study Guide: essential reading for anyone planning to take the 'Life in the UK' test in order to become a permanent resident (settled) in the UK.

Making a Living: Comprehensive guides to self-employment and starting a business in France and Spain.

Renovating & Maintaining Your French Home: The ultimate guide to renovating and maintaining your dream home in France.

Retiring in France/Spain: Everything a prospective retiree needs to know about the two most popular international retirement destinations.

Running Gîtes and B&Bs in France: An essential book for anyone planning to invest in a gîte or bed & breakfast business.

Rural Living in France: An invaluable book for anyone seekingthe 'good life', containing a wealth of practical information about all aspects of French country life.

Shooting Caterpillars in Spain: The hilarious and compelling story of two innocents abroad in the depths of Andalusia in thelate '80s.

For a full list of our current titles, visit our website at www.survivalbooks.net